THE 19TH CHAMBER

KILLER OF MEN TO HEALER OF MEN

"A Time to Kill and A Time to Heal"

Ecclesiastes 3

Written by

Special Agent Joe Bannon, Ph.D.

(The 19th Chamber – Killer of Men to Healer of Men)

ISBN (Paperback): 979-8-9905012-6-3
ISBN (eBook): 979-8-9905012-5-6

"And they overcame him by the blood of the Lamb, and by the word of their testimony; and they loved not their lives unto the death."

Revelation 12:11

This Book is My Testimony from Death to Life

From Cold Blooded Killer of Men

to

Peaceful Warrior and Healer of Men

"I will give you a new heart and put a new spirit within you; I will take the heart of stone out of your flesh and give you a heart of flesh."

Ezekiel 36:26

Born to Fight – Trained to Kill

"Born to fight, Trained to kill, Prepared to die, Never will, Keep low, Move fast, Kill first, Die last, One shot, One kill, No luck, Pure skill."

Special Agent Joe Bannon

THE 18 CHAMBERS

KILLER OF MEN

"Blessed be the LORD my Rock,
Who trains my hands for war, and my fingers for battle."

Psalm 144:1

THE 19TH CHAMBER

HEALER OF MEN

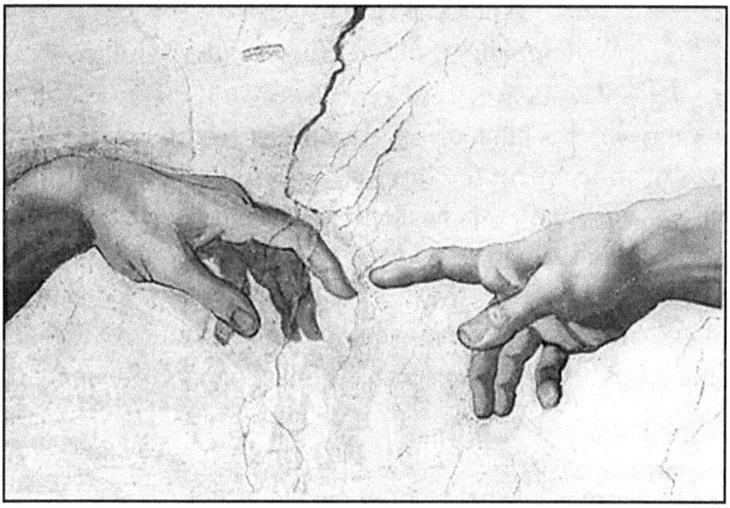

"By stretching out Your hand to heal, and that signs and wonders may be done through the name of Your Holy Servant Jesus."

Acts 4:30

The Hunting of Man

"There is no hunting like the hunting of man, and those of us who have hunted armed men long enough and have liked it; can do nothing else thereafter."

Ernest Hemmingway
Writer, Sailor, Soldier, Spy (1899 – 1961)

"As a man who has hunted armed men as a profession and has been hunted by armed men in return, I was convinced that, 'I could do nothing else thereafter' because *I liked it*. Hunting armed and dangerous men had become my primary predatory instinct. But God had greater plans for my life as a healer, as opposed to a hunter and killer by nature. Yes, we ***can*** do something else thereafter. God is not limited by the foolish or limited philosophies of man."

Joseph Bannon
Former Special Deputy United States Marshal
America's Most Wanted – Equal Justice Violent Fugitive Task Force

Declaration of Independence

"We hold these truths to be self-evident, that all men are created equal, that they are endowed by their Creator with certain unalienable rights, that among these are Life, Liberty, and the pursuit of Happiness."

Viewing this Declaration specifically from a mental, physical, and spiritual perspective, we can also extrapolate that the bodies, minds, and spirits of all men were also created equal by our Creator in their respective functions. This being the case, it would be accurate to state that all men are also 'equally' susceptible to physical and mental trauma, secret lifestyles, addictions, wounded emotions, and the like. The only difference would be the specific event that brings them about. Does the Post Traumatic Stress Disorder (*PTSD*) experienced by a soldier differ from that of a police officer? A sexually assaulted person? Child abuse? Or someone who has witnessed a horrific criminal act such as a mass shooting? Not necessarily. The end point is the same. We just acquire it from different events and life experiences. Unfortunately, we try to manage our pain and suffering by resorting to methods that can make our situations much worse. This is referred to as "self-medicating."

This book is written with a perspective relative to the warrior lifestyle. However, people from all walks of life will benefit from the spiritual lessons and encouragement found within it – as well as identifying the *hurts, habits, and hang-ups* that are common to all men and women. After all, each one of us was made in God's image and likeness living in a fallen world. This is the universal truth shared by all of humanity which is the great equalizer of us all.

May this book (*my testimony*) be an inspiration that gives you hope.

Table of Contents

Preface xiii
The Hidden Clause Within Our Oath of Service xvii
Dedication xxi
Acknowledgements xxiii
Disclaimer xxv
Introduction xxix
My Torn Canvas 1
Repainting My Torn Canvas 11
The Games People Play 19
The 18 Testing Chambers of the Shaolin Temple 25
My Personal 18 Chambers of the Temple of Life 31
Born Into Hell 35
Surviving My First Murder Contract 47
Body Slamming Through Macy's Plate Glass Door 51
Officer Down – Happy Birthday 61
Baptism by Sniper Fire 71
Legend of Mission Street 77
Saved by a Prostitute 83

Machete Man 89
Shooting a Brother Cop 97
Ordered to the Police Stress Unit.....................................103
San Francisco to San Juan...111
Living the Vida Loca...125
Back to Mission Street...147
The Drug Case That Ended My Police Career..........................169
DEA – Double Agent...181
Penetrating The Emerald Triangle.......................................189
The Resurrection of Lazarus...215
Taking my 'Mark of the Urn' of the Temple of Life.................239
Passing on my Sword of the 18th Chamber (1)..........................245
Passing on my Sword of the 18th Chamber (2)..........................251
Force on Force Range *("The Kill House")*..............................257
The Art of Hunting and Killing...263
T.R.I.A.D...275
The 19th Chamber of the Shaolin Temple...................................283
Midnight Confessions...315
Spiritual Warfare..329
Epilogue...341
Resources..349

Preface

"A Letter from a Police Officer"

"I have pulled dead, mangled bodies from cars. I have lied to people as they were dying. I said you are going to be fine as I held their hand and watched the life fade out. I have held dying babies. Bought lunch for homeless people who were mentally ill and hadn't eaten in a while. I have had people try to stab me and have fought with men trying to shoot me.

I've been attacked by women while I was arresting their husbands who had just severely beaten them. I have held towels on bullet wounds. I did CPR when I knew it wouldn't help just to make family members feel better.

I have torn down doors and fought inside of drug houses. Chased fugitives through the woods. I have been in high-speed car chases. Foot chases across an interstate during rush hour traffic.

I have been in crashes. Slowly squeezed the trigger about to kill a man when they came to their senses and surrendered. Waded through large angry crowds by myself. Drove like a madman to help a fellow officer who was outnumbered and screaming for help. Let little kids who don't have much, sit in my patrol car and pretend they are a cop for their birthday.

I have taken a lot of people to jail. Given many breaks. Prayed for people I didn't even know. Yes, and at times I have been "violent" when I had to be. I have been kind when I could. I admit I have driven to some dark place and cried by myself when I was overwhelmed. I have missed Christmas and other holidays more than I wanted to.

Every cop I know has done all these things and more for lousy pay, exhausting hours, and a short life expectancy. We don't want your pity; I don't even ask for your respect. Just let us do our jobs without killing us."

Thank You – Police Officers of America.

The author of this letter is unknown, but its words capture the essence of this book, as well as both my personal and professional life experience.

One element that the letter does not fully capture however, is the mental, physical, and spiritual toll that these experiences can have on the men and women who have chosen law enforcement, military, paramilitary, first responder, or similar vocations, as long-term professions as I had.

At least twenty-two military veterans commit suicide every day from PTSD (*Post Traumatic Stress Disorder*). Or "PTSd" (*lower case 'd'*) for those folks who do not wish to be stigmatized by the word "disorder." I articulate the later out of respect to those who choose to make this distinction.

Many law enforcement officers and other first responders take their own lives within five years after they have retired. Some of us tend to struggle with our post-retirement identity shift, the absence of psychological stimulation, feeling needed, and adrenaline withdrawal. In an attempt to offset this, some of us engage in self-destructive behavior such as alcoholism, workaholism, extra marital affairs, drug, sex, or pornography addiction, and the list goes on. My own personal list was quite extensive.

Then there are the toxic emotions that many of us swallow over the years such as our own unresolved trauma, child abuse, hatred, anger, vengeance, unforgiveness, inner secrets, low self-esteem, fear, feeling unappreciated, shame, regret, survivor's guilt after losing a partner in a gun battle, and many others. Many things not so foreign from the people that we deal with on a day-to-day basis.

The problem is that we bury these "emotional carcinogens" alive inside of us with no expiration date or automatic self-deleting program to dispose of them. Their roots grow deep within our soul and become part of our person until we learn how to get free from them. Until then, we just keep them suppressed, repressed, and or self-medicate ourselves the best ways that we know how. For me it was alcohol, sex, drugs, rock and roll, fatal attractions, adrenaline, and living life on the edge.

Based on our profession's high rates of suicide, addictions of all sorts, divorce, short life expectancy, and an infinite list of pre and post retirement degenerative diseases – I have to wonder if all of the emotional poison that we have swallowed over the years, compounded with adrenal gland burnout, could partially be the reason why?

My objective in writing this book is to show the *insides* of a soldier, a cop, a combat martial artist, and a first responder, that the public never sees behind our uniform or exterior persona. Our "personal lives" if you will; the parts that you don't normally see on television or in the movies. And yes, I have also included some high-speed police, military, and paramilitary war stories from my own, as well as other's very complex, violent, and intense careers. But these 'war stories' are not meant to be the 'headliners' of this book. Their inclusion is only to show the negative and destructive effects that they can have on us over time.

From the killing fields of the inner-city streets of New York, San Francisco, and Los Angeles; to the overseas Caribbean Islands and Jungles of the Colombian Drug Cartels – I share with you my testimony of how I transitioned from being a violent spirited-killer of men as a warrior, to a spirit-filled healer of men as a police chaplain, and doctoral professor of theocentric clinical psychology – and that there is life after combat, childhood traumas, addictions, loss of partners, and PTSD.

> *"Greater love has no one than this, than to lay down one's life for his friends"* (*'partners, missions, or people that they serve'* – added).
>
> **John 15:13**

The Hidden Clause Within Our Oath of Service

"I, Joseph F. Bannon, do solemnly swear that I will support and defend the Constitution of the United States against all enemies, foreign and domestic; that I will bear true faith and allegiance to the same; that I take this obligation freely, without any mental reservation or purpose of evasion; and that I will well and faithfully discharge the duties of the office on which I am about to enter. So help me God."

I have taken the above or similar oath six times under the badges and flags of six separate government agencies during my professional law enforcement, intelligence agent, and paramilitary special operations careers. Several of my brothers and sisters of the thin blue, green, white, and red line have done so as well. But the one thing I believe that we didn't consciously sign up for, was the onset of PTSD *and* how to deal with it. We were only told to, "Suck It Up Buttercup," or "Soldier The 'F' Up," while we destroyed ourselves by our attempts to quell our inner pain with our addictions of choice.

PTSD was just the "unwritten probability."

PTSD – "The Battle After The Battle"

Body, Mind, and Spirit

"Insights of a Police Chaplain"

I have earned college degrees in both health science and psychology with many research and continuing education units in between. The more I studied the physical and mental sciences, the more I learned that there was a missing aspect in the approach to the healing of addictions, wounded emotions, child abuse, PTSD, and the like. That would be the Holistic, Spiritual, and Faith-Based Aspect.

Senior Police Chaplain Joseph F. Bannon, Ph.D.

Local, State, and Federal Government Service (1975 – 2005)

Dedication

This book is dedicated to Military Combat Veterans, Law Enforcement Officers, First Responders, Government Special Operators, Mortal Combatants, Paramilitary Contractors, and Protective Agents, both foreign and domestic. The world is a better and safer place because of your sacrifice and service. Some of you sacrificed your minds to PTSD. Some of you sacrificed your physical bodies to dismemberment and brokenness. Many of you gave it all. **Thank you is not enough!**

Acknowledgements

There are several people, agencies, and institutions that I must honor and gratefully acknowledge before I go any further. Had it not been for them, I most assuredly would not be here today. Each one of these people, agencies, and institutions has added a part of themselves to my soul and skill level that makes me who I am today.

To God Almighty who has saved my life and my sanity on numerous occasions despite my high level of "kill-skill," and for "teaching my hands to war and my fingers to fight." **Psalm 144 verse 1.**

To the government agencies that I have served with, been attached to, have personally trained, and was trained by, in the overt and covert arts of Mortal Combat, Executive Protection, Undercover and Special Operations, while perfecting the art of being a Covert Intelligence Operative and "Gray Man."

To all branches of the United States Military and other foreign military, protection, narcotic enforcement, law enforcement, paramilitary, and ABC intelligence agencies that I have had the extreme honor to be a part of.

To all of my drill instructors, academy and field training officers, handlers, and college professors, whom I despised at the time. But when I was under hostile enemy gunfire, or fighting for my life, I could hear your voices screaming at me inside my head. Your prior words and training helped me to make the correct tactical choices for the battle at hand, which led to my survival, as well as the survival of my team and partners. Please don't teach this current generation to be politically correct or woke "paper tigers." Stay brutal and real, because being weak and politically correct will get them killed.

Thank You All

Disclaimer

The title of this book, "Killer of Men to Healer of Men" is not solely referring to the "*act*" of physical killing, although there is sufficient reference to that. It also speaks to the protraction of the lethal mindset, the lifestyle, the preparation, the vows, the memories, the emotions, the training, the tribalism, the passion for, as well as the study and teaching of the art of killing – and the emotional toll that this can have on us long after the war or necessary mindset has ended. "The battle after the battle."

We can kill in our hearts and never pull a trigger. It can become an attitude, a desire, a drive, a vengeance, a regret, anger, unforgiveness, or an intrusive bitter memory that has the potential to pervade every area of our lives. There is the justifiable external killing of another. But there is also the internal killing of ourselves by the short fuse of suicide, as well as the long fuse of holding on to negative emotions over time. Both fuses are lethal. These two fuses burn at different speeds but lead to the same explosive.

I am not an allopathic medical doctor. Nor is this book intended to diagnose, prevent, treat, or ameliorate any physical, psychological, emotional, or mental disorder. Please consult a licensed medical professional before implementing any of the information that I present and share within the pages of this book. Some of my statements are based on my opinion and findings as they relate to my more than forty years of education, research, self-care, and relative life experience regarding these subject matters.

This book is not meant to be a discourse or solution for PTSD or other related psychological challenges. It is a testimony to the power of God who shows up even in the middle of mortal combat. He certainly has for me and several others that I know. This writing is a call to conscience, and to challenge the already seasoned warrior, clergy, or layperson to rise to a higher spiritual level internally, as opposed to solely training and excelling in our physical and external realms. This is probably one of the greatest challenges to anyone. Even to a higher tenet than the Samurai Code of the Bushido, a Religion, or the Military Code of Conduct. I talk about the inner battlefield of a warrior, not only the outside physical terrain and related tactics and weaponry. I taught and lived by the Samurai Code of the Bushido for many years. But The Bushido, although respectfully altruistic, didn't offer me the greater and ultimate challenge that I encountered within "*The 19th Chamber*." The chamber that challenges us to face our inward selves that hide behind our outward achievements, status, and accolades.

Certain events in this book are not necessarily written in the chronological order as they have occurred. This is due to the multiple complexities and overlapping timeframes of those events. Not all chapters have a smooth transition between them, as some of them were meant to stand alone. I have also speeded up certain time-lapses of some events to simplify the information for the reader, while maintaining the factual integrity of each chapter at the same time.

I did change or omit the names of some people, classified operations, locations, and government agencies to keep them unidentifiable and safe. As well as keeping me and my family safe. The following information is a compilation of different but relevant subject matter, and violent personal war stories that have opened the gates of hell, addiction, self-medication, suicide, PTSD, adrenal burnout, and emotional pain for many of us.

Throughout this book, I will be sharing several opinions, philosophies, and Biblical scriptures that I felt were relative to the context. If you read something that you disagree with or don't feel ready to engage, that is perfectly fine. Just pass over it and keep reading. Take only what works or resonates with you and leave the rest. This book is my personal testimony, not a philosophical indoctrination.

> *"Absorb what is useful; Discard what is not; Add what is uniquely your own."*
>
> **Bruce Lee**
> (1940 – 1973)

Introduction

"God is Dead" – Nietzsche / *"Nietzsche is Dead"* – God

New York City 1963.

I was standing on the Jamaica train station platform in New York City waiting to board the train to Penn Station in Manhattan so that I could catch an underground subway to 23rd Street. It was winter and the temperature was below freezing. Jamaica was known for its very high crime rate and racial segregation tensions at the time. I had witnessed stabbings, robberies, and gang fights on more than one occasion. I not only had to be aware of criminals, but also the speeding trains and the slippery ice beneath my feet on the narrow cement waiting platform. One slip and a speeding train would eat you for breakfast.

One day while waiting for the train in Jamaica, I watched as a New York City Police car sped by on the street below with its lights flashing and siren wailing. I thought how exciting it must be to be a police officer. I whispered under my breath, "God, if it only be possible for me to become a cop someday." I believe that was the day that a seed was planted in me to become a police officer one day when I got older. But I had a long and hard road ahead of me before that would ever happen.

I was a young Catholic boy who had grown up riding New York City Trains and Subways to get in and out of Manhattan my entire child and young adulthood. Every subway car was completely covered with graffiti from spray paint and magic markers. It was just accepted as part of the 'artistic décor' of the very talented but misdirected youth of the inner city.

I weaved my body through many situations and all kinds of people from pickpockets, prostitutes, gang members, and winos; to armed robberies and purse snatches. I was always taught never to look anyone in the eye and to mind my own business. That was the safest way to survive a subway ride back in the day, "See nothing – Say nothing." But one thing that stuck in my mind, even to this day, was the aforementioned quote spray painted as graffiti on a subway wall: *"God is Dead" – Nietzsche, "Nietzsche is Dead"* – God.

I asked my father who Nietzsche was. He told me that he was a philosopher who held a certain amount of ambiguity towards religion. I couldn't understand that because I had grown up to believe in God while attending Catholic Catechism Training since elementary school. I thought it was kind of cool though that God had the last say by the closing words painted on the subway wall: *"Nietzsche is Dead"* – God.

I had no clue at the time that my simplistic childhood faith would eventually lead me to a seminary college, and ultimately, to become a police chaplain and theocentric clinical psychologist who specialized in addictive behavior and PTSD. But many "counter-culture events" had taken place in my life between the writing on that subway wall and the writing of this book.

Also, in the same year on November 22nd, President John F. Kennedy had been assassinated in Dallas, Texas by who knows who at this point? I watched the assassination play out repeatedly on our old black and white television. I found the job of a secret service agent fascinating when I saw one jumping onto the back of Kennedy's presidential limousine after the gunshot. "But why would someone be willing to take a bullet for the president?" I thought to myself. As fate would have it, that question was answered thirty years later when I stood next to the President of the United States myself, while assigned to his close quarter protection detail.

But well before I had been assigned to protect the president, I spent most of my childhood protecting my mother from her violent, alcoholic, Vietnam Veteran boyfriend who suffered with PTSD. When he was sober, he was a fun guy to be around. When he was drunk, he would attempt to kill my mother by strangling her inside of our small one-bedroom apartment. I tried to pull him off her to save her life, but he was too strong and wouldn't budge. I had no other choice but to grab a kitchen knife to stab him or smash him over the head with a glass flower vase. It was at this point in my life that I had become infatuated with various weapons and methods to kill him the next time he did this to her. I believe it was here that I had gotten in touch with both my protective and killer instincts. Instincts that kept evolving over time to the point that I had made a legitimate profession out of them. Long story short, I had become "the man" of our home by age eleven after my parents had gotten divorced. My role early in life was never that of a child, but that of a protector. A role that I did not choose but was thrust into by necessity.

I began to write this book in 1976 after I had gotten sober from alcohol and drugs. I wanted to share my strength, hope, and experience with others who struggled with similar addictions. I had gotten completely set free from alcohol and drugs in a Christian church service at age nineteen. This church service came just in time, because only a few days earlier, I had been sitting on the edge of my bed contemplating putting an end to it all. My entire life at this point in time made about as much sense to me as the following Picasso Painting…

"My Torn Canvas"

"Every act of creation begins with an act of destruction. For one to be truly creative, they must destroy their old knowledge and build on a new plane."

Pablo Picasso
Painter, Sculptor, Artist (1881 – 1973)

I was born into a life of absolute violent destruction and chaos all around me, only to eventually become a new creation through it all. If my earlier life was a Picasso Painting, it would have resembled a torn piece of canvas with unintelligible graffiti painted all over it, lacking any type of framework. It took many painful years for the Master Painter of the universe to restore me from the devastation of fighting, killing, teaching the art of killing as a profession, PTSD, multiple addictions, child abuse, violence, sexual identity confusion, and many other painful, negative life experiences.

Despite a severely abusive childhood filled with alcohol, drugs, violence, and 'other' violations; I had nevertheless become a sworn public official and district attorney investigator in New York for a couple of years back in the late 1970s and early 80s. Prior to that, I had been a store detective in one of the highest crime, and most dangerous areas in New York City – by myself, as a lone wolf. And over the course of many years to follow, I had become addicted to danger, high-risk missions, and fatal attractions. More about my New York Law Enforcement position and the several murder contracts that I had survived within the pages to follow.

I had also been a volunteer fireman between the ages of eighteen and twenty in the mid-1970s in a three-hundred-man fire department in New York – Badge Number 753. During this time, I had been inside many burning buildings and had seen many dead bodies. As a fireman or paramedic, you never forget the sight and smell of a fire charred body or a body that had been dead for more than a week. My severe alcoholism at the time had almost gotten me terminated from this job that I really loved. Fighting fires or carrying a critically injured body on a gurney while being intoxicated was not the smartest nor safest thing to do. The Board of Fire Commissioners didn't think it was too smart either. They relieved me of duty for ninety days so that I could check myself into an alcoholic rehabilitation center in New Jersey.

Based on how I had grown up, I had become very knowledgeable of the 'ways of the world' well before I had reached my twentieth birthday. A birthday, that many people predicted that I would be dead before I ever got the chance to celebrate. But despite their predictions of my demise, I made it past my twentieth birthday, and only because of the goodness of God, His perfect timing, and caring people who had intervened in my out-of-control and destructive lifestyle. A lifestyle of pre-teenage alcoholism, sniffing glue, taking prescription drugs, and becoming the epitome of a juvenile delinquent by the age of fourteen. Being the leader of a violent New York street gang was not necessarily the greatest reference to put on a job application either. I didn't like cops, although deep down inside I wanted to be one – a bit of a conflict I would say.

I was involved in numbers running and off-track horse race bookmaking rackets for a group of "New York Italian Men" as a very young teen. On any given day, I was either in the back room of a coffee shop taking horse bets over the phone, running numbers, or working at an illegal underground gambling operation in the back room of a funeral parlor. Dead bodies in caskets, flowers, and people crying in the front room; roulette wheels, slot machines, and card tables with people celebrating and cursing in Italian in the back room. I became friendly with the infamous "Teflon Don" John Gotti – who later became boss of the Gambino Crime Family. He referred to me as "Little Joey" and always tapped a twenty-dollar bill into my shirt pocket whenever he saw me. These and other activities got me expelled from public school and put in a military reform school at age fourteen, jail at sixteen, and again at eighteen. Not a very bright future to say the least. And not exactly the virtues that law enforcement agencies were looking for in their applicants either.

The fact that I eventually got into a very successful law enforcement career was a miracle in and of itself. But before my successful career, I was headed down a path in life that would have had a horrible ending if not intercepted by Divine Providence working through people who saw a spark of hope in me.

I had become the youngest member of Alcoholics Anonymous in my area at age sixteen and had been through a lifetime of family counseling. Despite all my secular, medical, and psychological attempts to unscrew myself, nothing had worked. I had even been put on tranquilizers in the fourth grade to try and stop my acting out in class. Some kids became the "teacher's pet." I had become every teacher's "worst nightmare." The truth was that I had been drinking alcoholically by age eleven and was thrown out of an alcohol rehabilitation center in New Jersey at age nineteen, as a "hopeless case." The director of the facility said that I was "the angriest young man that she had ever seen." This "title" was my only claim to fame at the time which I took a twisted form of pride in.

One day shortly after my banishment from the alcohol rehab center, I was sitting on the end of my bed with a bottle of whiskey in one hand, and a 38-caliber revolver in the other. I was contemplating which one of these two options to use first. Then in a twist of fate, God showed up again through an ex-girlfriend of mine and offered me another choice – *a third option.*

She invited me to a very different kind of church other than the Catholic Church that I had grown up in. But I said to myself, "If this doesn't work and I don't find an answer here, I'm done. I will just go back to the end of my bed and figure it out from there." But at this church service I was told that:

> *"For God so loved the world that He gave His only begotten Son, that whoever believes in Him should not perish but have everlasting life."*
>
> **John 3:16**

I accepted God's offer (*the third option*) at an altar call for salvation in this Christian Church. I received Jesus Christ as my Lord and Savior and after being prayed for, my life was never to be the same. The craving for alcohol and prescription drugs was immediately removed from me. I no longer felt that intense anger inside of me either. I wasn't just "surviving" anymore but felt hope and purpose for the first time in my life. It was a true miracle.

Unfortunately, this 'true miracle' experience had only lasted for the next two years until I allowed the attractions, sensualities, and glitter of the world to pull me back into their grip. I had again stepped through the tempting door of the devil's world just to take a peek inside. The lustful allurements of New York City, Miami, Los Angeles, San Francisco, Las Vegas, and other "sin cities" of the world had me mesmerized. I walked out of that same door of the devil's world forty years later, lucky to be alive. That "peek inside" almost cost me everything. The devil had taken me farther than I intended to go and kept me much longer than I wanted to stay.

I never drank alcohol again nor fully turned my back on God, but at the very best, I had become a lukewarm Christian with one foot in God's World, and the other foot in the lusts, pleasures, and achievements of the material world. I was serving two masters: both God *and* the golden calf. As the Bible states in Revelation 2:4, "I had lost or at the very least, compromised my first love." Nevertheless, despite achieving many very successful accomplishments in my life, I spent the next forty years trying to find my true self and purpose in the world. I remained in this half-committed condition for four decades until I finally "got right" with my Creator. My trial-and-error-based search had failed. I had only been brought to my knees again and again, asking the same God that I had given my life to at age nineteen for help – but only on my terms and conditions, not His. This became a relentless and repetitive cycle. My greatest driving forces during this time were to seek pleasure, avoid pain, attempt to love, and to be loved. In other words, I pursued anything that made me feel good inside whether it complied with the Ten Commandments or not. My flesh had become stronger than my faith.

But during my forty-year "wilderness experience," God never left me nor turned His back on me. He blessed and spared me continuously, despite my strong self-will, rebellion, and contempt for this fallen world and a severely screwed-up childhood. A fallen world and screwed-up childhood that I eventually began to blame God for. I even blamed Him when my heroin-addicted grandmother blew her head off with a shotgun after being released from an insane asylum when I was six years old. It was around this age that I had developed my first of many bouts with PTSD and mis-directedly developed a bitterness and resentment towards any concept of God. The fact that I was sexually violated as a small child didn't help much either with my ability to trust in God's so-called proverbial – 'hand of protection.'

"God, where the 'F' were you when I needed you and was too young to defend myself?" was my bitter daily mantra.

I became extremely angry and resentful towards God. I struggled with this ambivalent 'love-hate' relationship with God for most of my life. One day I prayed to Him, the next day I cursed Him.

> *"O Lord, though our iniquities testify against us, Do it for Your name's sake; For our backslidings are many, We have sinned against You."*
>
> **Jeremiah 14:7**

"Fast Forward 1982" – After narrowly escaping a murder contract on my life as a public official and living under police protection. I relocated to California from New York City and became a police officer in San Francisco. Fallen partners, both by battle, suicide, cancer, alcoholism, heart attacks, and AIDS. I had lost more than one hundred personal friends to AIDS at the time, while seeing people at their absolute worst on a daily basis. Riots, anti-police protests, and violent, full-on hand-to-hand street combat. Being shot at with both bullets and hateful words. Seeing some of the most God-awful, twisted crap that the human mind struggles to comprehend – I began racking up a few more cumulative PTSD points. But I remained very functional and in control psychologically. I had developed an incredibly strong spirit to survive and succeed against all odds. It must have been a God thing despite my ambivalence towards Him.

Although I hold doctorate degrees in both healing of the body and healing of the mind – for the sake of this book, I chose to put on my chaplain collar and focus more on the spiritual aspects of healing. Helping others to come out of the clutches of PTSD, its co-related addictions, and wounded emotions. Or at least point them in the same direction where I had found my own hope and healing.

But many years after graduating from college as a "healer," a diametric shift had taken place in my mind and practice. My life's research, passion, and work were now to teach the world's finest military warriors the art of Mortal Combat; making them efficient killing machines to destroy the mind and flesh of their enemies in a ruthless and brutal manner. I used my knowledge as a "healer" to enhance my teaching and training skills as a "killer." Today, I certainly have no regrets about that because unfortunately, war and its preparative training are necessary for the world that we live in.

It took several long and hard years, but I had finally become that "new creation," as Picasso's quote states. I eventually began to pursue the path of a spiritual warrior and healer of men, as opposed to solely a physical warrior and killer of men. Yes, some men only understand and respond to violence, I get that. But Chinese Military Strategist Sun Tzu stated in his writing, '*The Art of War*' that, "It is superior to achieve an objective without destroying it." Abraham Lincoln said, "The best way to destroy an enemy is to make him your friend." Ecclesiastes 9:18 articulates that, "Wisdom is better than weapons of war." In essence, these 'wisdoms' would make a former enemy an ally, thus strengthening our own forces. Even if only gathering intelligence information from them to better understand our enemy's strengths and weaknesses. So, it seems to me that if we can convert a man to a new understanding and way of thinking, that would probably be a superior tactic than just destroying him as an adversary. Unless of course he is an immediate threat and refuses to stand down and surrender his adversarial posture.

I believe Jesus also contributed to this concept in Matthew 4:19 – "*Follow Me, and I will make you fishers of men.*"

Yes – war, teaching war tactics, and training men and women to rise to the occasion of mortal combat both physically and mentally are necessary skillsets. Especially in an evil world where we have inherent enemies that want to do us harm and take away our God given freedoms. But no longer for me. I am now a retired veteran of that necessary dark world. I have been led back to the healing arts to help those who have been negatively affected by life's battles – whether they be from a war in a foreign land, on a city street, or from the clutches of self-destructive addictions. My mission now is to teach and help men and women how to overcome the battles within their minds. As a universally understood concept within the military circles, "*We never leave a buddy behind.*" I say, we don't leave them behind mentally either.

I surmise that after all my years of maintaining a lifestyle of violence and mortal combat, I had a similar 'epiphany' or 'mindset shift' like the Apostle Paul had during his 'Road to Damascus' experience. His epiphany however, took place only after Jesus had a chat with him through a blinding light. He eventually became a fisher of men as opposed to a hunter and persecutor of Christians. I believe I had my own personal "blinding light experience" within The 19th Chamber which was my final turning point back to God after forty years of compromise.

But up until that time of enlightenment, or in my case, "re-enlightenment." It took many more years before I would be ready to trade my killer's heart and machine gun in for a fishing pole to become a 'fisher of men' as Jesus spoke of. I guess there is a time and place for everything.

> *"To everything there is a season, A time for every purpose under heaven: A time to be born, And a time to die; A time to plant, And a time to pluck what is planted;* ***A time to kill, And a time to heal;*** *A time to break down, And a time to build up; A time to weep, And a time to laugh; A time to mourn, And a time to dance; A time to cast away stones, And a time to gather stones; A time to embrace, And a time to refrain from embracing; A time to gain, And a time to lose; A time to keep, And a time to throw away; A time to tear, And a time to sew; A time to keep silence, And a time to speak; A time to love, And a time to hate;* ***A time of war, And a time of peace."***
>
> **Ecclesiastes 3:1-8**

"Repainting My Torn Canvas"

"Therefore, if anyone is in Christ, he is a new creation; old things have passed away; behold, all things have become new."

2 Corinthians 5:17

The Apostle Paul
(55 AD)

I'm sure you have gathered by now that my life has been a spiritually "on again – off again," lukewarm series of compromising experiences. But somewhere within God's Grace and Mercy, He decided to consistently have my back and allow me to accomplish many great things despite my half-hearted inconsistencies as a so-called Christian man.

Following is a general overview and prelude to '*eighteen*' of my personal life stories and what God can do with a broken life when we even "half-heartedly" give Him the opportunity to "repaint" our torn canvases. The chapters that follow will expound upon this basic overview in much greater detail.

I have been in both the "physical trenches" of mortal combat as well as the "mental trenches" of PTSD. They both suck.

Unfortunately, the mental trench of PTSD can last significantly longer than the trench of a physical battlefield. PTSD is a mental, physical, and spiritual extension of a physical battle or trauma long after the physical battle or initial trauma has ended. According to many experts in the field of PTSD, a "moral injury" is the psychological, behavioral, social, and spiritual fallout following a traumatic event. Thus, the spiritual aspect of PTSD.

As a warrior, a first responder, a paramilitary officer, and intelligence agent, I have held many positions within the local, state, and federal governments as well as privatized military contractor organizations. These positions had all become part of my restored canvas and "new creation" as described by both Picasso and The Apostle Paul.

Despite all odds against me, I graduated from the San Francisco Police Academy. I earned the rating of "Top Gun" on the Police Counter Sniper Team tryouts and got into more violent street fights than I can possibly remember; some to the threshold of death – both mine and theirs. But by the grace of God, I had lived to fight another day in the police octagon. Riots, violent protests, taking sniper fire, watching my brothers and sisters take their own lives, and witnessing my former police partner die in the middle of a city street from being shot in the head by a deranged gunman. Yes, becoming a police officer was definitely a dream come true for me and part of my "new creation." But this "dream," did have its fair share of nightmares woven within it.

I went on to being assigned as an undercover narcotics sergeant, and violent gang enforcement specialist. The "Streets of San Francisco" had become my daily urban war zone. Yet I loved it – excluding the death of my ex-partner and similar events that followed.

I eventually became disheartened arresting people on the streets with nickel and dime bindles of cocaine folded inside of torn out pages from a magazine. This wasn't even making a dent in the city's major drug problem. I wanted to attack the problem at its source – Colombia, South America.

Between my desire to make a greater difference in the world, and my allurement to fatal attractions, I left the San Francisco Police Department and accepted a position as a narcotics agent and consultant to Interpol in the Caribbean / South American Theater of Operation. This was during the height of "Operation Snowcap" which was run by the DEA, the Military, and "other" Agencies.

In addition to beautiful beaches, great food, and hot Latin women, I experienced local police corruption, more death threats and murder contracts, as well as more armed confrontations. I had personally witnessed or had been graphically briefed on the most egregious forms of human torture imaginable by the Colombian Drug Cartels. Men being hung by the neck. People's bodies being carved and dismembered with a knife or machete while still alive. Narcotics agents who were ambushed and assassinated. Colombian Neck Ties (*slitting of the throat and pulling out the tongue making it appear like a necktie*), and of course, more PTSD. I struggle to get those sights and sounds out of my head. I barely made it back to the United States Mainland alive.

When I returned to the San Francisco Police Department after two years, my personal vehicle was assaulted by gunfire. I didn't know if this was a "welcome back" or a "good riddance" message to me from someone who I had apparently pissed off. Just one of the job's perks, I guess. But I was still living my dream and new creation as a police officer.

There are many more incidents that continued to fill my emotional PTSD ass bag, and I will get into more detail about them in the following chapters.

Over the course of the years to follow, I had been sworn into the United States Department of Justice – Drug Enforcement Administration (*DEA*). Repelling out of helicopters, low crawling in rattlesnake-infested wilderness, as well as snipers, booby traps, wild animals, and raiding organized crime and drug syndicate locations high up in the mountains within the infamous "Emerald Triangle" had become my new "nine to five."

Further down the road, I had been deputized as a Special Deputy United States Marshal on "America's Most Wanted" Violent Fugitive Apprehension Team. I was assigned to the FBI Witness Protection and Relocation Program, and the United States Secret Service – Presidential Protection and Protective Intelligence Details as a task force agent. During this time, I have had the honor of protecting three United States Presidents and First Ladies, Congressmen, Senators, Governors, Mayors, Attorney Generals, Foreign Dignitaries, and Heads of State, as well as several members of the Royal Families from around the world.

I was assigned to Pope John Paul II's protection detail during his visit to San Francisco in 1987. He held my arm as I assisted him down the stairs of his 'Pope Mobile' before he walked inside of Mission Dolores Church for a special ceremony. He put his hand on my right shoulder and smiled at me as he said, "thank you." Every Catholic that I knew wanted to touch my right shoulder after that. Pretty amazing for a former juvenile delinquent whose primary role in life was protecting his mother. I had come a long way since JFK's assassination in 1963, but then again – with God and hard work, all things are possible. Even as an "imperfect" Christian.

In 1996, I had become the lead undercover case agent on one of the most politically charged narcotics cases in the history of California. "Medical Marijuana" and the "large cash profit" of the organized crime syndicate behind it. I essentially was operating as a double agent behind the backs of the mayor, district attorney, and other elected officials within the political machine of San Francisco. I had become a lone operator working between two separate agencies that both had different agendas. I carried my DEA Badge in my left pants pocket, and my San Francisco Police Badge in my right, with my butt stuck somewhere in between the two. This case cost me my police sergeant stripes and any future advancement within the San Francisco Police Department. This drug case went all the way up to the Clinton White House where it was politically squashed. I became the scapegoat target of the fake news, politicians, and the pro-marijuana community. And yes, more death threats against me by members of the drug cartel. But my dream and new creation continued.

> *"But as for you, you meant evil against me; but God meant it for good, in order to bring it about as it is this day, to save many people alive."*
>
> **Genesis 50:20**

As a result of doing the ethically right thing in a politically wrong arena. I was personally offered a position as a special agent by California State Attorney General Dan Lungren and Bureau Chief Joe Doane with the Department of Justice – Bureau of Narcotic Enforcement, which was formerly led by the now – Vice President Kamala Harris.

Seeing that my career in San Francisco was basically over. I accepted the position, went through the academy at Beale Air Force Base, and relocated to Los Angeles to start my law enforcement profession all over again. In addition to being a state narcotics agent and VSU (*SWAT Team*) member. I was appointed Tactical Commander and Counter Assault Team Commander of a team of fifty-five special agents and sheriffs assigned to the Attorney General's Protection Detail during the Democratic National Convention in 2000.

After the 2001 attack on the World Trade Center in New York, I was reassigned to the Attorney General's Criminal Intelligence Bureau – Anti Terrorist Unit (*CIB*), in concert with the FBI Joint Terrorism Task Force (*JTTF*). Penetrating suspected terrorist organizations as an undercover intelligence operative (*spy*), surveillances for days on end, and going through suspected terrorist's garbage cans at four o'clock in the morning looking for phone numbers or any evidence of an attack plan, had become my new mission. I also had the opportunity to interrogate a top military general under the president of a Middle Eastern country. It was this agency that I retired from in 2005 after sustaining a permanent injury from jumping out of a helicopter.

I am currently a board-certified police chaplain who has dedicated his life to helping soldiers, law enforcement officers, and other first responders with issues of PTSD and co-addictions. I am licensed and ordained as a theocentric healer and clinical psychologist by the Commission on Religious Counseling and Healing.

I believe my most valuable credential comes from thirty years of "boots on the ground," under the flag of several local, state, and federal government intelligence, and law enforcement agencies. I am a retired mortal combatant who had more than his fair share of both childhood and professionally acquired Post Traumatic Stress Disorder.

In this book I present to you, what it is like to be a killer, a healer, and a minister, all in one person. The good, the bad, and the ugly of it all. God had certainly taken my destruction and turned it into a new creation. It was a very slow and challenging process, but it was all worth it.

I guess He really did hear my prayer on that Jamaica, New York City train station platform back in 1963 – and He had given me one hundred times more than I had ever asked Him for; good, bad, and ugly. But in the end, it was 'all good' nevertheless.

> "*Now to Him who is able to do exceedingly abundantly above all that we ask or think, according to the power that works in us, to Him be glory in the church by Christ Jesus to all generations, forever and ever. Amen.*"
>
> **Ephesians 3:20-21**

My New Canvas Painted by God

"*Yea, though I walk through the valley of the shadow of death, I will fear no evil; for You are with me; Your rod and Your staff, they comfort me.*"

Psalm 23:4

The Games People Play

"Our Inner Secrets and Emotional Wounds"

Everybody to some degree has inner secrets and emotional wounds. Some of us share them with only one other person in our life that we trust. Some of us take them to the grave. Some of them put us into an early grave.

As a police chaplain, I attended a men's Bible study one night at my church. I conducted an experiment and made an interesting observation. As we read scripture passages and went around the room and shared our personal perspectives, all the men praised God and exalted His wonderous virtues, and rightfully so. But when it became my turn to share, I presented the things that I was angry with God about such as child sex trafficking, war, combat PTSD, world hunger, and my own abuse as a child. There was suddenly a dead silence in the room. Then it got real.

These same men who were hiding their true feelings and taking cover behind their praises to God, suddenly got honest and began to share their own angst and struggles with their faith in God. The Bible study leader had to get the group to refocus and tune down their hostilities. I apologized to the group leader for doing this, but I saw that it was something that needed to be done to make a point. Sometimes we need to see behind the poker faces, the masks, and the outer "Glory be to God" facades of bullcrap if we really care about a person… Strong love!

There is absolutely no judgement nor condemnation in my writing, and if there ever is a perception of that, it is me exposing my own secrets and personal healing journey over many years from PTSD, violent anger, addictions, and other self-destructive behaviors. Oh, and yes, I served my country, my state, my city, and my church, but none of these so-called "honorable acts" insulated me from physical, mental, and spiritual trauma. Where was God's so-called hand of protection on my life as stated in "Psalm 91" when I was injured in the line of duty? Where was He when I was sexually violated and beaten as a child? Thrown through a plate glass door and almost bled to death? Survived three murder contracts on my life, and many other equally awesome events?

Well, the fact that I am still alive and somewhat sane today writing this book is proof of His intervention in my life. Maybe not the way I would have wanted Him to do it, but nevertheless – He was there through it all.

In the world of emotional survival, there is something called the "I got this" and the "I'm fine" syndrome. This usually presents itself after seeing or experiencing such things as dead babies, unexpectedly losing a loved one, being diagnosed with a terminal illness, seeing your military battle buddy blown up by an improvised explosive device, dealing with PTSD, or watching your police partner die in front of you from a gunshot wound to his head – while ultimately leaving his wife and children behind to fend for themselves. Events like these rarely leave us feeling "fine." It's more like, '*Whiskey Tango Foxtrot*' What The 'F' God? Are you too busy to give a crap about the people down here that have to clean up your mess of a fallen world that YOU created? You call yourself a God of love; REALLY? I have not only heard this from others on countless occasions, but I have shouted it from the rooftops myself.

As a law enforcement officer for several years, I don't believe there is much that I haven't seen nor personally experienced in my own life. I used to find it amusing watching hard-core bikers, gang bangers, varsity male athletes, priests, cops, firemen, supreme court judges, and military officers, sneak into a gay nightclub, a sex club, a pot club, an opium den, or a swinger's party when they thought that nobody saw them. Nowadays it's much more accepted, but several years ago it was considered a taboo "act of moral turpitude" that had to remain a deep dark secret or there could be hell to pay and much to lose. It all reminds me of a song by The Spinners, "Games People Play." And to varying degrees, don't we all?

Then there were the feminine and beautiful female bank tellers that looked like J-Lo during the day, but dressed like Jay-Z at night, and acted more masculine than many other men (*no disrespect – just an observation*). And how about the City Councilman who was held in high esteem for being the model husband and father within his community who got arrested for paying a transvestite prostitute for sex while driving drunk on Santa Monica Boulevard in Los Angeles at two o'clock in the morning? Or the man, woman, or even pastor of a church who acts out their wild "after hour" fetishes while hiding them from the public eye to protect their stellar reputations? The politician or Hollywood actor who visited Epstein Island a few times on the down low? The comedian at work who makes everybody laugh at the office during the day, but cries himself to sleep at night all alone with a bottle of whiskey? The noble first responder who works hard by risking his or her life to serve the public in the name of God, but cheats on their spouse by having affairs and going to strip clubs or massage parlors to relieve their job stress? Or? – Fill in your own blanks. I've seen it all.

Bottom line? Many of us just have that deeply hidden proverbial "freak side" or "alter ego" within us. I sure did. Again, no judgement intended. Many see it as the inherent human need to seek pleasure and avoid pain. I get it because I did it within my own life and profession for many years. I guess I had my own freak side and alter ego that I leaned towards to deal with my own inner pain and secrets.

"Freak Side" is defined by Oxford as basically 'very odd, strange, or eccentric.' "Alter Ego" is defined by Webster as 'a second self or different version of oneself.' The Bible refers to some of these aspects of our personalities and behavior as our "sin" or "carnal nature."

Sin means missing God's mark or His best for us. But God continues to love us through it all. He knows why we do what we do and never stops trying to help us. This is why we are instructed not to judge people. Only God completely knows the depth of a person's back story and "inner self." We are called to love all people, but not necessarily to accept their behavior, life choices, or thought processes, despite the modern political climate relative to certain matters. Nevertheless, God loves everyone the same.

After reading the following pages of this book and learning about my borderline insane life of "kill or be killed," and seeing how God patiently loved me through it all and miraculously saved me from the jaws of death, murder, and addictions on countless occasions. It is my hope that you would come to your own conclusion that if God loved and saved this 'minister of death' (*me*) with all my sins, faults, 'freak sides,' character defects, and riotous living – He will certainly do the same for you because, "God is no respecter of persons. What He does for one, He will do for another."

> *"But the LORD said to Samuel, "Do not look at his appearance or at his physical stature, because I have refused him. For the LORD does not see as man sees; for man looks at the outward appearance, but the LORD looks at the heart."*
>
> **1 Samuel 16:7**

God looks at our insides not our outsides, and He understands what He sees and where it came from. But at some point, He expected me to eventually deal with and give up, '*the junk in my emotional trunk.*'

The 18 Testing Chambers of the Shaolin Temple

"Fact or Fiction?"

I have been an avid student of the martial arts ever since I was five years old. I began my training with my father who was the chief combat instructor within his division of the United States Army during World War Two. He taught me many techniques that had their origins in the Japanese and Okinawan fighting styles. We even watched martial arts TV shows together every Saturday night. Studying martial arts offered me a sense of much-needed stability in my life at the time.

When Bruce Lee and the Chinese fighting art of Kung Fu became popular back in the late '60s and early 70s, I became so intrigued that I eventually followed that path. One day many years later, I was accepted as a disciple into a Chinese Taoist Kung Fu Temple, and during the following twenty-one years to come, I had progressed to become a lead senior instructor of the temple. Over the course of these twenty-one years, I had been put through many brutal tests and challenges to become proficient in this fighting art. Being a disciple and teacher at this temple was yet another incredible life experience.

Many martial artists have heard of the Legendary, "18 Chambers" of the ancient Shaolin Temple. This is where the student monk finally gets to prove his combative skills and tenacity by systematically entering eighteen separate chambers of testing.

One of the best modern depictions of this "legend" was probably the 1970s TV series, "Kung Fu" starring David Carradine as "Kwai Chang Caine" – a Shaolin Monk who traveled through the Old West as a peaceful man but could pull out a can of whoop ass in a nanosecond to dispense justice where needed.

The first chamber of the temple was difficult, probably by having to fight one or two formidable opponents. By the time the student warrior monk progressed to the seventeenth chamber, it is said he had to survive and defeat the hardest challenges he ever had to come up against in his life. To make it to the 18th chamber, the monk had to successfully survive the extreme challenges of the first seventeen chambers. I'm sure many of us can relate to this experience in one form or another within our lives by dealing with our own personal "18 Testing Chambers of Life." Military, Law Enforcement, First Responders, or just Life in General.

'IF' the student monk survived all the challenges of these seventeen chambers, he is then told that he may proceed into the 18th chamber, where he must carry a scolding hot urn of burning cinders that melt the temple's symbols into his forearms. He is now a tried and true, Shaolin Warrior Monk.

I have had the honor to meet and train with some Shaolin Martial Artists, and their skill levels were borderline, "superhuman."

Me in the middle of a group of incredible Shaolin Martial Artists
(I can only "pretend" to be as flexible and good as they are)

"Fact or Fiction" – Did these 18 Temple Chambers actually exist in Chinese History? Did they really carry a hot urn with their forearms? Honestly, I don't think it really matters. The metaphor alone makes a great point to present here. Whether true or not, it makes for good episodes of Kung Fu Theater as well as other entertaining martial arts movies, books, and verbal pass-downs. But if they did exist, all the better.

In our modern-day world, I believe it is accurate to say, that this concept of receiving the burning urn marks on our forearms, even simply as a metaphor, is still relevant to today's proud tribal warriors and achievers.

The U.S. Navy SEAL is presented with his Trident to wear proudly upon his chest after successfully passing through BUD's School. The Special Forces Commando places his hard earned *('urned')* Green Beret on his head. The U.S. Marine passes through the "36 Warrior Stations" (*Chambers*) of the Crucible. The successful graduate of Special Unit Training gets "Blood-Wings" pounded into his chest. The Martial Artist ties on his first black belt. The doctor graduates from medical school. The alcoholic accepts his milestone chip after remaining sober for 30 days (*chambers*) in his recovery program. Whatever the case; this concept of struggle, defeat, and victory is metaphorically universal, no matter how you may fill in the blanks of your own path (*chambers*) in life.

What does the path of your eighteen chambers of life look like? Good? Bad? Ugly? Filled with a combination of failure and success? Or by looking back and changing our perspective, did we learn from them? Did we become stronger? And can we use our experience, strength, and hope to help others? How we choose to see our past life experiences is a choice we all get to make – one way or the other.

In this book, I will be sharing not only my own eighteen testing chambers, but the testing chambers of several others who also had to make the choice of how to perceive their past lives. We either get stuck in our past experiences (*distress*), or we use our experiences to make us more resilient, help others, and live our lives to the fullest (*eustress*). I had been stuck in "distress" for many years with PTSD and wounded emotions until I found the direction and power of choice to see it all from a more positive viewpoint. My hope is that this book can help you make the same transition in your own life no matter how difficult the journey through your eighteen chambers may have been. And when you are ready, The 19th Chamber of Enlightenment, Challenge, and Healing awaits you.

Following are pictures of the Chinese Kung Fu Temple where I was both a teacher and a disciple for twenty-one years.

My Personal 18 Chambers of the Temple of Life

In the beginning pages of this book, I introduced a summary of my life's experiences to give a preview of what was to follow – similar to a movie trailer. And in the pages that follow, I expound upon some of those experiences in great detail, while some others I never mention again. I wanted to present some highlights of both my great achievements, contrasted by my even greater challenges and failures. I would never wish to repeat them, but as of today, I choose to view them all as good, and just part of my life's mental, physical, and spiritual "boot camp." By the grace of God, I was blessed to overcome most of them, and the ones that still try to hold on, I have a fairly good grasp of them as well, one day at a time. However, I can certainly attest to the fact that spiritual growth and enlightenment are lifelong processes.

Following are some of the highlights (*testing chambers*) of my life – many of which contributed to my personal experience with PTSD and my good, bad, and ugly attempts to manage it.

There are several missions, deployments, and specialized government training locations that I am not at liberty to put into writing but will allude to them. Others I will articulate in specific detail. But that is not the sole purpose of this book. My objective is not to tell you how much of a bad-ass I am, although my students refer to me as that quite often. My objective is to testify to how many times and ways God has intervened in my life and has spared me from some of the most impossible tactical equations and personal challenges imaginable.

I also had to make several ethical decisions that were not necessarily the best for my career. Like Abraham in the Old Testament of the Bible, I too had to lay down and be willing to sacrifice things that were near and dear to me. My very childhood dream of becoming a police officer was one of them. I was given the choice to choose a path between being *spiritually correct* in the Eyes of God and lose my job, or *politically correct* and keep my job and get promoted. The choice I made cost me my childhood dream. But what I received in its place was greater than anything I could have ever imagined or asked for.

My purpose in presenting the following stories is not just for entertainment value, or to attest to my invincibility – quite to the contrary, as many others have experienced and survived much worse. My purpose is to show the hand of God's Grace, Power, and Mercy on my life despite my training, hardness, and skillsets. My skills alone would not have been enough in and of themselves to cause me to survive my battles. That is my core objective of writing this book; **"God is great, and I am not."**

Like Lazarus, God has literally raised me from my physical deathbed on several occasions. I had also been dead spiritually, but God gave me a new life in that arena as well.

Many people wanted me dead, and they had tried to make it so. But like it stated on that New York City subway wall back in 1963, "*God is dead*," Nietzsche. God again had the final say in my life. "*They are dead or in prison*," God.

"When the wicked, even mine enemies and my foes, came upon me to eat up my flesh, They stumbled and fell. Though an host should encamp against me, my heart shall not fear: Though war should rise against me, in this will I be confident." (God is able) added

Psalm 27:2-3 (KJV)

MY CHAMBER ONE

"Born Into Hell"

I was born on Long Island, New York in 1956. The end of World War Two and the Korean War were not too far behind me. The Vietnam War was just ramping up.

My birth was a challenge. As my head came out of my mother, I somehow twisted my body and got stuck, clogging up my own birth process. The doctor used forceps to yank me out, leaving scars on both sides of my head. Okay, not off to the greatest start in life, but it was about to get much worse. Maybe he dropped me on my head too? I don't know, but that would certainly explain a lot of things.

It was November 22nd of 1963 when the school bell rang, and my second-grade class was dismissed early for the weekend because President John F. Kennedy had just been assassinated. I only lived three blocks from Public School (*PS*) #3. As I walked closer to my house, I saw a scene that by this time in my life, had become all too familiar to me. The police ambulance was in my driveway again, and paramedics were rushing my mother out of our house on a stretcher. My mother was unconscious and white foam was frothing out of her mouth and running down the side of her face. This was just another one of her many suicide attempts by swallowing a bottle full of sleeping pills and chasing them down with a bottle of whiskey. On several other occasions later in life, I had to perform the Heimlich Maneuver on her when she began to choke on her food when she was drunk.

She had just recently returned home from Florida. She and her married boyfriend had taken my father's car and ran away together for two weeks. I thought that maybe I had done something wrong to make her do these things. It was only a short time before this, that her heroin-addicted mother (*my grandmother*) had committed suicide by blowing her head off with a shotgun. "Like mother – Like daughter," I guess.

My father worked in Manhattan and was gone all day. This is when our home became like a carnival. Married men came over to have sex with my mother. On several occasions, the wives of these married men also came over with their friends and began banging on and trying to kick down our front door. Once they got in, they brutally beat my mother while screaming, "You stay away from my husband you lousy bitch." I was just a small child and was terrified at what I had observed. Nevertheless, I had always grabbed some type of weapon to defend her. I knew my mother was wrong for having these affairs, but I couldn't just stand there and not do something to protect her. So, I did what I could.

On other occasions, different types of women would come to our home. They were lesbians. They sat around drinking and smoking with my mother. When they left, one would usually stay behind and go into the bedroom with my mother to have sex. If I interrupted them by knocking on the door to ask my mother if I could have lunch – her lesbian lover came out in a rage and began to punch and kick me right before she locked me in a closet. I learned never to knock on my mother's door again.

Between the married men, and lesbian women who came over to have sex with my mother; her bedroom was a busy place while my father was at work in Manhattan. I was told never to say anything to my father, or I would be put into an orphanage. That threat came true one day when my mother and one of her lesbian lovers put me in a car and drove me to an orphanage in Pennsylvania. While there, I was speaking to some of the other kids while my mother was speaking to the orphanage administrator. I don't know what they spoke about, but my mother suddenly came out of the administrator's office and said, "Let's go, we're leaving." We got back in the car and headed home to New York.

Several years later when I was eleven years old, my parents got divorced. My mother and I moved to East Rockaway into a one-bedroom apartment. I was a little bigger and stronger by this time but still no match for her violent, alcoholic Vietnam Veteran boyfriend who had severe PTSD.

When this one particular boyfriend got drunk, he would beat my mother and try to strangle her to death. As I observed that she was turning blue and gasping for air, I kicked and punched him but my efforts to protect her were of no effect. I then ran into the kitchen and grabbed a steak knife to stab him off of her before she died. We eventually had to put a metal bar across our apartment door and blocks in the windows in an attempt to keep him out long enough to give us time to call the police. Once the police showed up, the fight was on. It took several officers to subdue this guy after they beat the crap out of him with their nightsticks. There was even one night where he had taken my mother hostage while holding a knife to her throat screaming that he would kill her unless she agreed to marry him. The police SWAT team showed up and was able to take him into custody alive. We both knew that he would be out of jail soon, so we began sleeping with knives under our pillows and I was able to build a zip gun to kill him if he ever came back. Luckily for him, he didn't. We ended up moving to a different town before that ever happened. These types of scenarios became all too frequent and common during my childhood. My own childhood trauma got added to like bank deposits on a daily basis.

Between being sexually molested by my babysitter and her two friends when I was only a few years old. To witnessing my mother getting beat up by the wives of the men she was committing adultery with. To men beating her and trying to kill her. I would say that by the age of eleven, I had a pretty fair amount of PTSD. But I just swallowed it all and got used to this twisted, violent, but "normal to me" homelife.

In addition to my mother getting beaten, I took some pretty good physical and emotional beatings myself. When my mother got drunk, she became extremely violent. If I did the slightest thing to piss her off, I got beaten with anything that wasn't nailed down. Coat hangers, broomsticks, belt buckles, having hot plates of food thrown at me, and on several occasions, being chased around the house while she had a steak knife in her hand. My body had the redness and swelling of the exact shapes of the objects that I had gotten beaten with. My body had become a canvas of differently shaped artistic scars and images. Modern Day Artwork at its finest. More of a Picasso Abstract than a Rembrandt Portrait I would have to say.

While still a very small child, my mother brought me to bars with her. I learned bar talk, how to play pool, bar dice, pinball machines, and shuffleboard through the thick cloud of cigarette smoke. The old 50s and 60s songs playing on the jukebox took the place of the Walt Disney tunes that other kids my age were learning at the time.

Bar fights were common, and watching my mother become progressively drunker and more promiscuous was a daily occurrence. Oh, and then there was the drunk driving on the way home where I had to grab the steering wheel to keep her car out of the oncoming lane to the left of us while preventing us from smashing into the parked cars on the right. It became quite a balancing act. I guess I should be grateful for learning how to drive at a very young age – and from the passenger seat at that. Now that's a skill. This "skill" probably helped me ace my government vehicle escape and evasion driving courses in my future profession to come.

Both of my parents were bisexual, and my conception was more of a scientific experiment than lovemaking. My parents only had slept together three times during the twelve years that they were married. And the times that they did have sex, were very "textbook calculated." I guess they thought having a kid would make them a heterosexual couple, and if that were the case, their scientific hypothesis had severely failed.

My father took my mother's temperature and picked a day on the calendar when she would be most fertile. After he did his thing, he raised my mother's legs in the air and voila – after one of those three times, I was conceived. I literally feel like I was conceived in a laboratory setting. Who says you need love to have a kid, biology seems to work fine all by itself. I wish they had never told me that though. It made me feel more like a clone rather than a naturally "born out of love" human child.

My father had his own freak show going on as well. He had a boyfriend that he referred to as his "business partner." One Thanksgiving, seated at the table were my father and his boyfriend (*I mean business partner*), my mother and her lesbian lover, me, and the turkey. My mother had her freak show going on, as did my father. They just seemed to be ok with it all. I guess they had made some form of a sick, twisted agreement.

As I got older, I began to question and struggle with my own sexual identity. I fought and prayed hard not to be like my parents in any respect, but unfortunately, the fruit didn't fall far from the tree.

My parents fought violently just about every night. I would cringe at their screaming. Their fights were over the most mundane things. My father screamed at her not to wear another man's engagement ring on her finger while she was still married to him. I guess that was a reasonable request. Then there was the time he found a condom wrapper on the floor next to his bed. At this point in my life, nothing really made any sense to me, but I just accepted the fact that this was my life and there wasn't anything I could do about it. I closed myself off emotionally and lived in survival mode for the first nineteen years of my life. I sniffed model glue and paint thinner every day since the age of eight, just to escape my painful emotions. Self-medicating my post trauma stress and horror, I guess.

But on Sundays, the three of us went to Catholic Mass like one big happy, religious family. During the sermon, the priest spoke Latin. I didn't have a clue what he was saying, nor did I really give a crap. I did however always say a prayer under my breath for God to help me and my family to become normal someday. But that never happened. It just kept getting worse. Sometimes the only person I had to talk to in life was my imaginary image of God. But did He speak Latin or English? I had no idea.

My father didn't treat me much better than my mother did. He was a World War II Army Veteran. After returning from Germany, he achieved the rank of captain and was the commanding officer of the US Army Defensive Tactics Unit in his division. He began to train me how to knife fight at the age of five. I liked learning these skills, but he was extremely rough with me. When he either flipped me onto the floor or punched me, it was full force. When he disciplined me, it was either with his fists, feet, or his belt buckle. He even broke my nose with his fist on two occasions. But otherwise, I liked the martial arts training, "*in theory*."

My father treated me more like a boot (*soldier in training*) than a son. He taught me how to march, stand at attention, and other military positions. He had me join the Sea Cadets with the intent of being disciplined in the way of the Navy. I really liked it. I made it onto the rifle drill team and excelled in the training. I couldn't wait until I was old enough to join the military so that I could escape my home life by going to Vietnam. "Vietnam had to be better than this," I thought to myself. But unfortunately, I still had many years until I would be of legal age.

Everything he did to me was to "make me tough," he explained. Being tough was important, especially growing up in New York where a skill like that was necessary to survive not only the streets, but also the bullies and gangs within the public school system. Some of these gangs, which I had also become a member of, fought rival gangs with belt buckles, chains, and baseball bats. It looked like a scene out of the Broadway Musical, "West Side Story."

I had a lot of dental problems when I was a kid. In another attempt to "make me tough," my father wouldn't allow me to take the Novocain that the dentist always offered me. My father told me to just grip the armrests on the dental chair tightly and take it like a man. I did. It sucked, but I did it.

I was a severe behavior problem in school and in the neighborhood. I was very destructive and disruptive. Always getting in trouble in the classroom during school, and with the police after school. I was eventually expelled from public school as a juvenile delinquent and put in a military reform school when I was fourteen. I hated this place with a passion. It was filled with other kids from Brooklyn and the Bronx with behavior problems like mine. The mentality of segregation and racism was very prevalent. Puerto Ricans against Blacks, Blacks against Whites, and so on. I did however like the Army ROTC (*Reserved Officers Training Corp.*) classes. I again made the rifle drill team and was a shining star anytime I held a rifle in my hands. Maybe this is why I eventually came in first place on the counter sniper specialist team years later with the San Francisco Police Department. At least something positive came out of my childhood.

Speaking of rifles. At the military reform school, we were issued M-14 rifles. The Vietnam War was at its peak, and I still couldn't wait to get there when I turned seventeen in three years.

The punishments in this reformatory were not only brutal but illegal. We were forced to hold our M-14 at a horizontal position at shoulder level with our arms stretched out in front of us. After a while, you would begin to shake and slowly lower the rifle no matter how hard you tried to keep it in a perfectly horizontal position. Once the drill instructor saw one of us weaken, he would smack us across the face or hit us with a horse crop whip. Now that crap hurt like hell. But if you complained, you only got it worse.

Another highlight of this place was being forced to eat red hot Chile Peppers if you ever got caught cursing. The drill instructors would silently stand outside of the group showers and wait to hear one of us speak a curse word. Once you got caught, you had to eat the red hot pepper. If you either made a face, choked on it, or spit it out; you got to feast on another one. I ate a lot of peppers in those days. That's probably why I can't stand them now as an adult. "Hot Pepper PTSD." LOL.

Now, for the grand finale. When you did something stupid and broke a rule, they not only punished you individually, but they also punished your entire squad. That same night, as a result, there would be a "blanket party."

A blanket party was when the higher-ranking officers snuck into your room late at night. They would hold down all four corners of your blanket so that you couldn't move, and then they would proceed to beat you with belts, shoes, broomsticks, or a sock that contained a bar of soap in it. We just laid there until early the next morning when the bugler blew reveille, which was really a horrific sound to wake up to. Then, the start of another day in paradise.

One Big Happy Group of Boys – (*1971*)

One night this Puerto Rican dude who lived in the Bronx and I escaped from the facility. We timed our escape right at the changing of the guards. We ripped the patches off our grey uniforms that identified the facility, ran through a wooded area, and walked several miles before we were caught and immediately returned to the facility that we had escaped from. The drill instructors punished our entire unit for what we had done. The blanket parties and beatings that we took for escaping were relentless.

I could go on with the tortures, beatings, and other horrific events that took place in my childhood, but I think by now, you have a pretty good idea what my childhood was like. A far cry from David Cassidy and the Partridge Family.

Later in life, I watched both of my parents literally deteriorate from cancer brought on by their smoking three packs of cigarettes a day. You would think I would be happy, but I wasn't. I asked God to save them because although I hated both them and my life, I always prayed to God for a normal, peaceful home. But once they died, I knew there was no chance that would ever happen. It never did happen. They both died a painful death. I was sad that I never had the normal, loving family that some of the other kids my age had and that I always prayed to God for. I was now left to figure out certain things in life on my own. They both did however receive salvation on their deathbeds. But I am grateful because God sent other healthy adults into my life to help raise me and to be the compassionate surrogate parents that my biological parents had failed to be. Some of them were the group of Italian Men from the funeral parlor. A Black woman from a Baptist church who I came to know as "Mother Winfield," and the people who I had met in Twelve Step Programs. God uses who He chooses.

As I got older, I came to realize that my parents probably did the best they could with what they had. They hadn't been dealt the best hand of cards in life either. The saying, "*Hurt people – hurt other people*" couldn't have been truer in my life. To their credit, my father occasionally took me to baseball games and other events. My mother cooked for me and took care of me the best way she knew how – at least when she was sober and not trying to commit suicide. But it *always* turned into a crap sandwich shortly thereafter. Nothing was ever consistent in my childhood except inconsistency. In the morning, I was told that I was loved. By evening, I was told they regret that I was ever born. "*Hey, I never asked to be born. I am merely a product of your sex experiment, remember?*"

The only way for me to 'right the wrongs' of my childhood was to 'forgive it' and move on. Easier said than done, but I was eventually able to let it go.

It's amazing what we humans can adapt to and survive through. We accept as normal, things that were never meant to be normal. But that's how we survive and make the best out of a painful situation. My self-medicating with alcohol, drugs, and sexual behavior only made my life much worse. My attempted cures became more destructive than the malady I was trying to treat.

I was watching a religious program on TV many years ago. They interviewed a little African boy who had just lost his entire family. There were tribal wars and genocide taking place in his village. He literally was hiding under his bed while he watched his mother, father, brothers, and sisters get hacked to death by men with machetes. When the interviewer asked the little boy if he ever got angry or wanted to seek vengeance, he simply answered, "No – that would mean that those men who killed my family would have won." Wow, what a lesson I learned that day from watching that little boy's interview. I almost took it as a personal challenge, but I believe God had me watch that show to plant a seed of forgiveness into my own life. It took over fifty years for me to fully forgive my parents, those drill instructors, my molesting babysitters, and even God. Forgiving them was not necessarily for them. It was to free me from the prison of hate, terror, and anger that I was relentlessly stuck in basically since birth. If that little African kid who had experienced horrors far beyond mine could forgive his enemies, then so could I. There is life after child abuse and trauma.

> *"When my father and my mother forsake me, Then the Lord will take care of me"* (*And so, He did* – added).
>
> **Psalm 27:10**

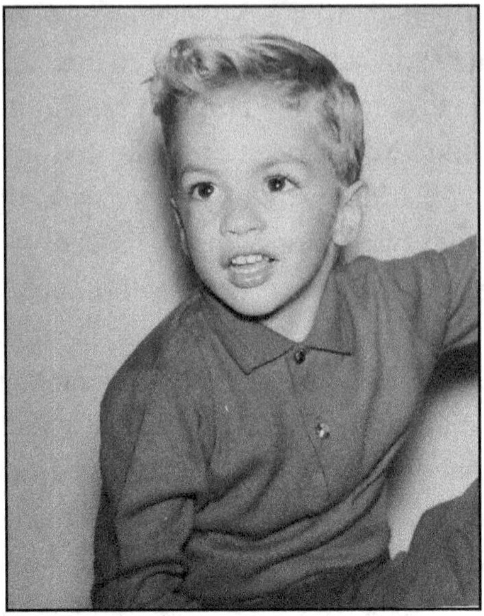

"Little Joey" 1960

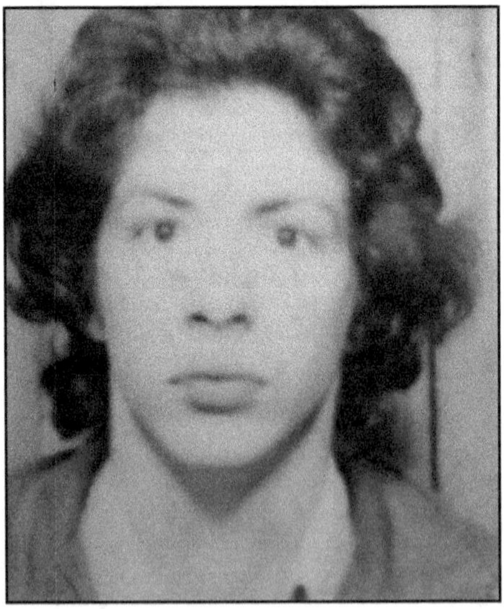

"Crazy, Angry, and Violent Joey" 1973

MY CHAMBER TWO

"Surviving My First Murder Contract"

New York – 1981.

"Fast Forward" – My mission now as a district attorney investigator was to collect evidence for the district attorney's office so that they could successfully prosecute their cases. Utilizing investigative methods such as surveillance, utility service checks, covert photography, interviewing witnesses, and interrogating suspects were all part of my job. It was a very challenging job, but I loved vindicating and protecting innocent people, and bringing justice to the criminals that preyed upon them.

Most of my cases involved underground illegal enterprises such as running numbers and gambling rackets (*something I knew a bit about*), cock and dog fighting arenas, human employment trafficking, code enforcement, slumlords abusing their tenants, as well as joint investigations with the fire marshal's office, and other related law enforcement agencies.

I had a very strong moral code and was dedicated to helping others and avoiding the corruption that was rampant all around me.

But to the contrary, I had lived a very corrupt and self-destructive life prior to surrendering my life to God and my entry into the field of law enforcement.

It's no secret that back in the 1950s, 60s, and 70s, some East Coast Police Departments and other public service agencies and officials were corrupt as hell. Taking bribes, looking the other way, sleeping in the same bed with the Mafia, and living by "*The Code of Silence*" was a way of life for some but not all public servants. Many books and movies have been written and produced relative to this dichotomy, so I'm not really disclosing any secrets. Read Serpico's story, or the book, "Buddy Boys" by Mike McAlary, which spells out New York Police corruption at its finest.

I never went down that road though. I maintained my values that, if you want to live the life of a criminal, then be a criminal, and if you want to live the life of a public servant, then there is no room for compromise. Choose one or the other, but not both. At least that was my personal conviction after I had gotten a bit of 'religion' in me.

I did however choose to live by "*The Code of Silence*." I kept my mouth shut and looked the other way when I saw things that violated my belief system. Taking on that "public official corruption monster" could get you killed fast. However, I eventually did take on that monster and was almost killed by doing so. I'm not claiming the tag of "Serpico," but I inadvertently inherited his title on more than one occasion.

I never directly went after corrupt public officials, as that would have been a death sentence. I chose to go after the kingpins that were compromising them. Unfortunately, this plan severely backfired on me, and I found myself in a battle to stay alive. The death sentence that I had tried to avoid, found me.

One day I was offered a bribe by a perp (*criminal*) to "look the other way" during one of my investigations. I tentatively accepted it. But before we committed the act, I went to my supervisor and presented my plan to him. He was a man I could trust. We met with the district attorney and put a sting operation in place.

I was equipped with a covert recording device that is nowadays referred to as a "wire." But a "wire" back then, was a miniature reel-to-reel tape recorder adhered to my body with duct tape. Not quite the sophistication of James Bond, but it got the job done.

I met with the perp who offered me the bribe. He handed me an envelope with cash inside. My cover team was covertly staged across the street taking pictures with a zoom lens camera. During our transaction, I opened the envelope and asked the perp, "Four hundred dollars, is this all you think I am worth?" I needed to get this verbiage on the tape recorder for the district attorney.

The perp stated, "What do you mean, that's more than I am paying Shapiro and McFarland."

I felt the blood rush out of my face and my heart sink, as I knew that statement had been recorded on my "wire." Shapiro and McFarland both worked in a different unit than mine and were already under investigation for corruption. They will never believe this was an "unplanned accident," I thought to myself. At that very moment, I knew that I was severely screwed and in deep shit.

Shortly after that day, Shapiro and McFarland were both indicted, and I "coincidentally" had a murder contract placed on my life. Was it from the perp who had been arrested? Or was it related to Shapiro and McFarland? To this day, I don't know.

There were drive-by shootings that took place at my home. Bullets flying through my bedroom window at night. A heat-sensitive car bomb was placed in my car that blew up in my driveway and nearly incinerated me. Shot at with a flare pistol. Telephone threats, and an attempt to light my house on fire. Eventually, I received police protection, but could I really trust them? My pride and mistrust caused me to stay and defend my own home and not rely on cops who might be dirty. I started to become paranoid and didn't have a clue who I could trust. I got to return fire a few times but was never able to confirm a hit or a kill. These incidents took place when my so called, "police protection" just happened to not be available on those particular nights.

I pulled into my residence driveway one night and by the time I exited my vehicle and walked up the steps to my front porch, my vehicle violently exploded. If the explosion had happened ten seconds earlier, I would have still been inside the vehicle. God had spared my life once again.

Doing my best to survive this murder contract and keeping my full-time job was wearing me down to nothing. Physical sickness and PTSD started to get the best of me. Now, I was not only carrying around trauma from my childhood, but I was racking up more emotional trauma stress points from my adult law enforcement profession. I didn't envision it at the time, but there would be much more to come as the years pressed on.

I eventually relocated to San Francisco, California to try my luck at becoming a cop out there. "Go West young man." And so, I did.

I Was Supposed to be Inside of This Vehicle When it Exploded

MY CHAMBER THREE

"Body Slamming Through Macy's Plate Glass Door"

I had watched San Francisco Police Shows on TV growing up as a kid in New York such as "Dirty Harry," starring Clint Eastwood. "The Streets of San Francisco," with Karl Malden and Michael Douglas. The police car chase scenes were awesome to watch as cars went airborne as they launched over the incredibly steep streets that San Francisco was known for. To me, it was an iconic and exciting city to be a cop in. That was my new dream; to become a San Francisco Police Officer. I wanted nothing more to do with New York Law Enforcement for obvious reasons.

While waiting for the police hiring process to take place, I got a job as a store detective at Macy's in San Francisco's Downtown Union Square. I already had experience working as a store detective years prior in New York City. I had always wanted to be a store detective at Macy's during the Christmas season as it was a "target rich" environment for shoplifters.

In New York, I had knives and guns pulled on me, and had gotten into many street fights in an attempt to arrest the shoplifters. No matter how big they were, or how many of them there were, I went after them and took them down. Many nights I came home with blood on my clothes. Sometimes it was mine, sometimes it was theirs, sometimes it was both. I was hoping that San Francisco would be a bit calmer. But at least here in San Francisco, I had a whole team of partners.

I reflected back to one of my last shoplifting arrests in New York City which ended up in a violent street fight. It was me against two of them. And those "them" were very big and strong. I chased them across the street dodging traffic as cars blew their horns at us and screamed obscenities out of their windows like only New Yorkers can do.

One of the shoplifters told me that he would kill me before ever going back to jail. While one of them hit me with a metal garbage can, the other body slammed me into a cyclone fence when a sharp pointed barb on top of the fence pierced its way into the back of my shoulder. As they were both attempting to take me out, I pulled out a billy club from my inner coat pocket and smashed one of them over the head. He began to bleed profusely and fell to the ground screaming. The other one had a knife in his hand and stated, "I'm gonna carve my name on your face whiteboy."

As he came at me slashing his knife towards my face, I threw a forward kick into his abdomen and knocked him through the plate glass display window of a department store. I was grateful for the years prior that I had trained in the martial arts with my father and under a Korean Tae Kwon Do Master. My legs had become fairly lethal weapons.

The police ambulance finally showed up and took both men to the hospital. The guy I hit over the head with the club almost died but he pulled through. The guy that I kicked through the window had sustained many cuts on his body from sailing through the glass. I was cleared of any wrongdoing or criminal charges, and my actions were deemed as, "justified self-defense." That would surely never fly in this day and age. People said that I was extremely brave to do this job. I don't know if it was "brave" or stupidly insane, but I always had a strong sense of justice and an extreme fatal attraction to danger.

If I was given a mission, then I would be true to that mission, no matter what it took. I don't know where this, "allegiance to my mission no matter what it took" came from. Maybe it was placed into my nature by God based on His foreknowledge of what was to come in my future. Come to find out, that trait within me would seriously come into play in my future missions where the stakes would be much higher.

The Christmas season was not only busy for stores and shoppers but also for shoplifters, boosters, pick pockets, and various other criminals. The Macy's San Francisco store that I worked at was a particularly busy store because of its downtown Union Square location. In addition to Bay Area shoppers, tourists from all over the world frequented this store.

We had our own detective office and prisoner booking area. When we arrested a shoplifter, we would prepare a report and the police would come by and pick up the subject. They were referred to as, "The Retail Detail." I soon got to know a lot of the police officers and began to become familiar with California law and criminal procedures. This job was a great preparation for me to become a police officer. I experienced many of the same situations I knew I would someday face as a uniformed cop.

We got into some great foot chases and fights, often pursuing suspects through five-star hotel lobbies, and into the underground train system. I was shot at one time from the upper level of a parking garage while I was pursuing a shoplifter. The police got involved in a lot of our chases as well.

The two-way mirrors and observation booths were great. Often a shoplifter would stand in front of a mirror trying on an expensive leather coat while surreptitiously ripping off the price and sensor tag. These people had no idea that I was sitting on the other side of the mirror watching everything they did while stimulating my inner predatory instinct. The feeling of *hunting and tracking another human being became addictive*. I guess I was experiencing some of what Ernest Hemmingway wrote about in his "Hunting of Man" quote at the beginning of this book.

Throughout this time, I continued my college studies at night, received my bachelor's degree, and began working toward my master's degree. A full plate indeed, but I was intent on reaching my goals.

One afternoon while working at Macy's, I spotted a guy stealing a leather jacket. He started to run out of the door leading to Union Square and I had no choice but to call it out over my radio and chase him by myself. I ran after him up the escalator. As the shoplifter ran out the door, he flung the large glass door back at me. I was running too fast to stop in time. My entire body crashed through the glass and I fell onto the sidewalk. I immediately got up and kept running after the shoplifter. As I ran, I noticed a long stream of blood pulsing out of my left wrist, which was sliced open to the bone. I could see blood squirting out of a sliced artery. I immediately sat down and put pressure on the artery with my other hand. A bystander took off his belt and tied it around my left biceps. By this time, I was covered with blood. I put out a "*Code Three*" over my radio which meant either "Agent Down" or "Agent Needs Help."

As my partner was pursuing and apprehending the suspect, I was rushed to the hospital in an ambulance and injected with morphine for the pain. I had shards of glass impaled into both my chest and arms. After 13 hours of microsurgery, my wrist had been reconstructed by a top trauma surgeon.

When I awoke from the anesthesia, I had a big heavy cast on my arm and my fingers were all tied back with nylon strings and rubber bands because my tendons had been completely severed. I was told by the surgeon that I would probably never regain the full use of my left hand. This bothered me greatly, especially with the police physical test coming up in a few months.

I told the doctor, "You watch. My left hand will be as good as new, I promise you that."

"Don't get your hopes up too high Joe," he told me.

I was sent home with a long list of instructions and a bottle of strong painkillers. I had to elevate my arm when I slept and kept my arm on top of a large stack of pillows to take away the pounding pain. The only problem was that during the night, my arm would fall off the pillows and hit me in the head.

It was like being hit with a baseball bat once an hour. I had a choice of tying my arm to the pile of pillows with a rope or wearing a football helmet. I chose the rope over the helmet. I had no feeling in my left fingers, but I was determined to fully recover, no matter what it would take. I traveled across the country to be a cop, and nothing was going to steal my dream – not even the loss of a hand.

I prayed every day for my hand to heal. I even refrained from promiscuous sexual encounters in an effort to obtain God's love and approval – also known as "bargaining with God." After getting sober from drugs and alcohol, promiscuous sex was about one of the only major vices I had left. "Come on God, how much more do you want from me? At least let me enjoy something," I thought. I eventually came to realize how futile and ignorant that thought was.

After several weeks my doctor removed the cast and discovered that my arm had severely atrophied. I couldn't move my hand at all. A new cast was put on, but when they removed the second cast two weeks later nothing had changed; I still couldn't move my hand.

Finally, my hand was put into a soft cast, and I was told to try as often as I could to squeeze a sponge. I tried again and again, but I just couldn't do it. I became incredibly frustrated, but I was still determined to regain full use of my hand. I had to, or my dream of becoming a San Francisco Police Officer would have been shattered. There was no way I could go back to New York. "God, I need a miracle," I shouted.

I prayed and struggled every day to squeeze that sponge. Eventually, I was able to barely move one of my fingers and this gave me hope. For weeks I spent all my days and many of my nights working on moving my hand. Each doctor's visit was depressing to me as the physicians continuously cautioned me to prepare for the worst.

"I will regain full use of my hand," I insisted stubbornly. "Nothing will stop me."

After a few weeks of intense, non-stop effort on my part, I could squeeze a sponge with three of my fingers. My determination made believers out of my doctors, and they stopped telling me to prepare for the worst. Instead, they told me that, "If anyone can do it Joe, you can."

Each week I progressed more rapidly and was soon squeezing a rubber ball with all five fingers. My physicians were astounded at the pace and scope of my recovery. One doctor took a picture of my hand for inclusion in a medical journal. "This is a true miracle," said the hand surgeon.

During my recuperation, I received a letter from the police department telling me that my physical agility test was scheduled in a few weeks. I took a deep breath and started to stress, for I had promised myself that I would pass that test. My doctors insisted that it was still too soon and that I shouldn't risk the rigorous physical exertion. I ignored their advice, prayed, and exercised both my hand and my faith harder than before. "Faith without works is dead."

Then came the day of the test. I knew that I only had two and a half strong fingers and that these would have to provide whatever strength I'd need in that hand. Halfway through the test, my hand and wrist started to swell severely. I was hoping that my wrist wasn't bleeding internally.

I kept the jagged scar and swelling on my wrist hidden from the police instructor as best I could and miraculously somehow passed the test. The next day, the swelling started to go down, which was fortunate since I had my medical exam a few weeks later.

During the medical exam, the doctor handed me a grip tester and told me to squeeze it as hard as I could. The objective of the test was to push the needle on the grip meter past the number 60 on the scale in order to pass. I purposely squeezed a 65 with my right hand. Although I could have squeezed a lot harder, I didn't want to create a big difference between my right and left hand.

I was then told to squeeze the gripper in my left hand. I took a deep breath and silently asked God for a miracle. Drawing on sheer willpower and faith, I squeezed my left hand as hard as I could, trying to use my two strong fingers as much as possible.

"Good," said the doctor. "Sixty-two, you passed."

On my way home I thanked God for this miracle. Now I only had the psychological and the lie detector tests to pass. I could only hope that the sins of my past would not emerge to haunt me during these last two tests, for I was only two steps away from realizing my childhood dream of becoming a uniformed cop. A uniformed cop that I had prayed to become on that winter day at the Jamaica Train Station as I watched that NYPD car speeding down the street with its lights flashing and siren blaring.

That was a very serious injury. But between my faith in God and my hard work, I was able to miraculously pass both the police medical and physical exams, as well as the psychological and polygraph exams (*another miracle*).

For several years after crashing through the glass door. I had developed a phobia of touching glass doors or windows with my hands. I relived the incident over and over in my dreams. Since that day, the sound of glass breaking sent chills up my spine. When I would walk down the sidewalk past that same glass door on the Geary Street side of Macy's, I could see the large stain of my own dried blood on the sidewalk in front of the door. As I looked at my blood, I felt butterflies in my chest and could hear the sound of shattering glass inside of my head. It was creepy and it lasted for a long time. Nevertheless, I passed my background investigation, and was sworn into the San Francisco Police Department in July of 1984 – Academy Class Number 158 – Badge (*star*) Number 431.

I prayed to God to help me with my PTSD. I prayed to God to heal my wrist before the police physical and medical exams. But if I had not put in the effort to do my part by getting counseling, changing my behavior, and squeezing the sponge and the ball, I would have been left with relentless PTSD and a useless left hand to this day.

I have lived most of my life by the following saying – "Get on your knees and pray as if it all depended on God. Then get up, and act as if it all depended on you." This has always been my 'preparation meets opportunity' experience where God has always met me at the halfway point. But I must say that there are those times when God does perform miracles instantaneously, like He did when He removed alcoholic drinking and other destructive things from my life when I was nineteen. Today, my left-hand functions perfectly. I still bare a jagged, nasty scar on my wrist, but to me – I see it as God's miraculous fingerprint and signature on my "torn canvas."

"Faith Without Works is Dead"

> *"What does it profit, my brethren, if someone says he has faith but does not have works? Can faith save him? If a brother or sister is naked and destitute of daily food, and one of you says to them, "Depart in peace, be warmed and filled," but you do not give them the things which are needed for the body, what does it profit? Thus, also faith by itself, if it does not have works, (squeezing a rubber ball) is dead."*
>
> **James 2:14-17**

Me and my Store Detective Partner Bobby, Who Eventually Caught the Guy Who I Was Chasing

San Francisco Police Department

Joseph F. Bannon

Successfully Completed the P.O.S.T.
Certified Basic Recruit Training Course
at the San Francisco Police Academy

from July 30, 1984 to November 28, 1984.

TRAINING MANAGER

CHIEF OF POLICE

MY CHAMBER FOUR

"Officer Down – Happy Birthday"

I graduated from the field training program of the San Francisco Police Department in early 1985. I had trained at Central Station which covered Chinatown, The Tenderloin, Fisherman's Wharf, The Downtown Financial District, North Beach, and of all places, Union Square where Macy's was located. I also trained at Park Station which covered Golden Gate Park, and The Haight Asbury District which was infamous for its drug and hippie movements back in the 1960s. Many rock and psychedelic bands got their start here. I was now a "real cop" but still considered a rookie until I "proved myself" on the streets, so to speak.

I received my orders for my first permanent duty station – "Northern Station" (*Company E*). Northern Station covered a very diverse sector of the city. We had some very nice areas which included The Marina, Pacific Heights, and Lombard Street ("*The Crookedest Street in the World*"). We also had some severely nasty areas such as the housing projects just off of Haight Street and Laguna Street. We could usually count on a good foot chase, a knockdown-drag-out fight, or getting shot at from one of the high-rise towers of the housing projects where the residents hated cops.

One of the first partners that I was assigned to was named Officer Jim Guelff. Jim was born on February 27, 1956, and appointed to the San Francisco Police Department on his birthday February 27, 1984. We were both born in the year 1956, but as time would tell, we had two very different fates.

Jim had already proven himself as a great, hard-working cop. The first one in, and the last one out. He was very well-liked and respected by his fellow officers. I was grateful to work with a cop such as Jim. Besides being a great cop, he was an extremely nice and respectful man. However, like most of us, he knew when to be gentle and polite, as well as knowing when it was time to rumble. Jim and I worked together very frequently. We made good arrests and had each other's backs all the time.

Time had passed and I had the opportunity to be transferred to "Mission Station" (*Company D*) which is where I spent most of the rest of my patrol career. Mission Station at the time was known as a hell hole and many of the cops assigned there were trying to get out. I was the only cop trying to get in. The other cops at Northern Station thought that I was crazy putting in my transfer request to The Mission District, but I wanted the greater challenge, the greater adrenaline rush, and the greater danger. And as time would tell, I would certainly get it.

On my last night working at Northern Station, Jim took me out for "Code 7M" (*dinner*). We ate at one of the greasy spoon crap holes that we normally ate at. The next day, I started my tour at Mission Station.

I partnered up with a cop who was in my police academy class named Chris. He was a great guy to work with. No one, and I mean no one could outrun Chris. So, when we got into foot chases, I let Chris chase them and I would show up for the 'catch and clean' ceremony to follow.

Again, as fate would have it, Chris needed to change his hours for his school commitment. He put in a transfer request and eventually transferred to Northern Station where his time needs could be better accommodated. Strangely enough, he became partners with my former partner, Jim Guelff.

As I mentioned in my introduction, I left the San Francisco Police Department to take a job as a narcotics agent in South America and the Caribbean Islands. After two years, I returned to the San Francisco Police Department in an effort to survive yet another murder contract put out on me by the Colombian Drug Cartel. (*Details to follow in a later chapter*).

During my waiting time to be reappointed, I was staying at a hotel on Franklin Street in San Francisco. I had bought a brand-new Nissan 300ZX and drove it up from Los Angeles where my plane had landed from the Caribbean. My new car was parked at the curb on Franklin Street as I went to bed. Suddenly there were several gunshots outside of my window.

I had been involved in a number of shootings in New York, as well as down in the Caribbean, and was hypersensitive to gunfire. After I pulled myself off the ceiling, I peeked out the window. My car alarm was blaring, and I just thought that it was in response to the gunfire. Well, it was. But those gunshots were fired directly into my new sports car. Somebody was either not happy to see me back in San Francisco or, somebody was trying to send me a message from my prior assignment overseas. I never did find the suspect or the motive behind the shooting of my car. I drove to the police station for that district, which just happened to be my former assignment – Northern Station. The officer who took the report was none other than my former partner Officer Jim Guelff. It was great to see him, but not really under these circumstances. For the years to come, I drove my sports car around with five bullet holes in it. If anything, it made for a great pick-up line or conversation.

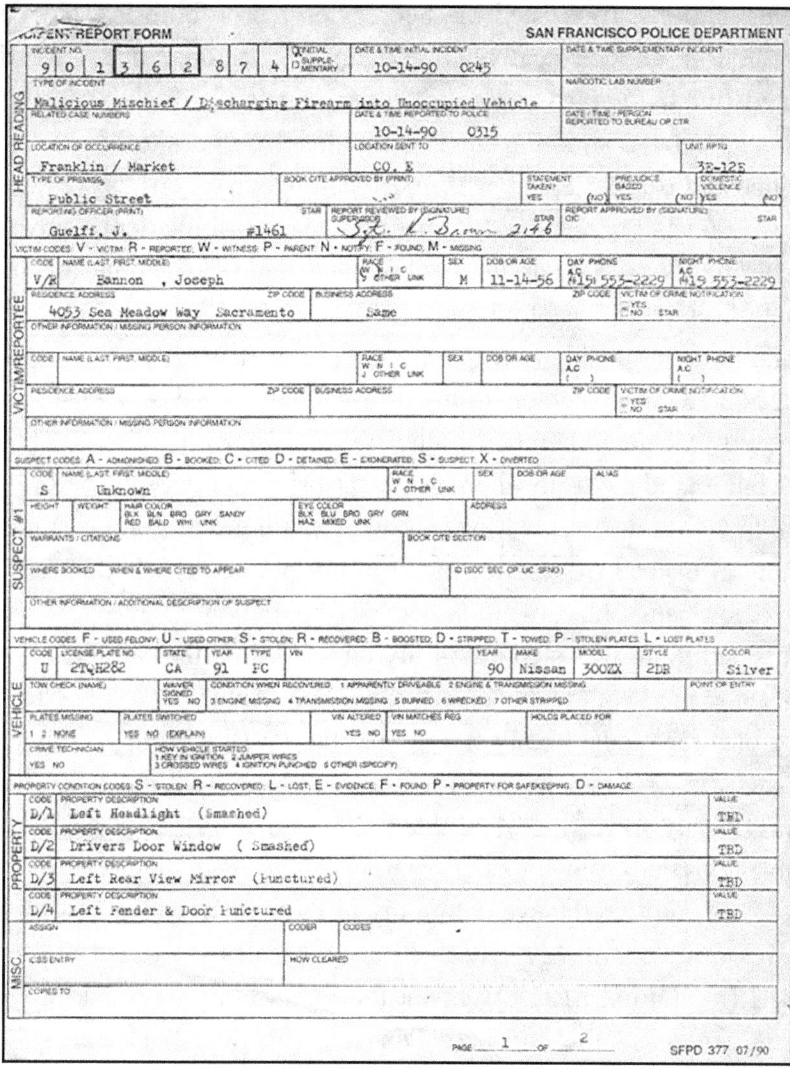

INCIDENT REPORT FORM — SAN FRANCISCO POLICE DEPARTMENT

INCIDENT NO. 9 0 1 3 6 2 8 7 4 — INITIAL
DATE & TIME INITIAL INCIDENT: 10-14-90 0245
TYPE OF INCIDENT: Malicious Mischief / Discharging Firearm into Unoccupied Vehicle
DATE & TIME REPORTED TO POLICE: 10-14-90 0315
LOCATION OF OCCURRENCE: Franklin / Market
LOCATION SENT TO: CO. E
UNIT RPTG: 3E-12E
TYPE OF PREMISES: Public Street
STATEMENT TAKEN? (NO) — PREJUDICE BASED (NO) — DOMESTIC VIOLENCE (NO)
REPORTING OFFICER (PRINT): Guelfi, J. STAR #1461
REPORT REVIEWED BY (SIGNATURE) SUPERVISOR: Sgt. L. Brown 2146

VICTIM CODES: V - VICTIM R - REPORTEE W - WITNESS P - PARENT N - NOTIFY F - FOUND M - MISSING

CODE	NAME (LAST, FIRST, MIDDLE)	RACE	SEX	DOB OR AGE	DAY PHONE	NIGHT PHONE
V/R	Bannon , Joseph	W	M	11-14-56	415 553-2229	415 553-2229

RESIDENCE ADDRESS: 4053 Sea Meadow Way Sacramento — BUSINESS ADDRESS: Same

SUSPECT CODES: A - ADMONISHED B - BOOKED C - CITED D - DETAINED E - EXONERATED S - SUSPECT X - DIVERTED

CODE	NAME (LAST, FIRST, MIDDLE)
S	Unknown

VEHICLE CODES: F - USED FELONY U - USED OTHER S - STOLEN R - RECOVERED B - BOOSTED D - STRIPPED T - TOWED P - STOLEN PLATES L - LOST PLATES

CODE	LICENSE PLATE NO.	STATE	YEAR	TYPE	VIN	YEAR	MAKE	MODEL	STYLE	COLOR
U	2TQH282	CA	91	PC		90	Nissan	300ZX	2DR	Silver

PROPERTY CONDITION CODES: S - STOLEN R - RECOVERED L - LOST E - EVIDENCE F - FOUND P - PROPERTY FOR SAFEKEEPING D - DAMAGE

CODE	PROPERTY DESCRIPTION	VALUE
D/1	Left Headlight (Smashed)	TBD
D/2	Drivers Door Window (Smashed)	TBD
D/3	Left Rear View Mirror (Punctured)	TBD
D/4	Left Fender & Door Punctured	TBD

PAGE 1 OF 2 — SFPD 377 07/90

I was reappointed to the police department shortly after this incident. After about one year of working again as a uniformed patrolman, I was assigned to the Special Investigations Division (*SID*), which was considered one of the most elite units within the police department. SID was formerly called the 'Police Intelligence Unit.' This unit handled very sensitive as well as organized crime investigations. It assisted the Secret Service on both Presidential Protection and Protective Intelligence Missions, and investigated threats against police officers, other city officials, as well as gang-related shootings and homicides. I was assigned my own police radio and kept it with me twenty-four-seven, as we were always on call to respond to some type of critical incident or investigation. My primary assignment was the Gang Task Force, and my first official case was to figure out who stabbed a sixteen-year-old gang member through the heart with a screwdriver.

I spent eighty percent of my time back in the Mission District. I knew all the gang members in the area, and they not only respected me but feared me from when I walked a prior foot beat and enforced the law with an iron fist. Now, I wore plain clothes and carried a shotgun instead of a police baton in my police vehicle due to the drive by gang shootings that occurred just about every night. All I needed to do was step out of my unmarked police car, and all of the gang members would drop to their knees and put their hands on top of their heads. I had conditioned them well since my foot beat days. They referred to me as "New York" and believed that I was crazy. They were right, and that's the reputation that I wanted to have with these violent gang bangers.

One night on the eve before my birthday: November 13, 1994, I was out celebrating. I received a radio call of, "406 – SHOTS FIRED – OFFICER DOWN" at the intersection of Franklin and Pine Streets in the Northern District. This was the same street where my personal car had been shot up and Officer Jim Guelff had taken the report. I sped to the scene where a heavily armed gunman was firing multiple rounds at civilians, paramedics, and incoming police backup units. I listened to my police radio for the safest avenue of approach.

The gunman was armed with two assault rifles, and several handguns including an Uzi automatic pistol. He was wearing a Kevlar (*bullet-proof*) helmet and vest. Needless to say, he was a hardened target, and it was almost impossible to deliver a kill shot to him. Two police officers had already been shot and critically injured by rifle fire. One had been shot in the abdomen and the other in the head. There was nonstop gunfire being exchanged between both the police and the gunman. I didn't know it at the time, but the officer lying on the ground with a gunshot wound to the head was my ex-partner – Officer Jim Guelff.

It is a horrific feeling being pinned down under gunfire behind cover (*parked cars and cement walls*) knowing that a brother police officer had been shot and is either dying or already dead. Everything inside of you wants to run into the hellfire and save him but that could have only produced a third officer down and severely complicated the tactical equation.

A friend of mine who was on the SWAT Team managed to get up on the roof behind the gunman and place a surgical shot into the back of the gunman's cervical spine which killed the gunman immediately. Great shot Al.

The ambulance that was standing by around the corner out of the line of fire finally was able to move in and transport both officers to the hospital where we all followed.

The waiting room at the hospital was filled with cops standing by to hear the prognosis. We were waiting for a very long time when the doctor finally approached us. He told us that the officer who had been shot in the abdomen was stable and was expected to make a full recovery. But as far as Officer Jim Guelff was concerned – Jim had died on the operating table.

It was approaching midnight and officially my birthday. My birthday meant nothing to me at this point. Fellow officers began to cry and scream. I was too much in shock to display any emotions. As a collateral duty, I was a Critical Incident Response Team member, and it was now time to help other cops deal with their grief over the next several weeks. It was quite a challenge debriefing other cops when I was dealing with my own intense grief and survivor's guilt. But putting all emotions aside, I went to work and got the job done. It sucked and was horrible at best for the many officers who had been involved in the incident over the course of the weeks that followed. Many of us were dealing with Post Trauma Stress and the inner brokenness from Jim's murder.

Officer Jim Guelff died a hero. He didn't know it at the time, but he had stopped a deranged gunman from Santa Cruz, California with a vehicle full of ammunition and explosives from committing an even greater atrocity.

At that time, we were issued six shot 357 Magnum Revolvers. No match for the artillery that Jim's assassin was armed with. Jim had fired six shots into the gunman but couldn't penetrate the gunman's armor. While Jim was reloading his revolver, he took a rifle round to the head. It just so happened that Jim was working alone that night. "If he had a partner, would he have survived?" "If he had a semi-automatic pistol, would he have survived?" "If I had never left Northern Station and was his partner that night of my birthday, would he have survived?" If, If, If ???? Those "Ifs" played in my head for a long time thereafter, as they do many of us.

It's a very uncomfortable and earth-shattering feeling to lose a brother or sister of the Thin Blue Line. Especially one that you shared a certain time of your life with. As unreasonable as this may sound, you start to blame yourself and play the scenario over and over in your head trying to see if something different could have been done. But even if there was a different or better way, it wouldn't bring Jim back. Hindsight is always 20-20 but it doesn't have the power to raise the dead as Jesus did with Lazarus during His time in this F'd up world.

Officer Jim Guelff was appointed to the San Francisco Police Department on the day of his birthday, February 27, 1984. He died on the eve of my birthday, November 14, 1994. And ever since that day, there hasn't been a birthday that the memory of Jim's death and that horrific firefight hasn't forced its way into my thoughts. I can still see Jim's face and remember the sound of nonstop gunfire. I have it memorialized not only in my head, but also on a VHS tape recording from a news channel that I keep stashed away in my storage.

Standing at attention during Jim's funeral and saluting his flag draped casket with tears in my eyes, while thinking back on all the times we had worked together, made his death seem almost unreal. Listening to those God-awful funeral procession bag pipes playing, "Amazing Grace" is also a haunting experience. It seems that we must endure that song at every military, first responder, and police funeral that we attend. I've come to hate that song. It means only one thing to me – "Death of a partner." Nevertheless, Rest In Peace Jim. The anniversary of your death has been honored every year since you have been gone.

Side note: Two years later the San Francisco Police Department began to issue semi-automatic pistols to its officers in "reaction" to Jim's death. How freakin sad that positive change had come only after an officer was killed in the line of duty. Near the same time-frame, the idea of sergeants carrying rifles in their cars was struck down by public advocacy groups stating that they didn't want rifles in police cars because innocent citizens might be injured. But it's ok for cops to die at the hands of criminals that are better armed on the street than we are? I get it, we are expendable as long as others are protected by us. Very Sad!

Officer James Guelff
End of Watch – November 13, 1994
RIP Jim – Miss you Buddy

MY CHAMBER FIVE

"Baptism by Sniper Fire"

Due to department budget cuts, I had been reassigned back into uniform to my former patrol station in the Mission District. It kind of felt like home being back in the "Devil's Quadrangle" named after its rectangular patrol sector shape and over-the-top violent crime rate. Just about every day, there were gang turf wars, murders, armed street or store robberies, bank robberies, knife attacks, suicides, drug overdoses, reports of shots fired from the housing projects; and maybe once in a blue moon, a cat stuck in a tree. But it all made the day go by fast.

My patrol partner Josh was Jewish and from the Bronx in New York. He wasn't nearly as brazen as I was, but he was a great cop, a great partner, and a great friend who always had my back, as I did his. We argued about stupid stuff all the time in the patrol car. But when the crap hit the fan and the police radio blasted out a critical incident in progress, we put our differences aside and took care of business as a team. Josh and I didn't even need to speak to each other during an incident, it's like we could just telepathically read each other's mind. This is very common among tight-knit military and law enforcement small teams. It's an amazing thing that just seems to happen over time when you work with the right likeminded people. It's like we become a "well-oiled machine" that just seems to operate intuitively.

Josh was more of a "by the book" kind of cop, whereas I tended to be more of a "throw the book" kind of cop while getting in the criminal's faces. I conducted several 'come to Jesus meetings' out on the streets. Nothing too serious. Just ruffled their feathers a bit to gain their respect and put the fear of God into them for intimidating innocent people. If a cop on the street doesn't have respect, he has nothing and can't do the job. After my "counselling sessions," many of the disrespectful street criminals began singing Patti LaBelle's hit song, "*I Got a New Attitude*." It almost seemed like a miraculous conversion had taken place. I guess I just had "people skills." But nevertheless, Josh and I made a great team, made great arrests, received many accolades from the community for cleaning up the streets, and commendations from our command staff for good police work.

One day we got a call on our police radio; "3 David 13 – 902 and 904 with 3 David 200." Which meant to return to the station and meet with our lieutenant.

"Oh crap," I said to Josh. "I wonder what we did now?" Josh just shrugged his shoulders as we returned to the station. I was the senior officer, so I walked into the lieutenant's office first to take the hit.

"Hey 'LT' (*short for lieutenant*), I'm sure I can explain what happened." The lieutenant started to laugh. "No, you're good this time Bannon. I have a special assignment for you guys. I need you to go to City Hall and pick up three members of the City Board of Supervisors and take them for a ride along. They want to see the diversity of the community in our district." I immediately showed a look of despondency on my face.

"No problem 'LT,' I'll give them the ride of their lives."

"Joe, please, these people are elected officials, and we need them on our side. Take them to Noe Valley or the Castro District," stated LT.

Both Noe Valley and the Castro Districts were fairly low-crime areas and heavily populated with special interest groups, upcoming politicians, neighborhood merchant associations, and political activists who all had the mayor's ear.

"Sir, they are in good hands. We got this," I replied as I left LT's office. LT just shook his head and had a nervous look on his face. This was a common look on his face whenever I walked into his office. But he really liked me despite my sometimes, "*unconventional*" ways of cleaning up the streets.

As Josh and I drove downtown to City Hall to pick up these left-wing political liberals, I told him, "Josh, these people need to see what you and I deal with on a daily basis. Not the sterilized areas that LT wants us to bring them to. Let's give them a dose of reality."

Josh agreed, as long as we at least drove them through the areas that LT requested first. "Done," I responded.

We picked up the three supervisors at City Hall and greeted them very respectfully. Two of them were very hospitable to us, but "Left Wing Karen" seemed disgusted that she had to lower herself to be in a police car with two 'low life' police officers. I learned in San Francisco that left-wing politicians really didn't like the police. This was way prior to the "Defund The Police" movement that we see today.

We drove them through the areas that they wanted to see, but on the way back to City Hall, I took a shortcut through the David 3 and David 5 Patrol Sectors which were both located in the heart of hell. I covertly peeked at them in the rear-view mirror and could see a look of curiosity and a bit of fear appear on their faces, as we entered the bowels of the Devil's Quadrangle.

As we drove through the intersection of 24th and Folsom Streets, one of the supervisors nervously asked, "What is that tall green building with all of those people standing around staring at us?"

"Oh, that's the Army Street Housing Projects that we work in every day," I replied.

"Housing projects," one of the supervisors responded with a shocked voice and look on her face.

"Yes Ma'am, that place is full of parolees, drugs, organized crime, guns, and just about anything else you could imagine," I added.

Just then, before I could get another word out of my mouth, there was a loud sound of rifle fire. One round creased the hood of our patrol car, and another sailed through my driver's side window, past my chest, over my partner Josh's lap, and penetrated through the passenger side door.

"Get your heads down," I shouted, as Josh and I slouched down in our seats to make ourselves smaller targets so the sniper couldn't get a fix on us. They immediately complied and were visibly very shaken if not craping in their pants. As I accelerated the patrol car into an evasive driving maneuver out of the line of fire, Josh grabbed the police radio and broadcasted, "3 David 13, Code 33, we're taking sniper fire from the 24th Street side of the Army Street Housing Projects." By this time the three city supervisors in our back seat were screaming for us to get them out of the area and back to City Hall.

The police dispatcher rebroadcasted over the radio, "Headquarters to all Mission and Ingleside Units, Code 33 – 3 David 13 is taking sniper fire from the Army Street Housing Projects. To all backup units, red zone of approach is the 24th Steet side of the building."

Sirens from backup units could be heard from all incoming directions. Josh and I held our position a few blocks away until we could get a ride for the terrified supervisors back to a place of safety. There was dead silence in the car. After transferring them into another police unit, I told them to have a nice day as Josh and I headed back to the housing projects to assist in locating the sniper. The other unit got to take the three "*enlightened*" supervisors back to City Hall. Hopefully with a new appreciation for the police.

The sniper was eventually located through one of my confidential informants, arrested and brought to jail via Mission Emergency Hospital. He had fallen down a flight of stairs while trying to escape. After all ends were tied up on the shooting, Josh and I went to lunch at a taco joint on Mission Street. Josh and I were laughing so hard that we had tears in our eyes thinking about those three supervisors who looked like they had seen a ghost. Our laughter eventually turned into a creepy solemness as we realized how close that bullet had come to the both of us. I knew I would have some explaining to do to LT. but it eventually all worked out. I had escaped disciplinary action from LT., but I did not escape from the sound of rifle fire in my half dream state that kept waking me up at night in a startled state. In my dream, I actually experienced the feeling of getting hit in the side of my neck by the sniper's bullet. I both heard it *and* felt it. This became a recurring nightmare. My dread of going to sleep at night that I had experienced since childhood just kept getting worse as time passed. But eventually, even my un-comfortability of going to bed at night turned into an apathetic numbness. I just dealt with it as long as I kept the TV on all night while I was sleeping. Usually a Christian channel. To me, the loudest noise in life was, 'dead silence.'

Every day as police officers, we all deal with scenarios like this and either laugh or just shrug them off as part of the job. But I honestly believe despite our laughter or shrugging off these types of incidents, that at least subconsciously, these incidents get stored up in the depths of our minds. Whether they become single-event PTSD, PTS (*short term stress*), or cumulative PTSD over time, I guess that depends on each individual officer and what type of baggage that we are already carrying around inside of us before we experience a critical incident.

One thing I do know for sure. This job changes us and the way we see life forever. If it makes us more vigilant, then that is probably a good thing. If it haunts us in our dreams or becomes an intrusive thought in our minds while we are on a dinner date, or it creates a feeling of avoidance to not want to drive passed the housing projects ever again – that's not so good.

> *"Yea, though I walk (drive) through the valley of the shadow of death (housing projects), I will fear no evil; For You are with me; Your rod and Your staff, they comfort me."*
>
> **Psalm 23:4**

MY CHAMBER SIX

"Legend of Mission Street"

Many cops in San Francisco still to this day refer to me as, "The Legend of Mission Street." They still tell what they call, "Joe Bannon Stories," referring to how I was a unique "one-man police force" and all the "*unconventional tactics*" I deployed to "take back the streets" from the criminal element back in the day. To me, I was nothing more than just a missionary spreading the Gospel of Peace. After all, I was considered a "*Peace Officer*" of the law.

Working on the violent streets and in the low-income housing projects of the Devil's Quadrangle for many years, I had been in a countless number of fights and used "guerrilla warfare-like tactics" to control the highest violent crime area of the city. But I have to say one thing in all honesty. Although I may have been able to hold my own as a street fighter and had confidence in my fighting abilities. There were many nights that I got into severe violent confrontations with drugged out, cop-hating parolees much bigger and stronger than myself. This included multiple opponents and criminals with guns, knives, and broken bottles. And looking back, I just know that it was not only my skill and fighting abilities that kept me alive. There were just some situations that there is no way

I can explain how I had survived them, other than an "Act of God," "Help from an Angel," or a similar intervention. I just know – it wasn't all me.

Why did I do things the way I did? Unconventional police tactics? Because after a while of being a street cop and "playing by the rules," I eventually saw the futility in it. Left-wing, liberal district attorneys letting criminals get out of jail and committing another street crime before I even finished writing the first arrest report. Little old ladies beaten down for their coin purses. Children being abused. Victim after victim – criminal defense lawyer after criminal defense lawyer. An innocent person hurt after innocent person hurt. Criminals having more rights than their victims. Good innocent people helping the police by doing the right thing, and then being retaliated against for doing so. All the while the police department and district attorney stating that, "they could do nothing to help, nor protect these good Samaritan witnesses and reportees." Then why the hell should anybody risk their safety by helping the police if no one would be there to protect them was my question?

What pissed me off to no end was when I had to read a criminal who was not even a citizen, his Miranda rights to make sure I didn't violate any of the murderer's or kidnapper's constitutional protections. This almost tipped it over the edge for me but not quite. I still respected and played by the rules – to a certain extent.

However, I began to lose it when I saw little kids get shot during drive-by shootings because of a stray bullet or bullets coming through their bedroom windows at night. When the drug dealers and gang members completely took over the housing projects and public parks; forcing parents to keep their kids inside behind locked doors and away from windows with no safe place to play. This is where I had drawn the line.

There were "no trespassing" laws in place, but the spineless district attorney's office would not allow us to enforce them without an additional crime being committed during the trespassing violation. Gang members and drug dealers from Oakland illegally hung out in these housing projects all day long selling drugs and guns. They made life for the legal residents of the projects hell on earth. "Screw this," I said to myself. This is where I took the problems within the Devil's Quadrangle into my own hands and declared war on these scum bags. If the legal system would not do what was necessary to protect these innocent people and their kids from this filth of society – then I would.

Using physical force to drive them out when necessary. Putting dog crap and pepper spray on the public telephones that they used to score drug deals. Shooting fireworks at them from the roofs of the housing projects to disperse them. Or tormenting them to the point that I had become the most feared cop in the Mission District – they began to leave the area. They now had something to be frightened of – 'me.' I had declared war against them, and the battlefield was the streets and the housing projects that they tried to take over. But not on my watch.

I was one of the only cops who could walk into the courtyard of the most violent housing projects, or down the worst streets in the city at night, when even the worst of the worst criminals would run away just at the sight of me walking towards them. It had to be this way. The kids and the innocent people on my beat needed someone to stand in between them and the ruthless criminals that plagued them. And I was that someone.

One thing was for sure. They all thought I was crazy and that is exactly what I wanted them to think. Maybe I was crazy. But the residents of the neighborhoods I patrolled, as well as the business owners, loved me and appreciated the interest that I had taken in their community to protect them.

Whatever it took to clean the streets of this cesspool and war zone, I was willing to do it. I got my share of complaints from these criminals and liberal onlookers, but none of them ever stuck. I really was trying to do the right thing in a politically wrong climate.

It was on this one particular night that I was working by myself, that this fear and respect that I had developed was not working with a certain parolee who had just been released from San Quentin State Prison. As I walked through the Valencia Gardens Housing Projects as I normally did, I observed a huge man beating a woman in the middle of the courtyard. I began to approach him ordering him to stop punching this woman who was bleeding from the face. He shouted back to me, "Fuck you pig" and began to run deeper into the projects. I chased after him up a stairwell that led to one of the higher floors. As I turned a corner in the stairwell, he turned around and jumped on me, causing us both to tumble backward down the stairs. I hit my head hard on the concrete and immediately became dizzy and a bit disoriented. I told myself that if I lose consciousness, I'm going to die in this stairwell. Things began to move in slow motion inside my head. Despite my altered mental state, I knew that I was in a fight for my life. He spat in my face and shouted, "I'd rather kill you pig than go back to prison." So much for the useless police academy taught, "verbal judo and de-escalation" techniques.

As we were wrestling on the urine-ridden stairway, he had gotten on top of me and grabbed the handle of my firearm and was trying to rip it out of my holster with the intention to kill me. I fought to keep my firearm in my holster with one hand while attempting to break his fingers on the concrete step with my hip and body weight. I pulled his head towards me in an effort to gouge his eye out, bite his face, or crush his trachea with my other hand but this guy had superhuman strength and wasn't budging. It was later determined that he was high on crack cocaine.

I was always taught that if a pit bull bites and locks his jaw on either you or your partner, to stick either your finger or a pencil up its butt and it will let go. I couldn't reach this guy's butt, instead I buried my finger up his nose and that seemed to weaken his grip. I used my chin to key the microphone on my police radio to call for help. "3 David 41 – 10-25 Code Three (*officer needs help*), Valencia Gardens Housing Projects – middle courtyard stairwell."

I could immediately hear the sirens of the backup cavalry coming as I continued to fight for my life while waiting for my backup to arrive. No matter how fast they come, in a situation like this it's never fast enough. I fought as hard as I could, but I could feel him pulling even harder on my firearm. My only plan at this point was either to try and turn the barrel of my firearm towards him and shoot him or try and release the revolver's cylinder lock and dump the bullets onto the stairwell so that my gun couldn't function. I wasn't even able to get to the knife hidden underneath my shirt to stab him in the eye or throat. As the sound of the backup unit's sirens got closer, I experienced a surge of strength and was able to get on top of him and began to head-butt him in the face while still attempting to maintain control of my firearm.

Finally, the backup troops arrived, and I don't know who received more knees, punches, and elbows – him or me. Nevertheless, my opponent was restrained, my gun safely secure in its holster, and he was taken to the hospital by ambulance. He must have gotten injured as we rolled backwards down the stairwell. I ended up with a concussion and some pretty good bruises. He on the other hand had a few very nasty boo boos.

> *"For he (police officer) is God's minister to you for good. But if you do evil, be afraid; for he does not bear the sword in vain; for he is God's minister, an avenger to execute wrath on him who practices evil."*
>
> **Romans 13:4**

Well, old homeboy definitely had "wrath executed on him that night," and it was back to state prison for violating his parole.

These types of incidents begin to weigh on you after a while. The constant rehashing of the incident to see if I could have done anything different or better. Playing out several different endings can drive you crazy after a while. Reliving these types of events in our thoughts can make it hard to sleep. Day after day, violent incident after violent incident, only separates and isolates us from other people, including our loved ones. We begin to emotionally harden and lose the ability to completely relax, even on our days off. Just an intimate touch from a spouse can become very uncomfortable at times especially when you're not expecting it. Life becomes "criminals versus us" in many respects. We can sometimes build brick walls around ourselves and begin to emotionally isolate from anyone who doesn't see life the same way that we do. Unfortunately, that could include our spouse or people who are close to us. We not only sometimes sacrifice our lives in the line of duty like Officer Jim Guelff had. But we always sacrifice a piece of ourselves as human beings the longer we do this job.

Defund and hate us all you want, but when one of these so called "underprivileged" or "misunderstood" people" attack you or a family member – call a social worker. Let me know how that works out.

Sometimes the acting out behavior of a person needs to be addressed before we can deal with the root cause. I'm sure the guy I fought with in the stairway of the housing projects had a bad upbringing or a hard life. I get that – so did I. But I wasn't going to let him just kill me in an effort to try and understand and counsel him. As far as I'm concerned, he got the counseling that he needed at the time. Maybe he will find God and or sobriety within a prison ministry. I pray that he does.

MY CHAMBER SEVEN

"Saved by a Prostitute"

It was another lovely day walking the beat on Mission Street. I got along very well with the store owners on my beat, and fairly well with the drug dealers, gang members, prostitutes, drug addicts, and alcoholics. We shared a weird respect for one another, but they knew what line never to cross with me. I had never forgotten how I had grown up back in New York. I always reminded myself, "But for the grace of God go I." So, I respected and tried to help the street people who are what I used to be.

I frequently bought lunch for many of these people, tried to encourage them to get off the streets, go to an Alcoholics Anonymous meeting with me, or to a drug rehabilitation center. Now and then I got one of them to accept my offer. There was one homeless alcoholic who was a Vietnam Veteran named Rodney. He too was a transplant from New York. I really liked Rodney and was grateful to him for his service to our country. Several times I bought lunch for him, and we sat on the cement stairway of a building and talked as we ate lunch. People walked by and gave us weird looks, as if a uniformed police officer and a homeless bum sitting on a stairway having a friendly lunch together was unusual. Maybe it was, I guess.

Everyone on the street called me "New York" and said, "New York is hardcore, but he is fair." And I believe that was an accurate assessment of me. I would administer justice to them on Tuesday and buy them lunch on Wednesday. That was just the way it was. I always addressed a person's behavior, never their race or status in society. That didn't matter to me.

One day I was walking down Mission Street when Rodney frantically ran up to me and shouted, "New York, it's Maria, I think she overdosed on herron (*heroin*)." I followed Rodney to the end of a filthy alley and there was Maria, a well-known drug addict and prostitute lying next to a pile of trash, unconscious, with a syringe sticking out of her arm. She had foam seeping out of her nose and mouth. For a minute I had a flashback of my mother when she had overdosed on sleeping pills while attempting to commit suicide. I tried to wake Maria up, but she was barely breathing and had a very weak pulse. I called for an ambulance which arrived a few minutes later. The paramedic on the ambulance was a friend of mine named Greg. He injected Maria with a drug called Narcan, which usually immediately causes unconscious drug overdosed people to wake up and become alert. Maria was not responding. The ambulance rushed Maria off to the hospital.

Later that night I saw my paramedic friend Greg eating dinner at a taco joint on my beat. I went inside and asked him how Maria was doing. He said, "Oh that piece of crap died at the hospital. They found rat poison in her system. No loss to humanity."

I began to feel very sad.

"Hey Joe, what's the matter, you act as though the bitch's death actually bothers you."

"Na, it's all good. You live by the street, you die by the street," I responded.

I then left the taco joint and continued walking down Mission Street. I became really troubled inside and took a seat on a stairway that led to an apartment building. I began to think of an incident that involved Maria about six months earlier.

I was walking my foot beat one night. As I passed a burrito take out restaurant, I noticed a Latin Man dressed in military camouflage fatigues. I got a strange feeling in my gut about this guy but I just kind of dismissed it and kept walking because I had my thoughts set on eating dinner. This was my first mistake.

I walked about a block or so further on my beat when all of a sudden one of my partners from a different foot beat (*3 David 42*) transmitted to me over my police radio, that there was a guy in military fatigues walking up behind me with a gun and was going to kill me. My mind immediately flashed to that guy I saw in the burrito joint that I got an eerie feeling about. I turned around and there he was coming directly towards me with his right hand in his coat pocket and a serious look of determination in his eyes. This dude was on a mission from hell.

I immediately jumped between two parked cars and used them for cover. I drew my firearm, pointed it at him, and ordered him to show me his hands. He did not comply.

"Come any closer and I'm gonna blow your freakin head off," I shouted.

By this time the second foot beat had triangulated him to avoid any crossfire between us. We continued to command the guy to show us his hands and drop to his knees. Seeing that he was outnumbered and that we were about a nanosecond away from lighting him up with gunfire, he finally complied. We handcuffed him, searched him, and located a fully loaded 357 Magnum revolver in his coat pocket. He was then transported to Mission Station and the gun was booked into evidence.

As I spoke to the other foot beat officers, I asked Mike how the hell he knew this guy was coming up behind me, armed with a gun with the intention to kill me.

"Well Joe, if it wasn't for Maria running up to us and screaming and pointing out that 'the guy in the army outfit has a gun and he was going to kill New York,' we wouldn't have had a clue. Maria saved your ass."

I walked over to Maria who appeared to be very shaken. I couldn't tell if she was "jonesing" (*withdrawing*) off of heroin, or if she was truly shaken by the incident. It really didn't matter at this point. God used this drug-addicted prostitute to save my life. I put my arms around her and hugged her.

"Maria, you probably just saved my life. But why?" I asked.

"New York, most people on this street really like and respect you even though you are a cop. You're hard, but you're always fair. You talk to us, try and help us, and even buy us food and give us breaks now and then. I didn't want to see you take a cheap shot like that."

"But how did you know the guy had a gun?" I asked.

"Right after you walked past the burrito place, I saw him pull a pistol out of his coat pocket. He checked to make sure it was loaded, put it back in his pocket, and said in Spanish, "I'm going to kill that cop." I then saw Mike and his partner and ran over and told them. I'm really glad you are okay New York."

I became flooded with emotions of gratitude, fear, anger, and vengeance all at the same time. I also felt stupid and angry at myself for not following my gut instincts when I first saw the guy in the burrito joint.

I thanked Maria again and returned to Mission Station. There was my potential assassin handcuffed to the booking bench talking to himself. I had an overwhelming desire to beat him with a baseball bat. I walked up to him and called him a pussy for trying to sneak up behind me as opposed to facing me head-on. I told him that if I ever see him on my beat again, it would be his last time. I was fuming with rage and vengeance inside. He wasn't even a citizen of the United States. He was here illegally and with a gun. But nevertheless, I thank God for Maria.

So, Paramedic Greg, yes, I was sad when you told me that Maria died in the hospital. That "piece of crap who was no use to society," as you called her – saved my life that night on the road to hell referred to as Mission Street. God uses who He chooses.

I must admit though, after Maria's death, I did feel a bit guilty and sad that here was a woman who had saved my life, and I was not able to save hers in return. I know this feeling of "survivor's guilt" is very prevalent in both the military and in law enforcement. I have counseled many soldiers and cops whose main stressor was that they wish they could go back and do something differently. Maybe if we were given a second chance to do it differently, our partners or loved ones would still be here? Most of the time, this is not the case. We did our best at the time and we just have to accept that that's as good as it gets. The rest is fate.

For me, I just needed to find peace in the fact that everyone has a specific destiny in life, and that "life isn't fair," at least with respect as to how we understand it now. I'm sure that it will all make much better sense in the big picture of eternity. Some people die, so that others might live. My life has been saved on countless occasions. That only means that I owe my life to my partners, people like Maria, and to God. The best way for me to pay them forward is by living the best most productive life now, and by helping other people wherever I can. I could no longer help Maria but I could help people like her, and I did wherever I could.

Maria was a drug addict and a prostitute – yes. But I am probably still here today because of her and other people that God had used over the years to spare me since my childhood.

Maria reminds me of a story in the Bible in the Second chapter of Joshua, where a prostitute named, Rahab the Harlot, hid two spies from the camp of Israel to save their lives from the searching army who would have arrested and probably killed them. They lived because of the actions taken by this prostitute named Rahab – (*in my case Maria*).

God can use anything or anybody that He chooses to get the job done. Throughout my entire life, God has shown up for me in countless faces and personalities. Everyone in life has a purpose, even if we may not understand that purpose at the time. People referred to me as a useless alcoholic until I got sober and met Jesus. We never know where someone may be on their path before the miracle happens. I was on the end of my bed with a bottle of whiskey and a pistol ready to check out right before my miracle showed up.

Where are you in your life, and how close are you to receiving your miracle? Are you asking for it? Are you expecting it? Are you doing your part? Do you believe you deserve it?

God says that you do – and that is a majority vote.

> *"For I know the thoughts that I think toward you, says the LORD, thoughts of peace and not of evil, to give you a future and a hope."*
>
> **Jeremiah 29:11**

MY CHAMBER EIGHT

"Machete Man"

It was the beginning of the swing shift (*2pm – 12am*) at Mission Station. We were all standing in formation in the "at ease" position being briefed by our lieutenant who was standing behind a podium in front of us. The purpose of these "lineups" or "briefings" was to update us on wanted bulletins of criminals that were being sought after, as well as any other administrative announcements.

This particular lieutenant was hard of hearing and wore double hearing aids. He would always ramble on talking about irrelevant, boring issues. I was holding a high-speed electronic dog-repellent device in my hand that was behind my back. The device put out a very high-pitched sound but not very noticeable to humans. I carried this device to repel dogs that came after me on my beat as a more humane method than using my gun or pepper spray.

But this day, I found a comical use for it. All the other cops in the lineup knew what I had planned to do. Every time the lieutenant began to speak, I would press the button on the device creating a high-pitched noise in his hearing aids. He tried to adjust his hearing aids to quell the noise, but this process just kept repeating itself every time he began to speak. The other cops were busting at the seams trying not to laugh. After about the fourth time, the lieutenant just released us to the streets, while still wiggling his finger in his ears. Yes, I am 'that guy.' I was always the class clown back in school and obviously, nothing changed when I became a police officer.

My partner Ed and I stopped into a few of the establishments and checked in with the owners to make sure everything was ok. We spoke to a few people on the street and literally helped a little old lady across the street with a bag of groceries who was on her way to her assisted living home. We went inside with her and greeted all the people who were there. Whether I worked alone or was with a partner, this was something that I made sure I did every day. I would go there to celebrate their birthdays and to just cheer them up in general. Somedays I brought them flowers for their dining room. They loved it when we came by to visit. We said our goodbyes and headed down to the bowels of Mission Street, where we were not so appreciated. As we were walking down 24th Street, a group of about eight gang members were sitting on a stairway. As soon as they saw me, they got up and left the area, leaving the name of a rival gang member spray painted on a brick wall with a line painted through the name. This usually foretold the next gang member who would be murdered within a few days.

"You're like The Grim Reaper Joe. Whenever you walk down the street these gang members run for their lives," said my partner, Ed.

"As it should be Ed. Those freakin pukes have no rights. All they do is harass innocent people, rob these elderly people from the assisted living home, and kill each other in drive-by shootings. They better move when they see me, or I will break my foot off in their ass and find something to take them to jail for. Nine out of ten of them have warrants for their arrest so that won't be hard.

I do this job as my service to God and to protect innocent people. Not to kiss politician's asses. This is my beat, and the taxpayers pay us to keep it clean and safe – then clean and safe it will be," I stated.

Me Having a Chat With my Gang Buddies as a Former Gang Detective

Ed and I finally reached the corner of 24th and Mission Streets. A popular hangout for gang bangers. There was a bar next to the underground train station. The bar's clientele were state prison parolees and the Mexican Mafia. They just loved it when I walked into this bar and interrupted their pool game by reaching into one of the pool table pockets and pulling out a bag of cocaine or methamphetamine, or sometimes a pistol. They hated it when I walked in but loved it when I walked out. They didn't like me, but they respected me. Many of them had past experiences of what disrespecting me felt like.

Suddenly, a guy frantically ran up to us. "Officers, there is a guy getting killed by the underground train station. He is being chopped up by a guy with a machete."

Sure enough, we crossed the street onto the train station plaza, and there was a guy chopping another guy to pieces like a tree trunk with a large machete. People were screaming in horror as this guy was hacking away at this other dude. Ed and I drew our firearms and triangulated our firing positions on the guy with the machete. I screamed at the guy to drop the machete, or I was going to kill him. The guy stopped for a minute and began to stare at this little girl frozen with fear near the bus stop. I repositioned myself in between "Machete Man" and the little girl. He then looked at me with a "focused stare."

"Ahh crap, this aint gonna be good," I thought to myself.

Just then, I had a very brief flashback to an incident I had been involved with two blocks away a few months earlier. A man had gone on a rampage inside of a family-owned restaurant. He was the deranged uncle of the family. He grabbed a meat cleaver and murdered all of the adults. Someone had called the police and said a murder was taking place. My partner and I ran to the location. When we entered the restaurant there was blood all over the place and dead bodies on the floor. There were two little children crying and shaking under a table. The guy with the meat cleaver had already fled the scene. We picked up the children and brought them to a safe place.

Even though this incident happened months ago, I was struggling to get this intrusive memory out of my head so that I could deal with the immediate threat at hand from the guy with the machete. I was experiencing two different but similar events in my head at the same time. It was like watching two different TV shows simultaneously. I began to focus on the man standing in front of me holding a bloody machete while doing my best to block out the memory of the prior meat cleaver event.

I had Machete Man lined up in my pistol sights and had already given myself the green light to shoot him.

Machete Man started to walk towards me as he raised the machete to strike me. As I began to press the trigger of my firearm to plant a bullet or two into his chest, I noticed a group of petrified kids standing directly behind him who were probably on their way home from school.

I eased my finger off the trigger. Neither Ed nor I had a clean shot at this guy because there were friendlies (*innocent people*) standing behind him. I had to do something very fast.

I re-holstered my firearm, moved off the line of attack, and drew my wooden straight-stick baton. As he took his first swing at me, I blocked his arm with my baton. He then pulled back to take a second slash at my legs. I wanted to smash him over the head with my baton but that wouldn't have saved my leg. Instead, I kicked the machete out of his hand, but the machete cut through my shoe and lacerated the top of my foot. I was then able to slam the guy onto the ground and handcuff him while Ed was covering my six (*watching my back*). Once the guy was handcuffed, he began to violently resist Ed and myself. Other backup patrol units had arrived at this time to assist. It all happened very fast.

Ed and I tried forcing our prisoner into one of the nearby patrol vehicles, but he began kicking at us and continued his resistance. I was pretty amped up with adrenaline by this time and I was done with this guy. My adrenaline dump turned into anger. I put the guy into a wrist lock, pulled his hair back, and forced him to the top of the very steep stairway that led to the underground train station. I pretended to speak into my police radio. "Headquarters, I need an ambulance Code Three for a serious head wound. My prisoner tried to escape, and he fell down the stairway. He's hurt really bad."

"I'm not trying to escape," said Machete Man.

"Then if you don't calm the 'F' down, I'm gonna throw your ass head first down these stairs," I stated.

"No, I'm good man, I apologize officer."

He then allowed us to put him in the back seat of a nearby patrol car.

"You're crazy dude," he told me.

"You have no idea," I replied, and off to Mission Station he went. An ambulance took his bleeding and semi-conscious victim to the hospital as well.

Before I left, I got down on one knee to speak with the little frightened girl while holding her hands to make sure that she was okay. I asked one of the patrol units to take her home so that she would not have to wait for the bus and see the blood from machete man's victim on the concrete.

Seeing a pool of blood on concrete always takes my mind back to the day I sailed through Macy's glass door. I guess these memories are just things we must accept within our profession. We never know what will trigger the resurrection of these past memories into current feelings. But like they say within the Armed Forces Circle, "*Suck it up buttercup.*" Sometimes that is easier said than done. Many of us just go through our professional lives and try not to feel certain emotions. I get that. We just do our jobs and convince ourselves that "*feelings are for pussies*" and our personal feelings and stresses have no place in our job. And during a critical incident that may be true. When it's "game on" we must be strategic and tactical rather than emotional. But after the critical incident is over, we have a choice. We either consciously debrief the experience and let it go, or we stuff it down inside of us and let it rot over time.

But after twenty-five years of constantly stuffing emotions down our own throats, they become like a compressed spring. At some point the pressure of the spring starts to recoil and push back. Such as in our sleep, at a bar, in an addiction, during the excessive use of force that gets us fired, or in a divorce court. We must take the time to consider our feelings both during our career and after our retirement. Our goal must be to find balance through healthy activities or a holistic lifestyle that offsets our negative emotions and experiences. But like with Maria the prostitute's death. I told the paramedic that she basically got what she deserved and "*if you live by the street, you die by the street.*" That is what I said, but it was far from what I felt. I was very sad that the woman who saved my life ended up dying in a filthy alley with a needle sticking out of her arm. Many of us try to avoid these feelings at all costs. There can be a temporary benefit to this, but unfortunately sooner or later, it is like a double-edged sword that comes back to haunt us in one way or another.

We can be like John Wayne and tough it out. But I have known many of the "*John Wayne Type Personalities*" including myself, that imploded internally over time. The old saying, "we are what we eat" is true. But that also includes the emotional food (*feelings*) that we swallow over time. We become that as well. I sure did.

But back to 'Machete Man.' My supervisor put Ed and myself in for a medal of valor. I told him that I didn't really think that we deserved an award because on Mission Street, stuff like this happens all the time. It's really no big deal. My supervisor then said that the medal of valor comes with a $500.00 check.

"Well in that case sir, put us in for the medal," I said as we both began to laugh.

A few nights later I was eating what was supposed to be a romantic dinner with my date. I began to rehash this incident in my head. It wasn't the swinging of the machete, nor the guy who got hacked by the machete that kept replaying over and over in my mind. I've seen crap like that many times before. It was that frightened little girl's face that kept haunting me.

"What if I didn't use trigger discipline and accidentally shot that little girl?" I kept asking myself. "What if?"

"Are you ok Joe? You're somewhere other than here with me," asked my dinner date.

"Yeah, yeah, I'm ok. Just thinking about something that happened at work."

"Can you leave work at work and just enjoy our dinner together?"

"Yeah, I'm sorry," I answered as the "what if" thoughts kept rolling around in my head.

About one month later, I was awarded a Bronze Medal of Valor and Ed was awarded a Police Commission Commendation. This was one of many awards that I had received throughout my law enforcement career from several different agencies both foreign and domestic.

San Francisco Police Department

Medal of Valor Award

WHEREAS, the Award Committee of the San Francisco Police Department has carefully investigated the application for a BRONZE MEDAL OF VALOR, made on behalf of

Joe Bannon

WHEREAS, the said Committee has adjudged that this officer did manifest outstanding bravery above and beyond that expected in the line of duty on the 3rd day of December 1991, and, at great personal risk of life and with full knowledge of the danger involved, terminated the criminal career of person(s) who, while at large, had engaged in criminal activity inimical to the public welfare and safety of the inhabitants of the City and County of San Francisco; and,

WHEREAS, the determination of the Award Committee has been approved by the Chief of Police; therefore be it

RESOLVED, that the Police Commission approves the findings of the said Award Committee and the said recommendation of the Chief of Police, and the Police Commission hereby awards a BRONZE MEDAL OF VALOR on the 18th day of May 1993

CHIEF OF POLICE

PRESIDENT, POLICE COMMISSION

POLICE COMMISSIONER

POLICE COMMISSIONER

POLICE COMMISSIONER

POLICE COMMISSIONER

MY CHAMBER NINE

"Shooting a Brother Cop"

A former police partner of mine had taken a leave of absence from the San Francisco Police Department. He applied to another agency down in the Caribbean as a narcotics enforcement agent. This was definitely the "big time" of being a narcotics cop. This was the front door of the Colombian Drug Cartels, who stopped at nothing to protect and profit from their precious Cocaine that supplied the United States via Puerto Rico and Miami.

Killing or torturing cops and narcotics agents was like swatting an annoying fly to them. I spoke to my former partner via telephone about once a week. The stories he told me were horrendous. Judges, political officials, and cops were getting killed on what seemed like a weekly basis.

Sometimes, the Cartel would cut their victims into pieces, put the pieces in a box, and send the box to the family of the chopped-up victim. Kind of reminded me of "Machete Man" at the train station.

My former partner would mail me newspaper clippings and pictures of some of the stuff that he was experiencing down in Cartel Land. Some of the stories kind of grossed me out, but at the same time, they enticed me to leave the police department and join him. Which I eventually did.

One day, my former partner came back to San Francisco for a few days, and he brought three local Puerto Rico Police Officers with him who he had become friends with. Their intent was to apply to the San Jose Police Department in California which had a large Puerto Rican population. San Jose was about fifty miles south of San Francisco.

There was a Puerto Rican and Cuban Restaurant on my beat just off Mission Street that I suggested that we bring our visiting guests to. I was off duty, so we all met at Mission Station and walked a few blocks to the restaurant.

For some strange and very unusual reason, I decided to carry a different off-duty firearm tucked in a shoulder holster with me that night under my shirt. I don't have a clue why I did this. I hardly ever carried this large frame .45 caliber semi-automatic pistol with me on my days off. But for some reason this night, I did. Maybe it was to impress my dinner guests? I don't know.

As we were walking to the restaurant, we passed a small unlit parking lot on 24th Street known for its illegal drug dealing activity. Being that we were all cops, we seemed to see the same thing at the same time. There was a man standing behind a black car with its trunk open. Even though we were all off duty, it seems that our cop switch always stayed in the "on" position. We slowly approached the man and the car. One of the Puerto Rican Cops who spoke English shouted, "Hey, what the hell are you doing back there?"

Without notice, the man behind the car produced a handgun, pointed it at us, and shouted back, "Get the f—k out of here." My former partner and our out-of-town guests froze in their places. I instinctively jumped behind a nearby van for cover and reached behind my right hip where I usually carry my pistol. But there was no pistol. I then remembered I was carrying a different gun in a shoulder holster. I drew this pistol from my shoulder holster and pointed it at the guy who was pointing his gun at my former partner and our guests. I aimed carefully at his head and pulled the trigger.

Nothing happened. I suddenly remembered that this firearm had a safety on it that the gun I normally carried did not. I immediately flipped off the safety to take another headshot. Before I was able to get a shot off, I heard him speaking police codes into a radio. "Headquarters this is 5 Nora 120 (*a narcotics division sergeant*), I have a group of 917s (*suspicious people*) in the parking lot of 24th and Capp Streets. Can you have a Mission Station Unit do a roll by?"

"10-4, 5 Nora 120," responded the dispatcher.

"Holy crap, it's a cop," I said to myself as I identified myself to him. I then looked back over my left shoulder and there was a man (*his police partner*) pointing his gun to the back of my head getting ready to 'coup de grace' me. Thank God we all figured out what was taking place before one or more of us got killed. We exchanged a few words, blew it off as nothing, and shook hands. My former partner, the three Puerto Rican Cops, and I continued to the restaurant.

While at the restaurant, we sat there mostly in dead silence. We all knew what could have just happened and how close of a call it was for us all.

This was a difficult event for me to just let go because in my mind, I had just shot a brother police officer in the head. The only thing that saved him, was a tactical mistake on my part. I violated every tactical protocol in the book that night by carrying a firearm that I was not familiar with.

I know better. I came in first place as "Top Gun" on the police counter sniper team tryout list. I was a member of the Police Counter Sniper Specialist Team. We trained consistently. I was a "gun guy." I would not have missed, especially at such close range. The problem was, his partner who had his gun pointed at the back of my head, wouldn't have missed either. I was so focused on the guy with the gun standing behind the car pointing his gun at us, that I didn't even sense his partner coming up behind me. Another tactical mistake.

This one really broke the straw on the camel's back for me. I laid in bed at night for hours and pictured newspaper headlines reading, "*Cop Shoots Another Cop in Confrontation Gone Bad.*" I repetitiously asked myself, "what if, what if, what if." Finally, I had to tell my mind to shut up. It didn't happen so stop playing it out a billion times as though it had.

I just couldn't forgive myself for killing another cop (*at least in my head*) and me almost getting my brains blown out simultaneously by his partner. That night continued to haunt me for months.

It haunted me so much that I had to find that narcotics sergeant and tell him what really happened. He turned out to be a really cool guy until I told him that I pulled the trigger on him, and by the grace of God, my gun didn't fire. I could see the blood drain from his face as his smile turned to a very nervous look.

"I should have identified myself as a cop instead of just pointing my gun at you and telling you guys to, "get the 'F' outta here," said the narcotics sergeant.

By telling him what really happened that night, I finally felt some closure and relief for the first time since that incident had taken place in the parking lot. I never carried that gun again. I sold it to a gun dealership.

God works in very mysterious ways. If I was carrying my normal off duty gun that night, both he and I would be dead. Why did I decide to go Rambo that night with an unfamiliar gun in a shoulder holster that I hadn't worn for a very long time? I don't have a clue. All I know is that because of violating standard protocol, which I never did before, two cops got to live and see another day. Me being one of them.

"The steps of a good man (or a man trying to be good in my case) are ordered by the LORD, And He delights in his way. Though he fall, he shall not be utterly cast down; For the LORD upholds him with His hand." (words in parenthesis added).

Psalm 37:23-24

Does that scripture also mean that God led me to carry the wrong (*actually the right*) gun that night? Was He that involved and sovereign in my life that he could have me choose a different firearm for no known reason? Or did He just back up my mistake?

I was a backslidden Christian. I did just enough to keep a lukewarm relationship with God. Even in my backslidden state, God had my back. I never ever could have lived through that night if I had shot that sergeant, even if his partner hadn't shot me. I would have died inside one way or another.

I went right back to my "self-medicating" lifestyle to deal with the PTSD that at the time, I didn't really believe I had.

My stress-relieving techniques still consisted of praying, trying to relax and meditate through a rapid heartbeat and nonstop thoughts. Going to church on occasion, still staying sober in a Twelve Step Program, drinking Red Bulls, coffee, and ephedrine-laced gym drinks (*when they were legal*), and engaging in sexual encounters. I didn't really believe that I was "The Apple of God's Eye" at the time. Maybe a "road apple" (*horse crap*).

I refused to admit that I had Post Traumatic Stress issues. Neither from my childhood nor my chosen profession. "I was just in a profession where insanity is normal," I convinced myself. "I am a warrior, we don't get that crap. PTSD is for the weak. Just suck it up and push forward. As long as I can just suppress my feelings, I will be fine. I got this," is what I constantly told myself.

I had developed a great ability to control my emotions, especially my anger. The martial arts helped me to develop this ability to control my feelings. The problem was that it was all or nothing. I was able to control my anger and fear, but at the same time, I couldn't let anyone get too close to me emotionally, nor did I have the ability to be overly intimate with another person.

Promiscuous sex without any commitment seemed to work well to manage my stress and inner loneliness. The problem is that sexually acting out had become just as strong of a compulsive behavior as alcohol and drugs had been, back when I was nineteen. I didn't even ask God to take this compulsive behavior away, because I didn't know what life would be like without this form of an escape. I couldn't drink alcohol or take drugs, so sexual promiscuity had become my current form of emotional medication. But I would never come to terms with that until many years later. At the time, it was my limited way of expressing any form of love.

Thank God for His Grace and Mercy. He doesn't always give us the punishment that we deserve (*Mercy*). And He does give us things that we don't deserve (*Grace*). I'm glad that I was on His shortlist.

> *"He the LORD is merciful and gracious, Slow to anger, and abounding in mercy. He will not always strive with us, Nor will He keep His anger forever. He has not dealt with us according to our sins, Nor punished us according to our iniquities. For as the heavens are high above the earth, So great is His mercy toward those who fear Him; As far as the east is from the west, So far has He removed our transgressions from us".*
>
> **Psalm 103:8-12**

MY CHAMBER TEN

"Ordered to the Police Stress Unit"

I was making great arrests on the street and making life much safer for the business owners and innocent people on my beat. They wrote letters of appreciation to my captain stating that they appreciated my work and that life was better for them when I was on the beat.

My lieutenant (*LT*) called me into his office one day to offer me a new position. It was with the Community Police Officer Program (*CPOP*). The prototype for this program originated with the New York City Police Department and had proven to be very successful.

"Is this a punishment 'LT?' I asked.

"No Joe, you do great police work, but with the number of complaints that you have been receiving lately, I thought you might need a break. You will still do police work. You have a great personality and a natural way with people. I appreciate your hard work, as do the business owners and residents of the Mission District. I think you are ideal for this team. It's a little more 'using your brains as opposed to your brawn.' Its either this, or I put you inside for a while to cool off by working the front desk," stated my lieutenant.

"I'm in Sir, when do I start?" I asked.

Soon afterward I became a part of the "Community Home Security Program." The objective of the program was to teach the residents of my district how to make their homes safer and more secure. I attended a two-day seminar that presented a bunch of weak, politically correct, security techniques that stood no chance of success. I began meeting with the residents of my district and conducted security surveys of their homes and businesses.

I visited the home of an elderly couple who stated that they had been burglarized several times by cocaine and methamphetamine addicts over the past eighteen years. The man stated that the best locks that money could buy couldn't keep these burglars out of their home. I saw a photograph on a credenza of the man holding a fishing pole with some fish that he had caught.

"So, I see that you are a fisherman," I stated.

"Yes, I used to fish all of the time until my arthritis got really bad,"

"Well King Neptune, I have an idea. I would suggest that you nail some large fishhooks two inches apart around the inside frames of your back windows. I'll also show you how to booby trap the entrance to your basement if they try and get in that way," I added.

The man then showed me an old, rusted shotgun that he had since he was a kid (*based on his age, I'm surprised it wasn't a musket*). I helped him clean the shotgun and get it back into functional condition.

These were not exactly the tactics that I was taught at that security seminar but hell, these people needed tactics that work – not just look good on paper and have been approved by lawyers and weak politicians. I believed that these people had the right to be safe in their own homes. After all, the burglars didn't follow any rules, so why should the tax-paying home and business owners?

I continued to go from house to house, and business to business, teaching people effective security tactics that helped to keep them safe. I even helped them build some of my suggestions with my own hands on my days off.

There were community meetings each month where the residents and business owners got together to present their issues to the police department and the mayor's office. I was invited to this meeting. In attendance were the home and business owners of my district, the captain of my police station, and his chief of staff who was a sergeant and a good friend of mine named Ray. Also present at the meeting was a representative from the mayor's office.

After the snacks and coffee, the residents and business owners got up to express their concerns about crime in their neighborhood. As they spoke, each one of them brought me up by name.

"We especially appreciate Officer Bannon and his creative ideas to make us safer."

They went on to explain how I taught them how to make booby traps, place fishhooks around their windows, and how I repaired the fisherman's shotgun. On and on they explained how I had taught them these tactics that they were extremely grateful for. I noticed Sergeant Ray trying not to crack up laughing in front of the captain and the official from the mayor's office. I felt proud as I heard each resident compliment me in front of my captain. I did notice though that my captain had a very nervous look on his face, and the representative from the mayor's office looked like she had just seen the original movie, "The Exorcist" starring Linda Blair.

The next day I was called into my captain's office. I was prepared for him to tell me how great of a job that I was doing in my district within this new community security program. That's not quite how the conversation went.

"Joe, I just got a call from the mayor's chief of staff. She was appalled at what you have been teaching these people in our CPOP Program. I could hardly believe what I heard myself. This is supposed to be a "community program" that the mayor was proud to implement – not an act of "guerrilla warfare." You're a great cop who means well, but this isn't New York, and you're going to have to do things by the book. You're eventually going to bring a lawsuit against yourself as well as the department," said the captain.

"I'm only trying to clean up my beat and keep innocent people safe captain."

"Yes, Joe, but there are rules to follow."

"The rules don't work captain. The rules protect the criminals, not the victims."

"Make them work Joe," replied my captain in a very stern voice.

"Yes Sir," I responded.

As I left the captain's office, I ran into the captain's Chief of Staff, Sergeant Ray.

"So did you get your ass chewed out?" asked Ray.

I just looked at him contemptuously.

"You're my hero Bannon. That was the best community meeting that I have ever attended since becoming the captain's chief of staff. I'm sorry the captain doesn't share the same sense of humor," he added as he slapped me on the back.

A few days after my meeting with the captain, he got another call from the mayor's office from another high-ranking official.

"Joe," said my captain. "I need to deep-six you for a while until the mayor's office cools down."

I was placed on desk duty taking window reports and answering the phone for the next thirty days. I also had to see a counselor at the Police Stress Unit once a week. During my absence on my beat, the captain's office received several calls from the residents and business owners.

"Where is Officer Bannon? We haven't seen him in over two weeks and things are starting to get bad again."

The captain stated that I had been temporarily assigned to a "special project."

These mandatory police stress counselling sessions were pretty lame.

"Do you have any underlying stress or frustrations in your life?" asked the counsellor.

"Only that this city lets the criminals run the streets and that they have more rights than the tax-paying citizens. I hate to see criminals preying on innocent people in their own neighborhoods. What's wrong with that?" I asked.

"Nothing Joe, you just have to play by the rules."

"Screw the rules, they don't work. The criminals laugh at the rules. This system is a waste of taxpayer's money. They don't get the protection that they not only pay for but that they deserve. It's not about what's right or wrong. It's about politicians getting votes and defense attorneys making money. That's bullcrap. That's not why I became a cop. I think our society needs to reevaluate what we are willing to put up with and what we are willing to let these criminals get away with. We arrest these a-holes and the courts release them the same day so that they can go right back and victimize the same innocent people again. Where is the 'criminal justice' in that?

When I see some dope dealer on the street frightening some little old lady on her way home from the store, I'm not going to arrest him, I'm going to teach him respect. If the useless, backed-up court system can't solve the problem, then I will."

The counsellor then asked me if I had any conflict about having a religious background and being a tough, hands-on street cop.

"Not at all," I answered. "What I do out on the street is tough love and it's the only thing that some of these people understand. I'm not aggressive with everyone on my beat. Just the ones who want to challenge me, my job, and abuse helpless victims. It's my job to alter their behavior and to protect the rest of society from them. For example: I was walking my beat one day when I saw a guy punch an elderly woman, knock her to the ground, take her purse, and then fractured her ribs by stomping on her before he fled with her purse. I chased him for three blocks while my partner attended to the elderly woman. When I finally caught him, he began to resist arrest by fighting me. To me, I used justifiable force to overcome his resistance and arrest him. To others, some may say that he got his ass kicked just like Jesus would have done to him."

"Where in the Bible does it say that Jesus kicked anyone's ass, Joe?"

"When the traders were selling goods at the temple, Jesus referred to it as a 'den of thieves,' and proceeded to flip over their tables, pour out their money, made a whip, and drove them out of the temple," I answered.

"So, it's spare the rod, spoil the child?" he asked.

"Exactly" I responded. "The Bible also states, 'For he (*police officer*) is the minister of God to thee for good. But if thou do that which is evil, be afraid; for he beareth not the sword in vain; for he is the minister of God, a revenger to execute wrath upon him that doeth evil.'

I'm nowhere close to being a perfect Christian. I have my own sins that I struggle with. But, when I am working on the streets, I am serving God who is the ultimate truth, not political correctness and all of these one-sided rules that benefit the criminals and keep innocent people victimized."

"You really need to re-evaluate your perspective of police work Joe. Times have changed," said the counsellor.

"And not for the better," I stated. "Times may have changed but the Word of God and His principles of right and wrong have not. And it's not even about fantasizing God's words or religion. I'm not a religious fanatic. It's just about the moral and societal principles of right and wrong. If that guy was hard up for money, then just take the old lady's purse, there's no need to knock her onto the ground and stomp on her. So, to answer your question about 'sparing the rod and spoiling the child' – yes, he got just what he deserved."

The counselor suggested I talk to a certain police lieutenant. This lieutenant was a living legend in the police department. A former US Marine and Viet Nam veteran with the reputation of being a one-man army in his day. I admired a man like this, and I looked forward to meeting him.

I met with the lieutenant and found he agreed with some of the ways I viewed police work. But he also cautioned me that getting in trouble or losing my job over some dirtbag on the street just wasn't worth it.

"From what I hear, Joe, you're a really good cop who's made excellent arrests and a great name for himself. Don't burn yourself out by making this your own personal war," said the lieutenant.

"I just want to counter the freakin' injustice lieutenant," I answered.

"That's an admirable quality, Joe, but you'll never do it all by yourself. Trust me. I learned this a long time ago."

I had no clue at the time that years later, this lieutenant would be promoted to captain, and I would be working for him as an undercover narcotics sergeant on one of the biggest, most politically hot, drug sting operations in the history of the police department. A case that would change both of our careers and drastically change my life.

I thanked the lieutenant for his time and went back to Mission Station to finish my thirty-day prison sentence of desk duty. Actually, it wasn't all that bad because I used a lot of that time to complete my doctoral dissertation on Nutritional Medicine and Health Science in between my desk duties.

After my thirty days were up, I took some time off from the department. Part of the completion of my doctorate degree required me to attend a supervised internship and undergo a written and clinical examination process. I had passed with a very high-grade point average.

After eight years of hard work in addition to a full-time career, I was awarded my doctorate degree in Holistic Health Science. Pretty amazing for a guy who barely made it through high school. It was another stroke of God's Hand on my 'repainted canvas.'

I developed a health program for law enforcement officers called, "*Tactical Nutrition*," for cops on the go. It was a much healthier approach to a cop's general nutritional and mental well-being than the "donut and coffee diet" that many people always accused us of eating.

MY CHAMBER ELEVEN

"San Francisco to San Juan"

During my time off to finish my degree requirements, I had deeply pondered the words that the lieutenant had spoken to me – *"Don't make this my personal war."*

"But it is a war, and I am a warrior. This is a war between good and evil and I have been called to protect people who can't protect themselves. Maybe I need a new mission in life?" I thought to myself.

After much thought and prayer, I applied for and took the United States Treasury Enforcement Agent (*TEA*) exam which I aced. Passing this exam put my name on an eligibility list that opened several doors for me within the federal government. I then decided to leave the San Francisco Police Department and relocate to the Caribbean to join my former police partner in the "*War Against Drugs*." A war with no restraints, and no mayor's chief of staff bitching to my captain because I was trying to help good people survive. If it were up to her, she would have suggested putting pillows around the old man's window instead of fishhooks.

I previously had several phone interviews with the chief of the agency that my former partner was now affiliated with. I had also mailed the chief my resume. The chief showed enough interest in me and my background that he asked me to fly down to the Caribbean for a personal interview with him and if selected, go through an expedited hiring process. I flew down to meet with him in person and after my interview, he offered me a position pending a successful background check which I had passed. My former partner had vetted me and talked me up to the chief. Things were done much differently in that part of the world. Much less red tape. Basically, if the right person vets you or if the chief likes you – you're in. Luckily, I had both going for me. I flew back to San Francisco to tie up my loose ends.

The police department was no longer permitting leaves of absence like my former partner had been given. If I wanted to relocate to this new mission, I would have to resign from the police department with no guarantees of getting my job back if this venture didn't work out. This was a very hard and risky decision. But a decision nonetheless that I had made.

My fellow San Francisco Police Officers were shocked that I had decided to travel over four thousand miles to the unknown but agreed that I would do well as a Caribbean Commando battling the Colombian Drug Cartels. I was about to become a narcotic enforcement agent in one of the most dangerous and politically corrupt playing fields in the world. Another one of my fatal attractions.

My last day as a San Francisco police officer finally had arrived. A few days before, the cops that I'd worked with throughout the years had all gotten together to throw a party at an Italian restaurant in North Beach, which was San Francisco's version of Little Italy. Several of my closest male and female friends on the force had tears in their eyes as they said their goodbyes.

"Joe, we wish that you would stay," one of my old partners said. "It just won't be the same here without you. You've become a legend on Mission Street. Some of us looked forward coming to work just to see some of the creative things that you were going to do that day. You're really a good hearted man and the best backup a cop could ever ask for."

Afterward, an officer carried out a candle-lit cake with the words, "We love you Joe," written on it. Now it was my turn for teary eyes.

After the party, I said my final goodbyes and drove my car to the top of Twin Peaks, which is one of the highest points in San Francisco. I wanted to take one last look at the city that had played such a crucial role in my life. My mind started to wander as I scanned the "City by the Bay." I thought back to when I was a kid watching the TV police show, "The Streets of San Francisco" and remembered how cool it was to watch the shoot-outs and the high-speed car chases up and down the steep streets that I now personally knew so well.

What used to be a fantasy and a dream for me as a kid, had now become a reality that was about to become a fond memory. I recalled my armed confrontation scenarios and high-speed chases down some of the same streets and over some of the same hills that Clint Eastwood had chased his bad guys. I thought back on some of my crazy escapades and some of the close calls I had while out on patrol during the late-night hours of this wild city. Drug dealers, drag queens, gay life, pimps, prostitutes, gangsters, the violent riots, and protests – and the little Christian Apostolic Faith Church on the corner trying to save them all had become a big part of my world on a daily basis.

Several thoughts flooded through my head. I sincerely asked God to be with me and guide me in this "pseudo-insane" venture that I was about to embark on. But nevertheless, I felt a peace inside that I was doing the right thing. My former partner who I will now refer to as 'Airborne' or 'A' for short, had previously sent me several newspaper clippings about the Colombian Drug Cartels and the increasingly murderous drug war being waged in the Caribbean and South America. I knew this was about to get real.

What many people do not understand about the South American "Drug War" is the sophisticated and lethal network of drug traffickers that operate between Colombia, Bolivia, Puerto Rico, Miami, Mexico, Central America, and other points of entry. Puerto Rico and other strategic routes throughout the Caribbean are set points of resistance between South America and the United States Mainland in an effort to intercept large shipments of cocaine before making it to Miami or these other aforementioned points of entry. Many people get killed on both the South American and North American sides of these shipments.

Colombia judges, court workers start nationwide strikes

BOGOTA, Colombia (AP) – Judges and court workers began a series of nationwide strikes Thursday, a day after another judge and a congressman were murdered, apparently by drug traffickers.

In Medellin, where the judge was killed, federal justices walked off the job indefinitely until they receive more protection.

It is the third time judges have gone on strike in the last three months, with each walkout following the assassination of a federal judge. In the last eight years 222 court workers, including 43 judges, have been killed, most of them by drug traffickers.

In the latest slaying, federal Judge Mariela Espinoza was killed by submachine gun fire from two speeding cars as she arrived at her Medellin home Wednesday night with two motorcycle guards. One of the bodyguards and a bystander were wounded.

Espinoza, 43, was one of 42 federal appellate judges in Medellin, a city of 2 million people that is the cocaine capital of Colombia.

In the capital of Bogota federal Rep. Luis Francisco Madero was killed with a pistol shot to the head Wednesday night by a man who was waiting for Madero in the shadows outside the congressman's apartment.

Madero, a 27-year veteran in Colombia's House of Representatives, had supported extradition of Colombians to the United States to face drug traffickin[g] charges.

No one claimed responsibility for [ei]ther of the slayings, but governme[nt] security forces say that brought to 42 t[he] number of people killed by drug traffic[k]ers since a government crackdown beg[an] 11 weeks ago.

The deaths include the three fede[ral] judges, a congressman, a governor, [a] state leader of the leftist Patriotic Uni[on] and nine news media employees. T[...] newspapers have been bombed.

The traffickers are trying to force t[he] government to reverse its decision [to] extradite suspected Colombian drug tra[f]fickers to the United States. Five suspec[t]ed traffickers have been extradited [so] far.

The National Association of Co[urt] Workers, which includes 5,000 judges a[nd] 12,000 other court workers, declar[ed] a strike of two hours Thursday, four ho[urs] Friday, and all of Nov. 1 and Nov. 8

Judges, Court Workers, Cops, and other Government Officials are assassinated in Colombia, South America, and the Caribbean on a weekly basis.

(43) Colombian Judges Assassinated by The Drug Cartel in Medellin

My departure day had finally arrived. My plane left the San Francisco Airport and landed in San Juan, Puerto Rico via Miami where I was met by 'A' and an agent from Interpol. 'A' had made a lot of high-level police, military, and government agency contacts during the time he was living here on the island. After I picked up my luggage, the three of us walked outside to an unmarked police vehicle with a revolving blue light propped up on the roof. We arrived in the Condado area of San Juan and transferred my baggage to a different car.

By now, I was pretty tired and sick to my stomach from something that I had previously eaten in San Francisco on my way to the airport. While driving down a highway called the Autopista, 'A' brought me up to speed as to what has been going on in the drug world locally. He also told me that our first training mission was to tentatively start in two weeks and that most of it would consist of waterborne operations.

"That's great," I said, too tired and sick to pay much attention. "Just please take us home."

We drove through little towns, down dirt roads lined with palm trees and along the oceanfront. I looked at my watch and noticed that we had been driving for fifty minutes.

"A' this is just a joke, right?" I asked.

"We're almost there," he said.

"Bro, I used to vacation here in Puerto Rico back in the 70s' when I lived in New York. I've never been this far outside of San Juan. This is a pretty rural ass looking place," I said.

I knew that Puerto Rico's violent crime rate was horrific and began to feel a bit uneasy way out here all alone in the boondocks.

"I hope you have your gun on you," I said as we passed through an especially ghetto-looking area.

Finally, we pulled up in front of an elevated cement block house at the end of a dark street. There was an animal standing by the front gate.

"Bro, you didn't tell me that you got a dog."

"That's not a dog, you idiot," laughed 'A.' "It's the neighbor's pig."

"Ohh my bad. Out freakin standing," I said in disbelief.

"You've got all kinds of surprises coming, buddy," he grinned. "Sometimes the electricity goes out suddenly, the water shuts off in the middle of a shower, and the sewers back up. And if you don't keep the door shut tight, you'll find yourself sharing your bed with lizards and red ants."

"Nice, any other perks?" I asked.

"Well," 'A' replied, "The roosters start crowing about five o'clock every morning."

"Well, of course, you gotta have that," I said shaking my head. "Is it illegal to shoot them?"

"It may not be illegal, but I guarantee that whoever owns them would shoot you in return. These people live by their own rules out here."

"Why the hell didn't you tell me that you were living in one of those places that you see in a National Geographic Magazine?" I asked.

"Well, I figured you might change your mind about coming," he replied.

We parked the car behind a locked gate and carried my heavy luggage up a steep flight of stairs. Accompanying each step were the sounds of barking dogs, goats, and the loudest crickets I'd ever heard. Both of us broke into a sweat in the hot humid air as I asked 'A' where the air conditioner was.

"Right there," he said, pointing at a revolving ceiling fan.

I just shrugged my shoulders. "Of course, my bad again, what was I thinking? Hey, let's walk to the store so I can get something for my stomach," I suggested.

"Walk? The closest store is about fifteen miles down the road," 'A' replied.

By this time, I wouldn't have been surprised if he'd told me that I had to hunt and fish for my food and go to a well for water.

"I'm beat and I feel like I'm gonna puke any minute bro. I'm gonna crash before the roosters wake up," I said as I went to bed.

> ***"Spying Out the Land"*** – When Moses sent spies to explore the Promised Land, he told them: *"And see what the land is like: whether the people who dwell in it are strong or weak, few or many; whether the land they dwell in is good or bad; whether the cities they inhabit are like camps or strongholds; whether the land is rich or poor; and whether there are forests there or not. Be of good courage. And bring some of the fruit of the land. Now the time was the season of the first ripe grapes."*
>
> **Numbers 13:18-20**

To me, "bring back some fruit of the land" meant to go on a reconnaissance mission and gather intelligence information about my new neighborhood. And to this day, the CIA still uses this ancient biblical story as a case study for their mission protocols.

I woke up at dawn the following morning to what sounded like someone squeezing a rooster's testicles. I laid in bed for hours hoping they would shut up. I eventually got up, unpacked my suitcases, and toured my new crib. Not really much to tour. It was a two-bedroom house made from cinder blocks and elevated on four cement podiums in case of a flood. I decided to venture out and explore my new surroundings.

The family across the street was a Puerto Rican version of "The Beverly Hillbillies." They were all there, Granny, Jed, Jethro, and Elli Mae. Just like the TV show, they were friendly, happy, and content with their simple existence. I met them later and liked them immediately. Fortunately, I spoke fluent Spanish and could communicate with them. English seemed to be an unknown language on this part of the island that was out in the middle of nowhere.

The sun was already starting to get bright and hot, and everywhere I looked there were flowers, fruit trees and coconut palms. Kind of a cool place. Now I understand why 'A' had chosen this area to live and not just to keep a low profile.

About a quarter mile down the road, I came upon the most beautiful, secluded beach that I had ever seen in my life. Flocks of seabirds flew overhead, and local children were playing in the sand. Several young men were already out surfing, while the older men sat under shaded palm trees drinking rum through a straw from a coconut with the top chopped off.

There was a little bar opposite the beach that sold alcoholic beverages and cigarettes. From across the street, I could hear the sounds of pool balls clicking against each other and bar dice being slammed down on a hard surface. As the patrons saw me walking by, all the previous sounds had stopped abruptly, and all eyes were on me. I got an eerie feeling inside. The kind of eerie feeling a cop gets when something bad is about to go down. The same feeling that I got from that guy in military fatigues right before Maria the prostitute saved my life on Mission Street.

As I kept walking, I saw a man with a machete chasing a chicken through his yard. He finally caught it, brought it over to a chopping block and whacked its head off. "Damn! Well at least this time it was just a chicken and not another person like Machete Man's victim," I thought to myself.

I arrived back at the house and told 'A' what I had seen. He started to laugh and called me a "dumb white city boy who lacked a country education."

"That may be true, but there's something not right in that bar down the street," I responded. 'A' just shrugged off my suspicion.

'A' was black, and many people automatically assumed that he was a Cuban and spoke to him in Spanish. At first, 'A' seemed to be a little more accepted by the island people than I was. However, when they heard me speaking their language, some of them almost felt honored and this is what seemed to break the ice for me.

The children were friendly and even the dogs stopped growling at me after a while. We started to develop a nice rapport with the neighbors. 'A' had already known some of them for the past several months and had developed a close friendship with them. We were invited to go to barbecues and ate Puerto Rican food at neighbor get-togethers.

I enjoyed this island hospitality, but I reminded 'A' that we're on a covert mission and we have to be careful not to get too close to the "friendlies" as to compromise our safety and cover stories. We never know who's on the cartel's payroll – even just as "eyes and ears" (*lookouts*).

Two weeks later, 'A' and I received notification over a satellite phone to report to the Federal Building in San Juan for an appointment with the commander in charge of the Caribbean Drug Intelligence Task Force. When 'A' and I arrived, we were greeted by a government agent who escorted us to a waiting room. While we were waiting, I noticed a mirror on the wall over a table.

"I'll bet you any amount of money bro, that that's a two-way mirror and they're back there watching us and listening to our conversation," I said.

Just then the office door opened and a well-dressed older man with gray hair said, "Gentlemen, come in please." The man introduced himself as Colonel Luis Ortega and shook our hands.

"Please be seated," he said, lowering himself into a comfortable leather chair behind his large desk. "So, Joe, it's good to meet you. The chief told me that he was very impressed with you during your interview. 'A' has also told me a lot about you. You and 'A' scored at the top of the treasury enforcement agent exam nationwide; I am extremely impressed, but I'll get right to the point. I just got notification from Washington D.C. that due to a lack of funding your training at the Federal Law Enforcement Training Center (FLETC) in Glynco, Georgia will be delayed until further notice."

"How does this decision affect us, sir?" I asked.

"Your entire training plan will have to be revised. Eventually, you will have to go back to the States twice for schooling, once in Georgia, and then again in Miami. 'A' has been "consulting" with us for the past four months so I will let him brief you and bring you up to speed. But for the next few months, you'll be undergoing tactical training here and at other locations, including helicopter, heavy brush, and waterborne operations.

Once you complete your training, you will be introduced to a special team of narcotics agents known by the drug cartels as the "Policia Secreta" (*Secret Police*). This team's operational area covers the entire grid of the Caribbean Islands, so both of you will be moving around a lot. Joe, I've looked over your portfolio and you and 'A' both have very impressive qualifications. 'A' was an Army Airborne Lieutenant and you were the top gun on your sniper team. You speak fluent Spanish, that's definitely a plus. You also have experience in undercover operations and were an investigator in New York. That's good; I actually grew up in the Bronx.

But you must also become familiar with the drug world of South America. It's very different here than in California or New York. Muy peligroso (*very dangerous*)."

As the briefing continued, I recognized Colonel Ortega as being very sharp and intuitive, yet also friendly. We started to relax a bit as we got to know each other. We sat there for another fifteen minutes talking about different things. Colonel Ortega turned out to be a very religious man and was impressed with my own belief in God. He then emphasized how important faith was in a dangerous job like the one I was about to undertake.

Colonel Ortega then cautioned us that we would come in contact with very large amounts of cash and drugs and that we would have to have a strong set of ethics and considerable moral fiber to resist the frequent temptations ahead. He also said that the drug lords believed, and not without good reason, that everyone could be bought, and the only difference between men was their sellout price.

When the interview ended, Colonel Ortega asked us to meet with some of the other agents. We shook hands, then followed another agent to a large room filled with computers and other data processing machines. There was a huge map of the Caribbean Islands, Miami, and South America on the wall with several different colored dots on it. There were also straight lines drawn between Colombia, Puerto Rico, and Miami to indicate flight and boat paths taken by Colombian aircraft and watercraft delivering cocaine to the United States. This area was the command center of all South American Intelligence Operations. It was the epicenter of constant drug traffic monitoring.

We were then escorted into another room where we were introduced to several special agents representing different agencies within Federal, Foreign, and Local governments. This task force was involved in some high speed paramilitary operations that 'A' and I eventually got to associate with. But for now, our official titles were "*Consultants to Interpol.*"

One heavy-set agent pulled out a thick portfolio from a locked desk drawer and handed it to me. "Abrelo" (*open it*), he said. As I turned the pages, I saw that it contained dozens of photographs of bloody, chopped up, carved, decapitated, and otherwise tortured bodies. I saw pictures of "*Colombian Neckties*" – a form of execution in which the victim's throat is slit and his tongue pulled out through the opening so that it hangs down like a necktie. The heavy-set agent told me that this is what the drug lords did to people who snitched on their operations or were dumb enough to get caught by the police. And cops who get caught, get it even worse, including their families.

Every drug runner knew the horrible fate awaiting them if they got caught, so they have no second thoughts about shooting it out with the police. What the hell, a police bullet was a better fate than being tortured to death by the cartels. I put down the portfolio, only to be handed another book. What was contained in this book was even more disgusting than the first one. We were also briefed on some of the torture methods used by the cartels. Electric drill bits forced into a person's genitals, and every other imaginable torture one could think of. The bottom line we were told, ***"Don't Get Caught."***

"Some law enforcement officers sell out and work for the cartel," said the agent. "These sell outs are the most dangerous security leaks you will come across. If you ever get captured by the cartel, or cops that are on their payroll, we will have to assume that you will talk and give up the operation as no human being can withstand the creative tortures that they will do to you," he added.

After viewing these horrible photographs, we left to tour the armory. On the way down the hall, I looked into a room and saw a blue uniform police shirt draped over a chair that was covered with blood. "What's with the bloody shirt?" I asked our guide.

"It was taken off a police officer who was shot and killed during a drug arrest this morning," he said. "We have to wait for the blood to dry before we can book it into evidence."

"Damn!" I said. My eyes practically bulging out of my face.

"Agents and cops down here get it all the time," our guide said matter-of-factly. "Compared to California, you're gonna find this one loco (*crazy*) place to work."

We reached the armory and found it filled with police, military, and confiscated civilian guns. I was handed a large, heavy automatic weapon which I recognized as a Thompson .45 caliber sub-machine gun. 'A' and I looked over a wide range of other weapons before heading down to an underground garage where several different types of vehicles were parked. These, I was told, were the undercover vehicles that are used during drug operations. Several of them were stocked with some pretty high-tech equipment. High tech for the 1980s that is. We walked over to a jeep that was riddled with bullet holes. There was dried blood on both seats. The glass was also shattered.

"What happened here?" I asked.

I was then told that there were two agents inside of this vehicle on a stakeout when their cover was blown, and they were ambushed with automatic weapons.

"Were they killed?" I asked.

"One was killed, and the other was paralyzed," said the agent. "You can listen to the tape recording of the radio transmission from that incident if you like?" That tape recording of the ambush is something that any cop would never want to listen to. I regret listening to it myself but it did bring a certain reality to the drug war that we were getting involved with.

Later that day, 'A' and I were driven down to the harbor and shown a fleet of heavily armed Coast Guard ships used for drug interdiction on the high seas. I started to feel a little uneasy inside about the ocean operations, but also very hyped up at the thought of going to war with these drug cartel animals. We drove back to the Headquarters building and were set up to start our scuba diver training and underwater navigation courses.

As 'A' and I drove home that night, there was a dead silence between us. Finally, I looked over at him and said, "This shit is for real, dude."

"Roger that," 'A' responded. "Now you know what I've been involved in over the last several months before you got here and couldn't get into detail over the phone. It's not Mission Street Joe."

"I get that, but I'm down bro. You go, I go," I responded.

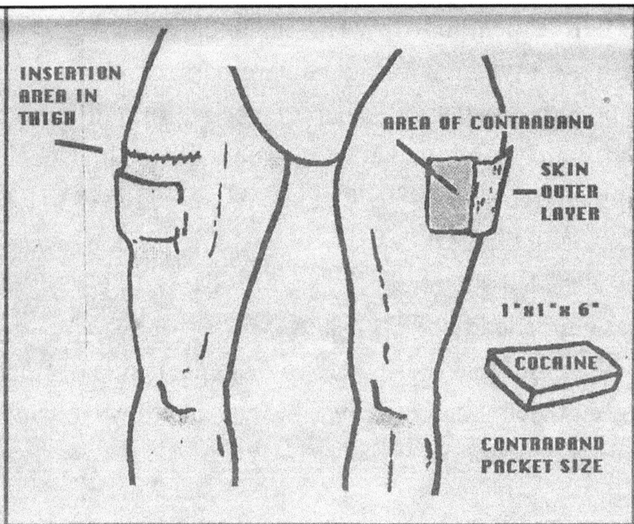

This artist's rendition, provided by the U.S. Customs Service, shows a man who had a pound of cocaine surgically inserted beneath the skin of his thighs. The suspect was arrested on Sunday at the Luis Muñoz Marin International Airport.

Drug Traffickers – "Dedication or Desperation?"

MY CHAMBER TWELVE

"Living the Vida Loca"

I wasn't too thrilled about watching videos of operations at sea. All it seemed to show were sharks, barracudas, poisonous jellyfish, and dangerous ocean currents. "We not only had to worry about the cartel getting us, but now these freakin sea monsters," I thought to myself.

As our waterborne training progressed, we spent half the day in a classroom and the other half in a large pool. Some of the exercises were extremely demanding and painful. The "*Current Pool*" became a daily challenge. This was a long narrow flume filled with running water. The objective was to swim against the current until you became exhausted. You would then be washed down the flume into an open pool. After a few days of this, it felt like my shoulders had been beaten with a sledgehammer.

After lunch, we were told that our next training would be in rougher ocean waters, and that eventually we would train at night. Our training became progressively more difficult. We traveled to different islands for different types of training and also spent a lot of time in the Interpol Office where we met several high-ranking government officials who apprised us of several operations that were going on in the Caribbean and South America. Normally after training, 'A' and I would drive straight home, waving to the local townspeople who hung out drinking beer beside the narrow dirt road leading to our house. They would always smile and wave back. On the surface, everything appeared normal, but one day I had another gut feeling like I did when I walked past that little bar on my first day here that something wasn't right. I told 'A' of my concerns, but he responded that I was just an overly suspicious cop.

"No way bro, my cop feelings usually never fail me," I said.

After that night I got the same feeling every time we drove down that dirt road. Living way out here in the country was supposed to be a safe place for us while we went through our training. There weren't supposed to be any bad guys around here, but I couldn't shake the uneasy feeling inside me. Nevertheless, 'A' and I continued our routine.

Four days out of the week we would go to the western side of the island for specialized training. The drive was about two and a half hours. We stayed in a little quaint town called Mayaguez. Puerto Rico had some beautiful scenic spots. We visited a phosphorescent bay where the algae glowed in the dark, caves, mountains, rainforests, and exquisite beaches.

There was a tall cliff with a lighthouse on it that overlooked the ocean called "Cabo Rojo." Sitting up on this cliff and watching the sun go down was a highlight of my week. Yet, as I sat there taking it all in, I would often get angry that an island this beautiful was so infested with drugs, crime, and murder. At the time, Puerto Rico had a very high murder rate which was mostly drug related.

After our training, we sometimes drove home via the southern route through the town of Ponce or through the mountains in the middle of the island. Telephones and electricity were unheard of in some of these places. Often the other agents, 'A,' and I would get out of our cars and a group of us would have a shooting match, picking a target and seeing who could demolish it first. The rules were different here.

'A' and I already had our gun permits and had worked with some of the other agents by this time. Being that we both had prior law enforcement experience, we didn't have to wait until our training had been completed before participating in some of these task force operations.

Sometimes 'A' and I also rode bicycles around the area where we lived. It was great exercise. One late afternoon, 'A' suggested we go for a bike ride. I agreed. We put our guns in a specially made nylon pouch attached to the crossbars of our bikes and peddled down the country road. Then suddenly while rounding a corner, we came upon a scene that was to drastically change our lives. Ahead of us and off to the side of the road was a marked police car parked next to a white Lincoln Continental. Both vehicles had their trunks open and uniformed officers were transferring large packages from the trunk of the police car into the trunk of the Lincoln. Before 'A' and I could turn around, we had made eye contact with the uniformed cops and the well-dressed guys in the Lincoln. It was obvious to 'A' and I what was going on, and based on their body language, they knew that we had made them. Peddling out of the area, 'A' pointed out what could possibly be a small, abandoned airstrip in the middle of a field.

"A," I shouted. "We're in a freaking hornet's nest. We're living right in the middle of a cartel drug operation bro." 'A' remained silent for a minute.

"It's probably just an isolated incident," said 'A.' "I think you're overreacting again."

We reached our house, jumped in a car, and drove to San Juan to report what we had seen. We didn't dare use the satellite phone for fear the transmission would be intercepted. Cell phones were not yet available. At headquarters, we were told to move out of the area as soon as possible because if the drug dealers or the dirty cops even suspected we were undercover cops they would kill us with no hesitation.

"This is not the States, fellas," one agent said. "A cop's life is not sacred here."

'A' and I listened to what they had to say but, despite stumbling smack into the middle of a drug operation, we felt the task force commander was overreacting. As far as we knew our cover hadn't been blown. The dealers most likely thought us merely to be two tourists out riding bicycles. Maybe we were "overreacting," or maybe we were just in denial as to the real danger that was creeping towards us.

Although 'A' and I weren't overly concerned about our own security at the time, we did worry about the safety of his sister and niece, who were about to visit us from California in a few days. I had known them both from San Francisco. Keeping our concerns to ourselves, we picked them up at the airport and drove them to our secluded home in the boonies. They couldn't believe that city boys like us had turned into hillbillies. 'A's niece loved the animals and played with the other neighborhood children, while his sister cooked us great soul food like fried chicken, greens, and black-eyed peas.

Over dinner one night, we were having a great conversation and laughing.

Having 'A's sister and niece there brought a change of atmosphere to our house, although 'A' and I couldn't forget the possible danger lurking beyond the door.

Every once in a while, 'A' or I would catch each other looking out the living room window, our eyes searching the road for suspicious people or cars. Neither of us wanted to admit it but we both sensed trouble headed our way. 'A's sister and niece returned to California, and we resumed our training.

A few days later, 'A' and I spotted several unfamiliar men just standing around about a block from our house. The neighborhood locals wore mostly tee shirts and shorts while these guys were conspicuously well-dressed. 'A' and I knew we couldn't approach the men, nor make any inquiries about them, for fear of blowing our cover. We had to continue acting like American tourists in Puerto Rico on an extended vacation. Our cover was that I was a doctor conducting research, and 'A' was a teacher on a sabbatical leave of absence. The agency that we were "consulting" with had developed proof to back our cover stories.

'A' and I went to the other side of the island for a two-day assignment. As we drove back home down the dirt road leading to our house, most of our neighbors waved to us as usual. But some of them didn't. They just turned their backs towards us. Then, as we rounded the corner near our home, we saw several uniformed police officers wearing flack vests and carrying machine guns standing in front of our gate. 'A' and I ditched our guns and task force ID behind the inside panel of the car door and got out.

"What happened?" we both asked.

An agent who identified himself as Captain Martinez from the local Police Intelligence Division told 'A' and me to have a seat in the back of his car after frisking us like two criminals.

Captain Martinez said, "We have to get you guys out of here. There are people who want to kill you both."

We drove for about twenty minutes until we arrived at a very secluded location. 'A' and I both knew we were in deep crap. When we arrived, we were directed into a small cement block room with a slowly spinning ceiling fan and greeted by a very rude police lieutenant and his assistant. Our wallets that contained our fake civilian IDs were confiscated, and the two men then began to interrogate us. We felt like we were in a third-world dictatorship, with no rights. We basically were.

"Who are you people?" the lieutenant asked with a heavy Spanish accent.

"We're tourists here on vacation," I replied.

"For several months?" he asked.

'A' became irritated and asked why the hell we were being questioned.

"You guys are either drug dealers or cops, and I'm willing to bet you're cops," the captain said. "I'm running your names through a computer search right now. Don't you realize that the local Colombian Drug Cartel has put a murder contract out on your lives? My informant told me that you, your wife, your daughter, and your white friend are going to be killed by the cartel because they think that you two are undercover agents," he told 'A.'

"They were my sister and niece visiting from California," replied 'A.'

"I saved your lives by bringing you here, now who are you?" demanded the captain.

I remembered back to our initial briefing when we were cautioned by the agent at headquarters that if we ever got caught by the cartel or the dirty cops on their payroll, that we would be tortured and killed. 'A' and I looked at each other believing we were about to experience both, then asked for our wallets. I took out a small piece of paper with a phone number written on it. We were to do this only in case of a serious threat to our lives. The captain studied the number for a moment, then picked up the phone and dialed the number.

"Who is this?" he asked the person who answered the phone. Suddenly his face turned pale, and he stammered, "Yes sir! Absolutely, sir. I fully understand, sir." The conversation was in Spanish, but I understood every word that was spoken. The captain then hung up the phone and came to his feet. He then told his lieutenant, "We have to protect these guys at all costs."

"Gentlemen, I apologize for any inconvenience. If I had known who you were, I would have treated you much differently."

"That's just it Captain, no one including you was supposed to know who we are," I stated.

He then ordered his assistant to return our wallets, drive us home and arrange police protection until we could move out of our house. To me, this was déjà vu from when I worked as an investigator back in New York when I had a contract put out on me for unintentionally fronting out two dirty public officials. I had very little faith in "police protection" and for damn good reason.

'A' became stubborn about moving out. "I'm not a coward," he shouted. "I'll be dammed if I'm gonna let a bunch of lousy drug dealers run us out of our home."

"Bro, it's got nothing to do with being a coward. We have to think like soldiers. You were a lieutenant in the Army. They have the tactical advantage. These aren't the dime a dozen, 'poo butt' San Francisco drug dealers that we used to arrest on the street. This is the Colombian Drug Cartel. What if they fire an RPG (*rocket propelled grenade*) into our house while we are inside? This rural area where we're living is their turf and they outnumber us. Besides, we can't trust the local police now that they know who we are. And I definitely don't trust our so called "police protection" outside either. I've never been a coward, but I don't want to end up on the next page of that photo album either. If we stay here, we're dead 'A.' We gotta get the hell outta here now. If we didn't give up the chief's phone number, those dirty ass cops would have killed us. These cops are owned by the cartel bro."

'A' finally cooled off and came to his senses. "You're right Joe, let's get the hell outta here."

We relocated to the metropolitan area of San Juan under an armed escort who we both knew and trusted. Living in San Juan made life much easier. There were stores, movie theaters, gyms, and just about every other amenity of modern life.

Things lightened up considerably for 'A' and me once we'd settled in with new homes and new identities. We still trained and went out on assignments together with the task force, but we constantly were looking over our shoulders. We also had much more time on our hands now that our local training had been pretty much completed. We were still waiting for the federal freeze to be lifted so that we could continue our training back in Georgia and Miami. As time passed, 'A' and I became involved with several task force operations. We continued to operate under the guise of "advisors" and "consultants" to the police anti-drug task force and maintained our relationship with Interpol.

When the other officers and agents heard how much money we made back in California they couldn't believe it. They asked why we would leave a job that paid us so much more a year than they were making here. 'A' and I both answered that we were unhappy in California and wanted the adventure of fighting the drug cartels in the Caribbean and South America. The local law enforcement guys just shook their heads as if we were crazy – an opinion I was fast coming to share.

"You guys have a fatal attraction," said one of the agents.

"Ya think," I thought to myself.

"Sitting on a Rock With my Gun" – One night, 'A' asked me to meet him for dinner. He told me that he had been living in Puerto Rico for just about a year and that his leave of absence with the San Francisco Police Department was up. He told me that he had decided to return there to resume his former job as a police officer. I was a little shocked, but I supported him in his decision.
"Damn bro, it's gonna suck being here solo. You lured me down here and now you're popping smoke on me (*military term for leaving in a hurry*)."

About three weeks later, I drove 'A' to the airport. Just before he boarded his plane, 'A' turned to me with a look like he'd never see me again.

"We've been through a lot together," he said.

"That we have," I said, swallowing my emotions.

"Watch your head and stay low bro," said 'A.' "This place is ruthless. Don't let them get you."

"I'll be alright. Say hi to everybody back in San Francisco," I replied.

We gave each other a sincere hug and he turned for his plane. On the way home I felt terribly alone. It won't be the same now, I thought. I felt like I had not only lost a partner but also the best-trusted friend I had in the Caribbean Islands. However, I realized that 'A' had to do what he had to do. I questioned my own sanity by staying behind.

The drug war was raging on. Every day, headlines in the Caribbean newspapers read, "Drug War Takes its Toll," "Another Cop Killed," "Police Station Under Attack," "Over 40 Judges Murdered in Colombia," "Drug Cartel to Take Over Colombia," and on, and on, and on.

To counter some of this violence at its source. A special task force team of narcotics commandos from several agencies was formed to assist in the counter drug and jungle guerrilla warfare efforts in South America. This was in addition to Operation Snowcap that was run by the DEA, the military, and 'other' agencies. I was told by the task force commander that the team needed a designated sniper, and because of my sniper skills and proficiency with a rifle, I was asked to join the team. The team would operate on 30-day deployment rotations after going through pre-deployment – mission specific training. I was handed a confidentiality agreement (*CA*) and was told to sign and return it within seven days if I decide to join the team. It was written in Spanish, so I had a trusted attorney review the 'fine print' so that I knew exactly what I was signing. I did a lot of soul searching over the next seven days and I believe that I had made the right decision about joining the task force. Only time would tell.

"Back to Being Solo in Puerto Rico" – I had recently been involved in a serious shooting incident that left me feeling very much in need of spiritual counseling, and I turned to a man I had met sometime before who lived on the floor below me in Puerto Rico.

His name was Albert, and he was the pastor of a nearby Christian Church. Albert and his family had always been very friendly to me, and frequently extended dinner invitations. Up to this point, I had always given them an excuse why I couldn't come to dinner. It had nothing to do with them; it was me. I was quite often invited to social gatherings but rarely, if ever, showed up for them. Normally, I felt much more comfortable socializing with only one person at a time for I was a very private man who rarely let anyone get too close to me. Besides, I didn't want anyone asking me what I did for a living. Albert offered to walk with me on the beach and just talk. I agreed to get together with him one day the following week when we were both free.

One evening a few days later, I was sitting on top of a large rock overlooking the ocean watching the rhythmic waves crashing on the beach. A flock of birds flew overhead, and I thought to myself how happy and carefree they must be. They appeared to be so much a part of nature.

"God," I said to myself, "Why couldn't you have made me a bird or a fish? They're blessed with a natural freedom that I sure as hell have never known."

I looked down at my fanny pack containing my pistol and imagined a bullet going through the roof of my mouth and out the top of my head. I wondered if I would feel any pain and how long it would take before my heart stopped. Would my soul leave my body the moment my heart stopped, or would it linger on in my dead carcass for a time while God figured out what to do with me? Or maybe if I floated out into the ocean with my inflated scuba vest and shot myself, the sharks would devour me and hide any evidence of my demise? As I sat on that rock feeling alone and depressed and dwelling on dark thoughts, I suddenly heard a voice behind me say, "Good evening, Joe." I quickly wiped the tears from my eyes and turned to find my pastor friend Albert standing there looking at me with his kind demeanor.

"Hi, Albert," I said, a little nervously.

"Whatcha doing out here all alone on this big old rock?" he asked.

"Oh, just watching the sun go down and enjoying nature," I replied.

We made small talk for a while, and then Alberts's voice got serious. "You've got a good heart, Joe. My wife and I both like you very much. But I sense there's something eating you alive from the inside out, and it's killing you." Unable to answer, I just sat there in silence.

"Would you like to talk about it, Joe?"

"I'm getting burned out on all the violence, crime, death threats, shootings, and paranoia that I've experienced and not being able to trust even some of the people that are supposed to be the so called "good guys," I answered.

Albert then told me that he believed that I had PTSD and that if I didn't do something about it soon, it would probably not end too well for me. During the weeks to come, I stopped by Albert's church and met with him in his office once a week. He counseled me and we read the Bible together. He gave me several pieces of literature to read, explaining that we could discuss their meaning on my next visit. Albert's views all seemed to make sense. He was a Ph.D. and really understood biblical theology and psychology very well. He told me that God loved me just the way I am.

"*B-but,*" I stuttered.

"Yes Joe, even with all of your sins," he said with a loving smile.

I shared with him my nightmares, waking up in a cold sweat from imaginary gunshots. My feelings of isolation and that I hated being around other people. I then finally confessed my self-destructive thoughts that I had been recently pondering. He always seemed to have the right words to say. I knew that God had put this man in my path.

"Joe, you have to do something. You're in a very bad place."

He urged me to go see a therapist named Mike, who specialized in counseling people dealing with PTSD. Mike was a former combat veteran who worked out of his house and lived only a few blocks away from me. Albert believed that Mike would be a good match for me and what I was dealing with.

I made an appointment to see him. Mike found it a little nerve-wracking that I always brought my pistol to our therapy sessions. Especially when my main issues were anger, rage, depression, and PTSD. He politely asked me not to come armed to our sessions anymore. I really didn't feel comfortable without my gun on me at all times, especially since I'd recently had a murder contract put out on my life. Nevertheless, I honored his request.

After some casual talk, Mike got right to the point. "So, Joe, how many shootings have you been involved in?"

I remained silent for a minute knowing that I was prohibited to speak to anyone about the specifics of my "consulting" missions.

"Will this remain confidential and off the record?" I asked.

"Yes, it will," answered Mike.

"Ok, confirmed kills, or just shootings in general? I asked.

"You choose Joe."

"More than a dozen and less than fifty," I answered.

"Just choose one to start," stated Mike.

"Including this last one that I shared about with Albert, or getting pinned down and overwhelmed by machine gun fire at a cocaine distribution center on another island last month? Or the time that? Or that one time when?" I unloaded on him.

"I see that you are emotionally wound up like a tight spring Joe. Let's try this. Tell me about the one that has been stressing you the most over the past several months."

I hesitated for a minute. "Well, I saw a car smash into a uniformed officer and pin him up against a cement wall crushing both of his legs. The officer began screaming in pain. The car that hit him was burning rubber in reverse trying to get away but crashed into a parked vehicle. I opened fire on him as he was attempting to flee. The car stopped but was still in gear. I reached in through the window, turned off the ignition, and put the car in park while he was slumped over the steering wheel. A group of local police officers that were eating at a nearby outdoor restaurant came running towards the scene with their guns pointed at me. I knew I was about to get shot so I placed my gun on the street and put my hands over my head. I was forced to identify myself by showing them my ID and gun permit. Once they identified the man driving the car that smashed into the officer, a uniformed cop got into the vehicle that I had just opened fire on and drove the car away with the guy still in it. One of the other police officers picked up the empty shell casings on the street that were ejected from my gun, handed them to me, and told me to leave the area and forget this had ever happened. No crime scene, no collection of evidence, and no asking me for a statement. I complied but was perplexed as to how and why they covered this incident up. I couldn't help but to wonder who this guy was that they were protecting. An ambulance arrived and took the injured officer away."

Did you report this to anyone?" asked Mike.

"Hell no," I replied. "I already had one murder contract put out on me and I don't need another one. I just figured, 'When in Rome, do as the Romans do' so I split. This is their world. I am way outnumbered. If that's how they want to roll then so be it. Maybe the officer that got hit was a snitch, I don't know. I just went away and kept my mouth shut. But unfortunately for me, these cops now know who I really am which wasn't supposed to happen. But I couldn't just ignore the injured officer and look the other way. Someone had to try to protect him. It was just my cop instinct. I can't just let another officer get killed right in front of me despite my cover story."

"I see," said Mike. "What else?"

"I mean, then there's all the shootings, the violence, never knowing who is on the cartel's payroll. Setting up mega kilo cocaine buys as an undercover operative and always being afraid you might be getting set up yourself. Always having to look over my shoulder every day can make you paranoid after a while. I just wish that there was a distinct line between the good guys and the bad guys. Never knowing who's who in the zoo is frustrating and freakin dangerous. It's not just here in Puerto Rico, but all throughout the Caribbean Islands and South America," I answered.

We spoke for a while longer until our session was over. Mike ended with these words. "Joe, war and killing are necessary evils in this world. You mentioned to me that you believe in God and that you try your best to serve Him. But you can't make this your own personal war. Nor can you live under the belief that this level of violence is God's mission for you to continue in very much longer."

"Those were the same words a police lieutenant told me back in San Francisco," I stated.

"Which were?" asked Mike.

"Not to make this my personal war."

"Mabey he was right Joe. Mabey you should get out of this personal war while you still can. If a cartel bullet doesn't take you out, PTSD will."

"But I came down here to make a difference in the world. I got tired of pulling syringes out of young kids "tied off arms" and overdosing while snorting this crap. I wanted to come down here and put a dent in the source."

"And are you?" asked Mike.

I just sat there in silence.

"Entire governments, the military, and other agencies, either can't or won't stop it. What makes you and your messiah complex think you can? Get back to serving God like you used to. Help your fellow man who has been through some of the same things in life that you have. Jesus said to be "Fishers of Men," not "Killers of Men," stated Mike.

"That's funny. That is the second time I've heard that as well," I responded.

I left Mike's office thinking how I could become a fisher of men as opposed to a killer of men. But as time would tell, I wouldn't be making that transition into a fisherman until several years down the road. But Mike's and the San Francisco Police Lieutenant's words stayed with me throughout that entire time.

"Hurricane Hugo" – The Weather Service Center in Miami began picking up signs of unstable weather off the coast of Africa, the origin of many Caribbean hurricanes.

As the days passed, the forming storm picked up momentum and headed our way. Most hurricanes that had started out on a similar track had eventually veered north and missed Puerto Rico altogether. Not this one though. As each day passed, the fierce storm drew closer to the island, and we were warned to be prepared for the worst and to start planning for survival. The media was now graphing the hurricane's movement. The newspapers printed a map of the area between Africa and the Caribbean and every few hours the San Juan radio station would broadcast the latitude and longitude of the hurricane. It became a game, drawing little hurricane position dots on the map and then connecting them with a straight line.

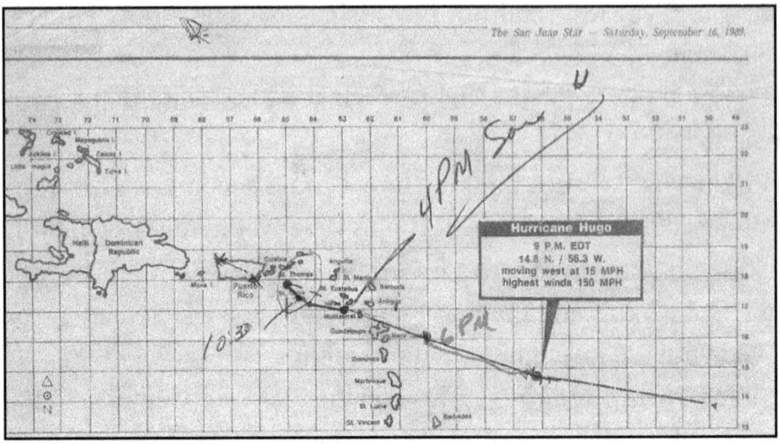

I stocked up on bottled water, canned food, and candles. But I didn't yet feel threatened because, in the past, most hurricanes had eventually turned north toward Florida or the North Atlantic.

As time passed, the weather service warnings became more serious. The winds were now above 150 mph, and the hurricane was not only expanding but also coming directly towards us.

At about 10:00 A.M. on September 17, 1989, "Hurricane Hugo" smashed into the island of Guadeloupe, several miles south-east of Puerto Rico. News reports said that the island had been devastated by fierce wind, rains, and flooding, and several people had been killed. By now, all the TV stations were broadcasting continuous updates on the hurricane in both Spanish and English. We were repeatedly told not to take the threat to the island lightly. The Weather Service warned that if Hurricane Hugo should strike Puerto Rico, everything within 50 miles of the eye would be totally decimated. Many people of faith on the island started to pray and conduct candlelight prayer meetings. As the hurricane warnings worsened, I filled the bathtub with water, and taped the windows. 'A' called me to wish me well as he had heard about the incoming hurricane on the news in California.

"Yeah, you bastard, you got me into this crap and now I'm here solo, and you're safe back in California. I wish you were here to enjoy this with me," I said jokingly.

I made my final preparations as Hurricane Hugo devastated the closer island of St. Croix. If the hurricane continued on its collision course with Puerto Rico, it would strike us in a little under twenty-four hours.

The next day the sky gradually became darker, the ocean rougher, and the wind increasingly strong. I saw the hurricane as an opportunity to witness nature in its fullest fury, and I headed for the beach. I climbed to the top of a tall lifeguard chair and looked up and down the empty beach, realizing that I was the only person (*idiot*) outdoors. Over the next hour, the waves became enormous, and the wind got intense. I finally decided that it was time to leave, and I ran back home and bolted the door behind me. For the next twelve hours, Hurricane Hugo bashed Puerto Rico with sustained winds and rain. Objects tumbled down the street and roofs were ripped from houses. Huge trees were uprooted and catapulted through the sides of buildings. The sound of the storm was terrifying: thunderous wind, splintering wood, screeching metal, and pelting rain. During slight breaks in the wind, I could hear human screams in the distance.

I realized that at this very moment people were being killed maybe even some of my friends. For hours, I laid on the living room floor face down listening to the fury of the hurricane buckling the windows and wondering if a tidal wave would sweep in from the ocean a block away and collapse my building. I was having a difficult time at this point practicing the "peaceful meditations" that Mike had taught me during our PTSD counseling sessions.

Finally, twelve hours after the full force of the storm struck, the winds began to abate. Listening to a battery-operated radio, I learned that at the last minute, the eye of the hurricane had veered away from the main part of the island and passed over the northeast tip near Luquillo. (*Luquillo was the place where I had met and played pool in a bar with Ricky Martin when he was younger*). There were no electricity or phone lines, so I had no way of knowing if my friends and partners were alive or dead.

The weather station called this last-minute northerly turn of Hurricane Hugo an act of God. If this had not happened the eye would have gone directly through the center of the island and most of Puerto Rico would have been totally devastated. Some considered this merely a lucky break. I believed it to be the answer to millions of Puerto Rican prayers.

When it was reasonably safe to go outside, I left my building for a look around. There was damage and flooding all over and a chill passed through me as I thought of how much worse things would have been if the hurricane had not changed course. For the next two weeks, we were without water and electricity. It was candle light only for a while.

On the day following the hurricane, I decided to challenge myself to swim in the ocean. The Weather Service warned the islanders to stay out of the ocean until the potentially fatal currents died down. This only made it more exciting and challenging for me. As I was swimming, I was suddenly pulled out by a very strong current. I was now about to face one of my greatest challenges – to swim back to shore against severe currents. My constant need for challenge, excitement, and adrenaline had finally gotten the better of me. I swam furiously towards the shore only to be pulled farther out. I fought against panic and fear. I put into use the tactical swimming techniques that I had learned during my training. I swam parallel to the shore instead of towards it as I used survival breathing and resting skills whenever I could. I was not ashamed at this point to solicit help from above. Eventually, I swam into a cross current which brought me back to shore but very far away from my starting point. I was never so happy to feel wet sand under my feet. I walked home a humbled man.

For days after Hugo hit, sleeping at night was difficult. Without electricity, we had neither air conditioning nor ceiling fans and the heat and humidity irritated my skin which was already raw from the salt water after my last "swim of death." The National Guard was activated throughout all of the Caribbean Islands to curtail looting and to keep the peace.

Breakfast consisted of fruit and bottled water. Lunch was a can of tuna fish and warm canned corn. Dinners, by contrast, were a treat. A friend of mine from church invited me and a few others to his house and we barbecued on a propane gas stove. We ate shrimp, veal, chicken, vegetables, and rice every night until electricity was restored to the island. We were all very grateful for these provisions from God, knowing that others on the island had little to nothing to eat, much less a stove to cook on. It's very humbling and even somewhat convicting when God was so good to me over the years; even during my rebellion against Him by continuing in a lifestyle of my own self will. During the aftermath of this hurricane, God literally provided me an 'oasis in the desert' so to speak.

There were boats shipwrecked on the beach, trees laying across streets, and the rain forest had also been heavily damaged. As soon as the phone service to the island was restored, many of my friends from the States called me to see if I was still alive or just a statistic. During the months to come, restoration through federal disaster funding became the island's priority issue.

The building that I lived in had been miraculously unscathed. It was hard to believe considering the damage everywhere else around me. The house directly behind me had its entire roof ripped off, and from my fifth-floor apartment, I could look directly down into their living room and bedrooms.

Not long after the hurricane, I believe I had a vivid moment of clarity when I had experienced a few more "*red flags of danger*" and a stern warning to get out of the Caribbean. This cat was already on his 9th life, and I wasn't going to push my luck or poke the tiger any further. I had decided to change my career plans and go back to California before someone or something else decided my fate for me. I wasn't sure which was a better fate: getting killed by a hurricane, tortured and killed by the cartel, or sold out by dirty cops. I wasn't going to stick around and find out. I reapplied to the San Francisco Police Department and because I had good friends in the Police Background Unit and Personnel Division, I was put on the fast track to be rehired.

"ESI – Bodyguard Training Academy" – During the waiting process, I attended an executive protection school in Colorado called, Executive Security International (*ESI*). The school taught the art of Intelligence Based Executive Protection comparative to the level of the United States Secret Service and Department of State. Surveillance, Counter Surveillance, Small Team Tactics, Gun Fighting, and Motorcade Operations. The training was very challenging and high speed, but I loved it. I had already completed the home study part of the course and was now ready to attend the residence training in person.

The shooting and driving courses were top-notch. We were required to drive through fire, ram each other off the road, and ram through roadblocks. One day my partner and I were taking our final test on the high-speed escape and evasion course. The scenario called for us to be chased and shot at by instructors acting the part of terrorists. Attempting to outrun our pursuers, we took one of the tight turns a little too fast. Our car rolled over several times, shattering all the windows, and crushing the roof down on us. By the time the car stopped rolling, there was smoke coming out from under the mangled hood. The entire event seemed to happen in slow motion. I can remember giving my partner the "high-five" hand slap as we were upside down still inside the car. "We're on a roll," he said in a calm composure.

By the time our instructors had caught up to us, my partner and I were already out of the vehicle waving at them. I was taken to a nearby hospital and treated for a mild concussion and had a piece of glass removed from my right eye. Late that afternoon I returned to the track and passed my final test.

My driving partner was a big former US Marine. We had become good friends during the training and that night we had dinner together.

"You know Joe," he said, "I think we would have been killed in that car wreck today if God or something else hadn't been there to pull us through."

This sounded strange coming from him. "I didn't know you were a religious man," I said.

"I'm not, particularly. But I felt like this weird supernatural presence as we were rolling upside down in that car today. The car was at a dead stop while we were upside down. Then it was as if something pushed it back onto all four wheels. I have never experienced anything like that."

I nodded. "Yeah, God has been pulling me out of close calls my entire life bro."

After a few weeks of long, hard days; I graduated as a Certified Protection Specialist (*CPS*). Receiving such a credential from this school was like getting a degree from Harvard University. In fact, ESI was considered in the security industry as, "*The Harvard of Bodyguard Schools*." This hard-earned credential would eventually change the course of my life, (*again*).

Some people believe that when God protects us, life no longer has stress, trials, pain, and tribulations. Just based on my time in the Caribbean, that obviously wasn't true. Although I had experienced much danger and many close calls; through it all – I wasn't killed, Colombian Neck Tied, or worse.....

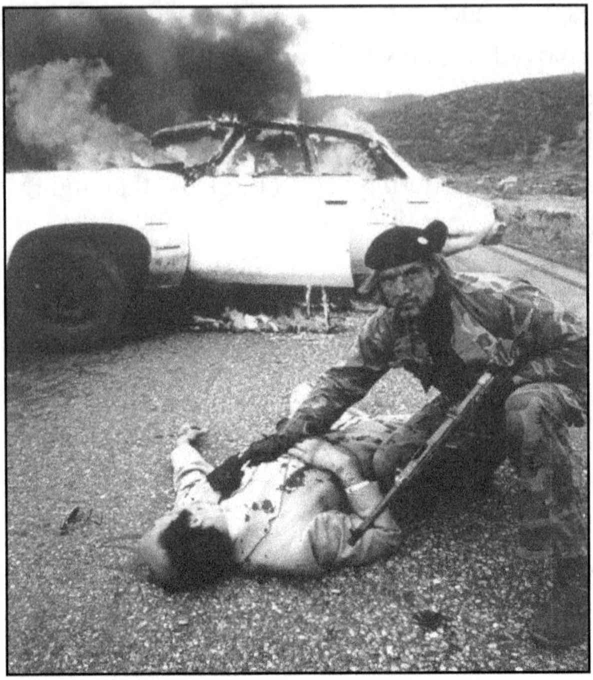

Executive Security International Ltd.

Certificate of Training

Advanced Executive Protection Program

This certifies that

Joseph F. Bannon

has completed 600 hours of training in:

Principles of Protection
Electronic Security
Profiles of Terrorism
Demolition Search & ID
Observational Psychology
First Respondent Medicine
Fundamentals of Defensive Shooting
Executive Protocol
Escape and Evasion Driving
Basic Combat Shooting / Combat Handgun Tactics
Unarmed Defensive Tactics

NHSC

President

June 6, 1990

Date

Considered the Most Coveted Credential in the Protection Industry
600 Hours of Combined Home Study and Residential Training

MY CHAMBER THIRTEEN

"Back to Mission Street"

My application and background investigation were finally approved, and I was again sworn into the San Francisco Police Department. No Counter Sniper Team, no permanent partner, just a uniformed street cop. As crazy as it may sound, I was ecstatic to be back at Mission Station walking down the streets of hell. But nowhere near the hell that I had just returned from trying to, "*make this a better world by fighting the drug war*."

There were some new cops that I didn't know and some old cops that just got a bit older and more jaded. Some of the new cops came up to me and said, "So, you're Joe Bannon? We heard that you were a living legend here in the Mission. Is it true that you choked a guy to death in the middle of Mission and 16th Street with one hand while he was trying to shank you with a knife?"

The questions went on and on, but it was great to be home. All I wanted was my foot beat back. There was one stipulation to my return as a police officer though. I was still having nightmares, grinding my teeth, and generally feeling on edge. I also had trouble hearing out of my left ear as the result of a gun being fired too close to my head while I was down south during one of my "consulting" jobs. The police stress unit told me that I would have to attend a formal PTSD debriefing. I was sent down to Southern California and met with Dr. Larry Blum who was a top police psychologist. He held a group debriefing session over the next few days and evaluated each one of us. He told me that I definitely had PTSD but was stable and functional. It was a valuable experience. I eventually was reappointed to the Police Behavioral Science Unit as a Peer Counselor and Critical Incident Stress Debriefer – especially now that I had been debriefed from my own PTSD.

Everyone loved my new sports car, especially all the bullet holes that were in it from when I had it parked outside of that hotel on Franklin Street shortly after I had returned from the Caribbean.

The familiarity and "good to be home" feeling I had experienced to be back on my beat was very short-lived. The war in the Middle East, "Operation Desert Shield" and "Desert Storm" had broken out and the anti-war protests and riots in San Francisco became extremely violent. The entire city was put on alert, and we were put into riot squads. All days off were cancelled, it was hand-to-hand combat at its fullest. It was them against us. I was assigned to a riot squad that had to face large groups of angry, violent people. The protesters threw rocks and bottles at us, and even cans of red paint. So much for my "familiar foot beat."

Some of the fights between the police and the demonstrators were fierce. Many protesters set cars on fire and trashed buildings and businesses as they also tried to set the Federal Building ablaze. It was a war zone again. Some of the mobs were trying to maim or severely hurt us. I was struck in the chest with a brick, but "payback" time came shortly after when I caught the guy who hit me.

The anti-war riots went on for several weeks. Each cop that had gotten hurt personally pissed me off. Our pussy political leaders made sure to keep our hands tied so that we wouldn't offend the protesters and their supporters. God forbid a special interest group might get pissed off at the mayor. That could cost votes. So, cops just kept getting hurt and the damage to the city continued nonstop.

The police force could have stopped the violence immediately, but the orders came down to just hold our position and not take overly aggressive police action unless it was for self-defense. This sickening time made me want to just throw my badge on the mayor's desk, but I had just gotten it back and I was starting to run out of places to go.

Several months later more rioting broke out after Governor Wilson vetoed the Gay Rights Bill. Gays took to the streets in great numbers to protest. They set the State Building on fire and damaged public property. Again, the politicians ordered us not to take aggressive action. Incensed by the passive stand of San Francisco officials, Governor Wilson threatened to send in the National Guard. When the protests finally subsided, I felt like I had just been through another war.

The next hurricane of civil disobedience came when members of the Los Angeles Police Department were accused of beating up a black man named Rodney King, and the extreme violence started all over again. I would compare this early 1990s incident to the more modern day "*George Floyd Riots*." The Rodney King incident was videotaped and shown just about every day on national TV. As a result, the rioters got an excuse to take to the streets again.

The violence this time was much more severe than the Middle East war or the gay rights protests. Countless people took to the streets of San Francisco looting, rioting, setting stores and police cars on fire as well as attempting to turn huge public transportation buses over on their sides. This time they were met head-on by an angry police department with a new police chief who had just recently been sworn in. A curfew was initiated and all police officers citywide were put on twelve-hour shifts. Still, the violence rapidly got out of control. The sound of "officer down" and "officer needs help" calls and screams from outnumbered cops became all too common over our radios.

Nothing jacks up a cop's or soldier's adrenaline more than hearing a fellow soldier or officer screaming for help over a radio.

The new chief of police warned the mob to disperse, but the rioters ignored the orders and continued to throw rocks and bottles at us as we stood in a disciplined skirmish line behind police barricades. The protesters were on the other side of the police barricade about six inches from our faces, spitting on us and screaming obscenities. One guy kicked the police barricade into us, and he got lit up by police riot batons. He was carried off into the crowd with what appeared to be a broken leg. Another idiot reached over the barricade to grab my riot baton and tried to pull me into the crowd of protesters. I voluntarily gave him my baton but not where he wanted it. This seemed to alter his behavior.

The next broadcast over the police radio was one that I'll never forget.

"This is the San Francisco Chief of Police. I authorize the use of force."

We all looked at each other in surprised disbelief. We were basically told to take back the streets by whatever means necessary. This was our chance to clean house and pay back all of those bottle and rock throwers. In a very short time, we had regained control of the city and made mass arrests. It just goes to show what can be done when riot control is taken out of the hands of the politicians and put where it belongs.

Although pride was once again instilled into the ranks of the police department, our hero chief was fired shortly thereafter for "stepping over the line" and a new police chief was appointed in his place. Politics and good police work just don't mix. Nevertheless, the city was back to normal. Normal for San Francisco that is.

Engaging in nonstop hand-to-hand combat day after day. Listening to chants of police hatred. Being pelted with rocks and bottles. Hearing your partners screaming over the police radio for help, "Officer down, officer down." It's amazing how it all replays itself over and over in our daily memories and pillow thoughts at night. It's like you never get to leave the job. We just learn to "suck it up" and move on. Ahhh, home sweet home.

With the streets once again relatively peaceful, I finally got to walk my foot beat on Mission Street. Some days I drove a police car, some days I worked alone, and some days I worked with a partner. I just had to use a softer gloves approach, and less unconventional guerrilla warfare tactics to crime abatement this time around. My captain made sure to brief me on that stipulation before my first day back on my beat.

Nevertheless, I was still glad to be home and not being shot at or having the Colombian Drug Cartel trying to kill me. PTSD??? Hell, by this time in my life I just considered it a normal "job perk."

"The Mayor and The Governor" – My recent certification in executive protection from ESI in Colorado had earned me an appointment as a bodyguard and driver to the Mayor of San Francisco. Granted it was somewhat of a political job, but it was definitely a step up. The committee that selected me was impressed with my credentials from ESI and my reputation as a street cop. I loved this type of work and, although I would miss working the streets of The Devil's Quadrangle, I couldn't turn down this golden opportunity.

My first job duty each morning was to pick the mayor up at his house and drive him to his office at city hall. The mayor's limousine was a dark blue Lincoln Continental, fully equipped with lights, sirens, radios, phones, and an array of other emergency devices. I loved gadgets and tested all of my new toys before I got to his house. When I arrived at the mayor's home, I got out and rang his doorbell. His small son answered the door, and I asked if his father was ready to go. This turned out to be a diplomatic no-no. The correct protocol, which I implemented on my second day, was to just pull up in front of the mayor's home and wait until he was ready to come out.... My bad. I followed his time schedule; he didn't follow mine.

I had heard some bad rap about the mayor. It was rumored that he didn't like cops all that much. As I waited in the car that first day, I half expected a modern-day version of Attila the Hun to come down the walkway. When he finally did come out to the car, I greeted him with a friendly, "Good Mornin Mista Maya."

"What part of New York are you from?" he grinned, recognizing my still strong East Coast accent. "You sound like a character straight out of Westside Story," he added.

"Long Island Sir," I said as we shook hands.

"I heard a lot of good things about you Joe," he said. "I'm happy to have you on my staff."

We pulled away from the curb and headed to City Hall. When we arrived, he invited me into his office and showed me around. I was quite obviously nervous and at one point he grabbed me by both shoulders with his hands and told me to relax. The mayor was a large, strong man who played on an all-star softball league. I didn't know why he needed a bodyguard. He looked like he could take care of himself just fine.

As time went on, The mayor became friendlier toward me. He even occasionally asked my opinion on mayoral issues that he was dealing with. He would often invite me to his house where his wife made lunch for me. On several occasions, the mayor asked me to drive his kids to special events on the weekends, and I often stood near the edge of the infield when he played softball. He was very energetic and a challenge to keep up with. He was like a big kid at heart and, although most of the police department didn't like him, I did. He treated me exceptionally well, and the job had certain perks. For instance, whenever I got on the police radio and used the mayor's call sign (*1-Mary-700*) to request something, I would get an amazingly fast response. Sometimes he would have to meet with the mayor of a distant city and during the drive we would have long conversations about different subjects. He also liked to tell me jokes during these rides, and we shared many moments of laughter together.

One day he was at a big affair honoring several Samoan Tribal Chiefs. The mayor was up on a stage in a receiving line with other city officials and the visiting chiefs were going down the line placing flowers around the dignitary's necks and blessing them. On a whim and in an effort to be closer to the mayor, I decided to get in the line as well. Everyone assumed that I was some kind of deputy mayor or other official. When the mayor saw that I was next in line to be blessed, he pointed toward me and told me to get off the stage and wait for him in the car.

Another time I was on the way to his house to pick him up when I heard a cop calling for help over the police radio. I was driving the mayor's limousine with lights and sirens going full blast as I careened around corners trying to get to the police officer's location who needed backup. Just my luck – one of the mayor's staff saw me while she was out driving to a meeting. When word got back to the mayor's office about what I had done, I was sat down for a little "talk." No more playing police officer in the mayor's car after that day. Although I wore a suit and tie, I was still a street cop at heart.

One day Arkansas Governor Bill Clinton visited the mayor's office.

"Joe, go downstairs and meet the Governor, bring him upstairs, and entertain him for a while. Tell him that I am on a very important call and will meet with him as soon as I can," directed the mayor.

I greeted Governor Clinton as his entourage pulled up in front of City Hall, then escorted the governor and his staff up to the mayor's office. While waiting for the mayor to come out of his office to greet him, I kept Governor Clinton company. We had a great conversation. Governor Clinton had an incredibly charismatic personality and we hit it off very well. He too commented on my

New York Accent. Later, I accompanied the mayor and Governor Clinton to a reception loaded with TV cameras and news reporters.

As we were walking towards the event from the parking lot, I heard a constant flapping sound. I looked down and saw that the sole had completely separated from the rest of my shoe. This couldn't have happened at a worse time. I tried to slide my right foot as I walked to stop the flapping sound. Finally, I got hold of a large rubber band and colored it black with a magic marker. This got me through the rest of the day.

I perceived something very special about Governor Clinton that I couldn't quite put my finger on at the time. For some strange reason that I just couldn't explain, I knew that I would connect with him again someday under different circumstances.

Several months had passed and mayoral election time was right around the corner, so I drove the mayor around to different campaign sites. Security was tightened up at this point. There were four other candidates running against him in the election. Some of the debates got heated up but the mayor held his own. He was under a lot of stress, and I prayed at night that God would give him the strength that he needed to get him through the campaign.

The mayor spent a lot of time speaking to minority and human rights groups. During the campaign speeches, I would sometimes see people in the crowd that I had arrested when I was a patrolman. I just hoped that they didn't recognize me and start a problem. The mayor didn't want security too close to him, so I had to keep a certain distance. This compromised my ability to react if something happened. It also frustrated me, but the mayor was the boss and I had to accept his decisions.

When the primary election night finally arrived, I joined the mayor, his family, and staff to await the results. The mayor was running against popular ex-Police Chief Frank Jordan, and the current mayor had lost the support of the police department and several other key groups. Things didn't look good. Sure enough, when the results came in, the mayor lost the election. When the outcome was certain, the mayor held his family close to him for a while, thanked his staff, then walked over and gave me a hug. He shook my hand and thanked me, and I expressed my gratitude to him for the kind way he had treated me despite some of the crazy stunts that I had pulled.

San Francisco now had a new chief executive, and I was out of a job. Mayor-Elect Jordan wanted a whole new staff which didn't include me. I remained on Mayor Jordan's detail for a short time until my replacement got up to speed. I went back on uniformed street patrol, working different assignments and making solid arrests.

Me (L) in the Background Protecting Mayor Frank Jordan (M) and Police Commissioner Wayne Friday (R)

"Promoted to Sergeant" – I was on vacation in Miami and called my home answering machine to check for messages (*modern* *technology at its finest*). I was surprised to discover one of my calls was from the secretary of the chief of police asking me to call the chief as soon as possible. I dialed his office from a pay phone near the beach.

"How are you, Joe?" the chief asked when I was put through. "What's going on with you?"

"I'm standing here on the beach in Miami returning your call," I answered.

"You didn't have to call me from Florida, Joe. It could have waited until you got back," he said.

"Well Chief, I just figured I was in crap again and I wanted to get it over with."

The chief laughed hysterically (*an immediate relief to me*). He had been my former Captain at Mission Station and we had developed a good relationship over the years. He told me that the reason that he'd called was to tell me that as soon as the next recruit class of cadets had graduated from the academy, that he was going to appoint me back to the Special Investigations Division and promote me to the rank of provisional sergeant.

"That's great Chief, thank you," I said.

"Enjoy Miami," he replied and hung up. I was happy that I would be returning to my old investigations unit, and this time as a sergeant.

One day after I'd returned from Miami, I was at police headquarters and happened to get on the same elevator with Police Commissioner Wayne Friday who was a very good friend of mine.

"Hey, Joe, how's it going?" he smiled.

"Great, Commissioner."

"I hear you're going back to the Investigations Bureau," he said.

I looked at him and asked, "Did you have anything to do with that Commissioner?"

He just smiled, silently shook my hand, and got off the elevator on his floor.

"Keep in touch Joe," he said as the elevator door closed in front of me.

"Appointed Detective of Narcotics" – The next two months passed quickly when one day I was called into the captain's office who was in charge of the Dignitary Protection Unit.

"Have a seat Joe," he said. "It looks like there's finally going to be some movement here in the bureau and we'd like to bring you back."

"Will I be returning to the gang unit captain?" I asked.

"No, Joe, you won't. We need you in the Narcotics Division which as you know is part of the Bureau of Investigations. If you accept the position, you'll start next Monday. On occasion, you'll be working joint task force operations with the FBI, US Secret Service, the Bureau of Alcohol, Tobacco and Firearms, and any other agency that needs our assistance. We'll still use you in dignitary protection when the need arises, but your primary assignment will be in the Administrative Narcotics Division (*ADNARC*) dealing with organized crime and the drug cartels."

"This has got to be a freakin joke," I thought to myself. Although I felt some reservations about working narcotics again, especially after my escapades down in the Caribbean, nevertheless, I accepted the assignment.

The next day, I drove out to the Narcotics Division and asked to see the captain. A few minutes later, I was ushered into his office. The captain was the commanding officer of the narcotics and vice division. This was the same man who counseled me years ago regarding my "*vigilante-style*" police tactics when he was a lieutenant.

"I'm delighted that you're coming aboard Joe," he said. "You've got a hell of a reputation, and your arrest reports are impressive."

The captain explained the structure of the division and the responsibilities of each different section.

"Joe, I'm going to assign you to the Major Dealer Section," he said. "You'll be on an eight-man team conducting criminal investigations of major drug dealers and organized crime. You'll be doing a lot of undercover operations, as well as stakeouts and surveillance. You'll also be serving search and arrest warrants. It's a very high-speed unit, Joe."

"Oh man," I thought to myself. All I wanted to do was kick back and relax a little. What am I getting myself into again?

I took a tour around the office and was shown my new desk. On the left side of a long hallway were several doors. I was shown through the unit's arsenal, a large conference room with pictures of drug dealers on a peg board, an interrogation room, and a room that was used to make undercover drug connections over untraceable phone lines. The final area I toured was the specialized equipment room. Inside were battering rams, door openers, sledgehammers, flack vests, and just about everything a cop would need to raid a drug house.

Our office was located in a secluded area out near the Hunters Point District of San Francisco, in the vicinity of many low-income housing projects. The division was so security sensitive that even other police officers, unless specifically assigned to the narcotics unit, were not allowed in our office without a special pass and escort. Some drug dealers did drive by shootings on our building on their way to the projects.

I knew a lot of the officers in this unit from working the streets in the Mission District. I spent the first few days familiarizing myself with the office and the operations of the unit. Everyone treated me well and I was made to feel very welcome and accepted. And wouldn't you know it, I would be working with the same narcotics sergeant that I almost shot in the head in that dark parking lot while escorting our Puerto Rican Cop guests to dinner a few years ago. To add to the coincidence; his partner who almost shot me from behind would be working on my team as well. Life can be one big circle of weird connections.

My new team and I started going out into the field to investigate complaints and ongoing narcotics cases. A lot of us wore disguises to fit into specific situations. Sunglasses, head rags, odd hats, and delivery-person uniforms all became popular attire. Some of us even dressed up like homeless people and pushed shopping carts around. We did a lot of surveillance on suspected drug traffickers in an effort to gather a certain amount of evidence before we could get a search or arrest warrant.

Normally, we would use five or six cars to follow the drug dealer, continuously switching the vehicles around so that the dealer wouldn't catch on that he was being followed. Some of our cars were ahead of the suspect, some on a parallel street, and the rest leapfrogging behind the suspect. We had special switches and electronic devices in our vehicles that would alter our headlight and taillight patterns so that at night, the suspect would not always see the same image in his rearview mirror, or the same taillights ahead of him. The surveillance was coordinated over our radio system. Many times, it got really hectic, especially when the suspect was driving very fast on a freeway and making sudden lane changes.

Often the suspect would drive around in circles just to see if he was being followed. This required us to take some rather imaginative maneuvers to keep up with the suspect without getting into an accident. I know I pissed a lot of innocent motorists off by suddenly cutting in front of them or doing something else outrageous on the streets.

Our surveillances were not confined to San Francisco. We went wherever the drug deal was going. One thing is for sure, we could always count on long, hard, tiring days and nights. Covering each other's backs was probably the most important part of this type of work. When one of your team members went in to make a "connect," or a buy, the rest of the team had to be close enough to react if the crap hit the fan, but not so close as to tip off the drug dealer. We used many techniques to accomplish this. Often, I would dress up like a street wino and pretend that I was sleeping in a doorway right next to the place where an officer was scheduled to make an undercover drug buy. I always kept one hand near my gun while I rested my head on a police radio hidden inside of a brown paper bag.

We had different types of non-verbal signals that we used, including a move-in signal when the deal went down, and a rip-off signal if the drug dealer tried to rob the undercover cop. We also had a distress signal to use if the undercover officer was in serious trouble and needed help right away.

One of the main dangers of this type of undercover police work was that, despite the phony identification we all carried, a lot of times the drug dealers would search you to see if you were wearing a hidden recorder, transmitter (*wire*), radio, bullet-proof vest, or gun. It was unavoidable at times, but we had to go into very dangerous situations with no gun, no vest, and no form of communication other than hand signals. It was up to the "close cover" officer to watch intently for any hand signals, and immediately radio a call for help to the rescue team if things went south. Miss the signal, and your partner could die. We had protocols for just about every possible scenario. If the undercover buy agent could not communicate somehow with his rescue team and needed help, the protocol was to throw a chair or other object through the window of the building he or she was in.

Many dealers would ask you to try some of the drugs that you were going to buy. This is where you really had to think fast and come up with a believable excuse why you couldn't use the drug. Sometimes, I'd show the dealer my phony undercover state parole card and say that my urine was tested every thirty days and that I couldn't use the drug myself but was going to resell it for profit.

My fellow narcotics officers and I would rotate our duties. Some days I'd be the cover agent. Some days I'd make the connection, and some days I'd make the buy. It was a bit nerve-wracking many times, when I shook hands with a drug dealer who was accompanied by armed bodyguards, ready to blow my head off if I screwed up. This was especially true down in the Caribbean on multi kilo undercover cocaine connections.

You really learn to be a good actor in this profession. If you don't, you could die. You could do everything right and still die. It's a life of living on the edge with no guarantee that you will see tomorrow. But the danger frequently brought on an adrenaline rush like no other. I think every one of us was an adrenaline junkie and lived for that same temporary high.

We also had to contend with what was called "counter-surveillance," during which dealers would have spotters out on the streets searching for us "narcs." They knew what to look for and they were pretty damn good at detecting undercover cops and surveillance teams. Many of them had police scanners and understood the usual police codes. Some dealers used little kids on bikes with walkie-talkies to spot us. We had to use special radio frequencies with scramblers and come up with our own codes to confuse the dealers who were familiar with the conventional police codes.

Whenever I was on a stake-out, whether sitting in a car or lying in a doorway disguised as a wino, I had to be certain that no one was watching me talking into a radio. The objective was to have a good enough disguise to fit into the situation but not bring any attention to yourself. A lot of the dealers that we investigated were from Latin America and it was no big deal for them to leave the country on a minute's notice. This meant that they could kill you and be out of the country before your body was cold. A lot of them used fake identification as well, making them even harder to trace.

One day not long after I had joined the division it was my turn to make the connect and buy some heroin from a well-known dealer. I made the connect in Spanish using one of our special phones. The call was being recorded as we negotiated. The dealer, Emilio, agreed to meet me in thirty minutes in a really nasty downtown area at Turk and Taylor Streets in the "Tenderloin District."

"Let's go guys, he'll be on the corner of Turk and Taylor Streets in thirty minutes," I said. "He's a Latin male with a ponytail, wearing green pants and a white shirt."

My surveillance team sped down to the area ahead of me. We used a plain-looking van with a periscope camouflaged to look like part of a sunroof. It allowed officers inside to scan a full 360 degrees. After my cover team was set up, I radioed that I would be entering the area from Taylor Street. As I approached on foot, I spotted members of my team. One was pretending to talk on a nearby pay phone. Another one was pulling aluminum cans out of a garbage can and putting them into a bag. They had to keep their distance but be close enough to react in case I got into crap.

I only had to wait about a minute before I spotted the dealer walking towards me. I also noticed his counter-surveillance set up around me as he neared. As he got close, he began to look a little unsure. I opened my left hand and showed him his phone number inked on my palm. That seemed to relax him, and he smiled for the first time.

I asked him in Spanish, "Is it hot around here?" Meaning are there any cops around?

"No, it's okay," he replied. "I'll go get the stuff."

"Okay," I said.

Shortly afterward, Emilio sent someone else back to do the deal for him. This second Latin male referred to himself as 'Emilio's partner.'

"Oh crap," I thought to myself. I didn't know if I'd been "burned" or what. I immediately thought of the gun that I had hidden down the back of my pants and the knife I wore strung around my neck in case a deal went south. As this other guy spoke to me, I noticed his counter-surveillance / bodyguards creeping a little closer to me. In situations like this, you really depend upon God and your cover team. The guy got to within three feet of me, looked around, and put his hand into his pocket. I was debating whether to reach for my gun or the money. He pulled his hand out of his pocket and handed me a bag of "tar heroin." I smelled the bag to detect whether it was heroin or bunk. I believed it to be heroin by its smell and consistency. I handed him the money and the deal was done.

The exchange itself took about ten to fifteen seconds. He walked toward the west, and I walked to the east, giving the "bust (*arrest*) signal" to my team as I went. They followed him back to a nearby hotel room where he was arrested. The marked money that I had given him was recovered, as well as a huge amount of additional heroin. We arrested the original dealer, "Emilio" a few days later.

This type of scenario went on every day. Some drug busts were similar, some much more intense. Kicking in doors, following people, making drug arrests, and confiscating large amounts of drugs, money, and guns were all just part of the job. We had a toll-free, 1-800 drug hot-line number where people could call in with anonymous tips on drug traffickers. Some of these leads panned out, and some didn't, but we followed up on each lead like a heat-seeking missile.

A few days later, I was pulled away from my narcotics officer role and assigned to the protection detail for the San Francisco visit of Gerry Adams, who is the leader of the Irish Republican Army's political wing, Sinn Fein. The security was very tight for him. Some people viewed him as a terrorist while others saw him as a freedom fighter. Some members of the British and other Governments would have loved nothing better than to see him killed. The rest of the security team and I took extra vigilant security measures against the possibility of a terrorist attack or assassination attempt.

I was assigned to drive the lead car in the motorcade which was considered the pace car. The name for this vehicle was "Escort One," and my responsibilities were heavy. One wrong miscalculation on my part and the entire motorcade could have been diverted. If I stepped on my brakes, every driver behind stepped on their brakes. If I speeded up, everyone speeded up. If I made a wrong turn, everyone would make a wrong turn. Radio communication between the lead car (*Escort One*) and the tail cars was crucial.

To add to the stress, the chief of police and deputy chief were sitting in the back seat of my car. This was obviously not the time for any of my crazy New York-style driving, nor to verbalize my opinion of the driving skills of others – an impolite tendency of mine.

We picked up Mr. Adams, and his Irish security force at the airport, then proceeded to San Francisco's Palace of Fine Arts where he would meet with the mayor, give a speech, and hold a news conference. After delivering his speech, he unexpectedly jumped off the stage and walked into the crowd of approximately five hundred people.

"Dang," I said to myself, this wasn't on the itinerary! Last-minute changes and sudden impulses on the part of dignitaries are very common in protective work. I jumped down off the stage and caught up with him. Many people of Irish descent wanted to shake his hand or get his autograph and we were soon surrounded by the crowd. All I could do was press my shoulder up against his and watch every pen, piece of paper, and hand that was coming his way. I looked into people's eyes to try and read their intent and scanned body movements and hands for any type of weapon that may have bypassed security. Meanwhile, we were being increasingly crowded by people who wanted to get close to Adams. I had to be a bit of a diplomat myself because I knew that he wanted to shake hands and sign autographs, and I didn't want to interfere.

A lot of times in protective details like this, the security of the VIP becomes compromised because dignitaries want to mingle with the people and press the flesh. There was little I or any other bodyguard could do. Flexibility is the key word in this profession.

This is referred to as "permissive protection" which meant that we could only protect the dignitary as far as he or she would allow us to. Unfortunately, this is the very thing that got President John F. Kennedy killed back in 1963 when he refused to follow Secret Service protocol.

The crowd started to press in a little too strongly and I locked arms with Adams and gave the signal to the team to move him out. His political adviser told him that it would be wise to move on to the press conference. The Irish leader was a good sport, though, and made some comical comments to me as I steered him out of the middle of the crowd.

We got to the press room without incident. If there had been trouble, the SFPD would have been ready. Behind the stage curtains, was a squad of SWAT Team officers with automatic weapons. The next day, as he was leaving for the airport, he walked over to me, shook my hand, thanked me for guarding him, and said if I was ever in Ireland to come and visit him.

I've noticed that a certain bond often forms between a VIP and a protective agent. Sometimes it's only the exchange of a meaningful look or touch, but it happens. I guess some VIPs feel a little flattered that someone like me would be willing to risk their life to keep them alive.

The next day I was back to work conducting narcotics investigations. I enjoyed the diversity between being an undercover narc one day, and a police bodyguard the next. Monday, I might be in a disguise making a deal with a drug dealer, and Tuesday, I could be wearing a suit and tie while guarding the President of the United States as a task force agent with the Secret Service. Or protecting a witness with the FBI Witness Protection and Relocation Program. My work was never dull. My career was blessed, to say the least.

"President Bill Clinton" – I was assigned to President Clinton's Secret Service Close Quarter Protection Detail. We attended several events all day long. We eventually brought him back to Air

Force One which was waiting for him at the San Francisco Airport. We got out of the motorcade and formed a circle around him as he was about to board Air Force One. Before he got on his plane, he walked around our circle and shook all our hands thanking us. As he shook my hand he said, "Joe, I met you in the mayor's office, nice to see you again." I had heard that he had an incredible photographic memory, and this only proved it. I was a bit flattered to say the least.

One week later, I was asked to assist in serving a search warrant of a hotel room being rented by two Vietnamese gangsters who were wanted for murder and serial robberies. We knew them to be in possession of two machine guns. We recovered both the gangsters and the machine guns.

A few months later, I received an order from my captain assigning me to a Secret Service protective detail during the upcoming weekend visit of both President Bill and First Lady Hillary Clinton. I was working the late shift and I arrived at the Secret Service Command Post on the 17th floor of the Fairmont Hotel. Before I went on duty, I was given a briefing covering my protective responsibilities and President Clinton's itinerary. Both Bill and Hillary would be together on this detail.

A Secret Service command post is a place of continuous activity. Computers, telephones, radios, and fax machines were in constant use. Operational orders were pinned up on bulletin boards, and different types of personnel were continually coming and going. There is an attaché case called "*The Football*" that went wherever the President went. It contained the United States nuclear missile launch codes. I thought it was cool when they allowed me to hold it.

I met my counterpart, Chuck, who would be my partner for the next eight to ten hours. Chuck had been a Secret Service agent for the past twenty-three years and had protected the lives of several U.S. Presidents and a score of other dignitaries. During our first night on duty together we became friends. He shared some very funny Secret Service stories with me, and I matched his tales with some of my equally hilarious police escapades. Our assignment was called "*protective intelligence*" and as part of our job, we viewed pictures of potential terrorists and other people who were suspected of wanting to kill the President. We roamed through the hotel lobby and the outside grounds, constantly on the lookout for any type of potential threat, then went up to the President's suite and made a final inspection before Mr. and Mrs. Clinton returned from dinner and went to bed. When the President and the First Lady were safely in their room, Chuck and I positioned ourselves outside of their door where we were available to intercept any threat while they were sleeping.

The next several hours were boring and tiring, but Chuck and I continued to find things to quietly laugh about. Finally, morning came, and we were relieved by another team. I went home and slept for the rest of the day. The following day, I went back to narcotics investigations and my team was assigned to a case involving the smuggling of 'Ice' (*chrystal meth*) into San Francisco from Hawaii.

Later that same night while at home, I walked out on my terrace overlooking San Francisco Bay and the Bay Bridge. I lived on the 23rd floor of my building on the Embarcadero. I probably had one of the best views in the city of the San Francisco Bay. I watched the boats go by and the traffic on the bridge. Off to the left, I could see Alcatraz Island with its bright spotlight. My living room also had a beautiful view of the downtown Financial District.

Seeing the City like this reminded me a lot of living in Manhattan. As I leaned against the rail of my terrace, I couldn't help but feel grateful for all the blessings in my life. More than twenty years before, I'd been a gangster and an alcoholic with a dark future. Today, I was a bodyguard to the President of the United States, a police sergeant, and a successful contributor to life. I finally felt good about the man I'd become. I also thought back to when I was a kid in New York standing on that Jamaica Train Station platform asking God if I could be a police officer someday. Looking back over my life's journey became almost overwhelming.

I looked up into the moonlit sky, smiled, and said, "Thank you God for the miracle of my life. You have given me more and delivered me from more than I could have ever asked You for, or even imagined."

Police Chief Anthony Ribera Promoting Me to Sergeant

MY CHAMBER FOURTEEN

"The Drug Case That Ended My Police Career"

In addition to those cases handled by my team, we all had our own individual narcotics investigations to pursue as well.

During the latter part of the year of 1994, I was assigned to work on a very sensitive case involving the sale of medical marijuana to AIDS patients by an organization called "The Cannabis Buyers Club." There were a lot of politics surrounding this case and I had to be very careful, reminding myself that in 1992, the City Board of Supervisors had passed a resolution directing the San Francisco Police Department and District Attorney's Office to place the prosecution of medical marijuana cases as their lowest priority – in other words, *don't even think of touching them.*

The Narcotics Division received an anonymous complaint that the "Cannabis Buyers Club was not what it appeared to be and that it was a front for an illegal drug enterprise." We were obligated to investigate "all" anonymous complaints.

My main objective was to find out if this organization was selling this so-called "*Medicinal Marijuana*" to people other than AIDS patients and people with catastrophic illnesses. Basically, was the

Cannabis Buyers Club legitimate or not? This Club was also eventually to become the headquarters for "The Compassionate Use Act of 1996," a ballot measure to legalize medical marijuana in California. The owner of the Club, and political leader of the medical marijuana movement, was Dennis Peron. Peron was a convicted drug dealer from the seventies. Peron claimed that his organization only sold marijuana to AIDS patients and people with other very serious illnesses.

I really didn't have a problem with people using marijuana in a medically prescribed manner. However, if someone was fraudulently advertising the compassionate use of marijuana for sick people with limited finances with the intent to hide an illegal drug operation, then that was a different story altogether. A blatant drug-selling operation, especially one that took advantage of the suffering of others, could not be tolerated and I vowed to myself to get to the bottom of it. At the same time, it made me uncomfortable to discover that a large percentage of the people who visited this operation were from the gay community. I really wrestled with the conflict of interest that I felt inside ever since I was assigned this case. Several of my friends and fellow police officers happened to be gay and some had died of AIDS, and if medical marijuana was helping people, I certainly didn't want to hurt them by taking it away. I kept an open and objective mind and let the findings of my investigation speak for themselves.

I was concerned that my investigation might end up hurting the legitimately sick people who went to the Club to help with their medical conditions. I didn't yet know the truth. I did know, however, that it was my job to prove whether this was a legitimate and compassionate organization, or a front for a major illegal drug operation.

If it turned out that the latter was true, then both the law and my own conscience dictated that I must do everything in my power to put the organization out of business. In any case, I knew that the final decision would not be up to me. I could only present the results of my investigation to my superiors and the district attorney's office and let them take it from there.

I had no idea at the time that this was to be the most controversial and highly publicized drug case of the decade. Ground zero for the legalization of marijuana; a case that would go right to the Clinton White House.

As part of my investigation, I began infiltrating the Club and making undercover buys of marijuana. It didn't take many of these trips inside to validate my suspicions. Many of the Club members weren't sick or suffering. Instead, the Club's rooms looked like a speak-easy, 1960s style, or an Amsterdam hash bar. Everyone was either sitting around getting high or buying pot "to go." There was also a huge menu on the wall listing different grades and prices of marijuana.

Everybody and his cousin could buy weed in this place. I now had no doubt that this was an illegal drug operation disguised as a compassionate place for sick people to obtain pain-numbing and appetite stimulating medication. The Club sold brownies, muffins, Rice Crispy treats, and even pizza laced with marijuana. 1960s music played in the background while people sat around getting stoned. I began to get stoned off the thick cloud of secondhand smoke myself. I couldn't imagine what this cloud of smoke was doing to the small infants that mothers had carried into the Club in their arms while purchasing their "*medicine*." This place was unbelievable, but kind of cool at the same time.

As part of my investigation, the Department of Justice agreed to make me a coat with a VCR Camcorder sewn into the lining, with a pinhole camera lens placed behind a breast pocket button. The next time I went into the Club to make a buy, I videotaped the entire operation. I didn't like staying inside too long because I would soon begin feeling high from all the marijuana smoke in the air. The first time I had left the Club and crossed the street toward my waiting partners, my legs felt rubbery, and I thought I was going to take a header onto the pavement.

"How did it go?" one of my partners asked when I wobbled up.

I just grinned at him for several seconds, unable to talk intelligibly. My hair, skin, and clothing all reeked from the smell of marijuana. "Damn Joe, we can get high off of you just being in the car with us," another partner laughed while calling me a "lightweight." I had been clean and sober since 1976 and my tolerance to drugs had obviously become very low.

I had purchased the so called "high grade" marijuana that was overpriced even by illicit market standards. Later analysis from the crime lab made clear that the stuff that had been sold to me was not that good, and definitely not of "high grade medicinal value." A "compassionate organization?" Yeah, right. The reality was that the Club was simply a sophisticated drug operation headed by one man who was daily raking in a lot of untraceable cash.

A police computer graphics expert was able to duplicate a batch of membership cards to gain entry to the Club. They were a perfect counterfeit. This was further proof that anyone who had basic computer skills could gain fraudulent entry into the Club for the purpose of buying marijuana for either personal recreational use or for resale. I handed out several of the counterfeit cards to different undercover narcotics officers, conducted a briefing and sent them in to purchase different amounts of marijuana. A covert surveillance van videotaped the undercover officers going into the Club. They also wore an audio device that electronically transmitted their conversations back to the van where they were recorded.

In my briefing I told the undercover cops that the reason we were conducting this investigation was to prove that the Club was selling marijuana to healthy people who did not have medical needs for marijuana, and not to deprive those sick people who had legitimate need of the drug – if there was such a thing. Each of the officers that I sent in, none of whom were pretending to be sick, successfully purchased marijuana.

I made several more buys wearing the coat-camcorder supplied by the Department of Justice and was able to videotape quite a bit of the inside operations. I recorded the sale of marijuana to young, school-age kids as well as the presence of several infants being brought into the Club by their parents, who were also buying marijuana. As I mentioned earlier, these young infants were being subjected to breathing in second-hand marijuana smoke in the poorly ventilated Club. Such irresponsible parents should be charged with "child endangerment."

I'd brought in a rolled herbal cigarette that smelled like marijuana when lit but didn't contain any of the drug and I fired this up as I sat in a chair, enjoying the 60s music and watching people get progressively more stoned. Then I left.

We conducted a surveillance and followed the sellers as they left for the day. We set up an undercover system to have them identified so that we could obtain arrest warrants for them later if necessary. The next day, we followed one female suspect as she drove over the Bay Bridge to Oakland and parked in front of a bank. Undercover agents followed her inside and observed her depositing huge wads of cash. Soon after, we had decided that we needed to investigate the possible money laundering side of this case as well. This "act of humanity" operation was literally hauling in a fortune. I also consulted with two special agents from the Criminal Investigations Division of the IRS and asked them to assist me in the investigation.

While waiting for their answer, I continued to work on the Cannabis Buyers Club Case with just my team. I decided it was time to try a different tactic. I typed up some phony doctor's notes, each with a ridiculous diagnosis, and sent undercover narcotic officers into the Club to become members. All of the officers were readily accepted and received their own membership cards. One female officer's note stated that she suffered from a '*vaginal yeast infection*,' hardly a terminal illness, but good enough to become a member. I had written this note for her on a napkin and signed it, "*Dr. Ovarian*" just to prove the sloppiness of this "*legitimate*" drug operation.

Meanwhile, I was inside covertly filming the operation. I saw people in the Club who I recognized from the street and knew personally weren't sick. They just wanted to smoke marijuana and get high as well. They used other member's cards or presented phony doctors notes like the ones that I had devised. This operation was out of hand. Sick or not, anyone could come in here and get all the marijuana they wanted, even enough to resell for a profit, which they did.

Many of these "customers" got into cars under the influence and drove off. The Club had to be shut down, or at least forced to return to its original mandate of furnishing marijuana only to legitimately sick people. The bottom line was that marijuana was an illegal substance. The problem with this case was the "fuzzy line" between the politically tolerated and illegal use of the drug.

A few days later, I was required to present the results of my investigation of the Cannabis Buyers Club to the chief and deputy chief of police. The chief couldn't believe what he was seeing when he viewed the video films that were taken with my covert camera. He really got upset when he saw a small child inside waiting for her mother to buy marijuana.

"These people don't look or act sick," said the chief.

"That's my point, Chief," I responded. "A lot of the people who frequent the Club are there solely for the recreational use of marijuana. There's not a damn thing medically wrong with many of them. At least not qualifying to the level stated within the Club's mission statement and regulations. I recognized many of them as street drug dealers. They're in there to get high and buy enough product for resale profit, and nothing else."

"How do they get to become members, then?" asked the chief.

"Easy," I said. "They just type up a phony doctor's note and they're in. I've already had five undercover police officers sign up as members by using bogus notes that I wrote for them. If I could do it, how many other people do you think are doing the same thing?"

The chief thought that over for a moment. "What are your objectives in this investigation Joe?" he asked.

"To expose the truth, Chief," I said adamantly. "The Club is nothing but a front for an illegal marijuana-selling operation. The owner, Dennis Peron, is out to make a pile of money, not to help sick people find relief from their suffering.

I have listed "***ten objectives***" to accomplish within this investigation. **(1)** – To show that there is in fact a Cannabis Buyers Club in existence here in the city and to identify its physical location. **(2)** – To show the direct involvement of Dennis Peron within the organization either by directing, supervising, facilitating, and accepting United States currency for the felonious exchange of a drug that is prohibited by law. **(3)** – To show that a person who is healthy with no objective signs of a "catastrophic illness" such as AIDS, cancer, etc. as listed within the Club's mission statement can purchase marijuana from the Club. **(4)** – To show that a person who is completely healthy with no objective signs of an illness can and does successfully become a member of the Club by the fraudulent presentation of a self-manufactured doctor's note. **(5)** – To show that a person can and does enter the Club to purchase marijuana by using another person's membership card. **(6)** – To show that persons under the age of eighteen years old are permitted to enter and remain within the Club while they smoke marijuana themselves and while marijuana is being sold to adults. **(7)** – To show that persons who frequent the Club, leave the Club under the influence of marijuana while walking, riding a bicycle, or driving a motor vehicle causing the risk of harm to themselves or to other people. This would also include bringing infants into the Club and exposing them to secondhand smoke. **(8)** – To show that several persons involved within this organization are acting as co-conspirators to violate numerous laws, ordinances, regulations, and codes of the State of California and the United States. **(9)** – To show that the co-conspirators within this organization are fully aware and cognizant of the fact that their participation and actions within the organization are prohibited by law. And by being aware of this fact, they continue to do so anyway. And lastly. **(10)** – To show that many of the people who are members of this Club and or purchase marijuana from the Club are not sick, suffering, or diagnosed with a legitimate illness that conforms to the stipulations of the "Compassionate Use Resolution" that was adopted by the City of San Francisco in1992. That many people are currently using the Club as a vehicle to purchase marijuana for recreational use, resale for profit, and to purchase marijuana for minors and their friends who are healthy and will probably continue to do so if allowed to. And as of today Chief, I have accomplished all ten objectives.

The Club is also a smoke screen and a funnel for organized crime marijuana growers to move their product. The whole thing stinks of abuse of trust and corruption, and I want to put Dennis Peron and his people out of business. This is all going on underneath the noses of the mayor, the district attorney, the board of supervisors, and the police commission."

"I'm impressed at your thoroughness, Joe." said the chief. "You have certainly proven to me that this operation goes way beyond just helping sick people who need marijuana as medicine. An illegal operation like this cannot be allowed to go on here in the City of San Francisco."

It felt good to have the support of the chief for I knew in my heart that taking action against the Cannabis Buyers Club was the right thing to do. The Club may have started out with the intention of helping sick people, but it had evolved into a money-making scheme with ties to marijuana growers and organized crime in the mountainous regions of Mendocino, Trinity, and Humbolt Counties; also known as "The Emerald Triangle." It was the largest Marijuana producing region within the United States – run, profited by, and protected by the Emerald Triangle Drug Cartel. They were raking in millions in untraceable cash and would take out anyone who got in their way – and did. Many people had disappeared up in those mountains over the years.

About a week later, the chief, my captain, and I presented the case to the San Francisco District Attorney, who declined to prosecute anyone involved in the Club – strictly for "political reasons." I'm sure he feared losing political support from his constituents. In light of the irrefutable evidence that I had presented, the district attorney refused to prosecute my case. Even after I showed proof of criminal resale of the product and child endangerment.

The district attorney said, "Find the money trail and we will then consider prosecution based on your findings."

"You mean to tell me sir that all of the improprieties that I have presented to you, including exposing infants to secondhand marijuana smoke and known convicted felons reselling this stuff for profit out of the housing projects are not enough?" I asked. "Besides sir, how will I be able to trace the money when all they use is cash for their transactions? You are tasking me with unreasonable and unachievable objectives."

"Find the money Sergeant Bannon," he answered.

As we left the district attorney's office, the chief told me he wanted some time to think about how to pursue the case further and that he would get back to me. I began to strategize how to move forward on this case.

"Death Threat Number Three" – A few weeks later, I received a call at home from my captain at the Police Narcotics Division telling me that he had just received a letter from an informant at the California State Prison. The informant had warned in his letter that there were two drug traffickers in California determined to kill me. The prisoner included the would-be assassin's names and descriptions in his letter.

"I wonder if the district attorney was behind it?" I thought to myself. At this point in my life, I didn't know what to think and nothing would have surprised me.

"Maybe he had a personal interest in the Cannabis Buyers Club along with the mayor, and the board of supervisors?" I imagined. It was stated to me through one of my confidential informants who worked at the Club that some high-level politicians were getting kickbacks from the Club. I was trying very hard to obtain enough evidence to prove it. I was now getting in a bit over my head. I was sailing out into some very deep waters by attempting to take down the political machine of the City of San Francisco. But I was willing to do it if I could prove it. This was yet another one of my, "David versus Goliath" moments in my law enforcement career.

The deputy chief ordered a full-scale investigation into my death threats and suggested that I wear my bulletproof vest under my shirt for a while, even off duty. Some of my partners asked me if I was nervous. I shrugged, remembering the death threats I'd been under in Puerto Rico and New York. I looked at my watch and said, "Right about that time, it's nothing I haven't been through before," I said laughingly.

I was temporarily transferred to the Inspector's Bureau as a hit-and-run accident investigator while another narcotics officer was assigned the Cannabis Buyers Club investigation. "How incredibly thrilling," I thought to myself. I now answered my desk phone, "Hit and Run, Sergeant Bannon."

The lieutenant from the Hit and Run Division put the pictures of the two men who wanted to kill me on the wall next to the secretary's desk in an effort to protect me during my death threat investigation.

Every day, I looked intensely at those pictures and had an extreme desire to locate and get them before they got me.

Memorandum

San Francisco Police Department

APPROVED YES NO

To: ALL HIT-RUN STAFF

From: Lt. Chris Weld, #1119
Hit & Run Section

Date: TUES., 03/07/95

Subj: **THREATS AGAINST MEMBER**

Issue:

Narcotics Division has received correspondence from a prison inmate/informer who wrote that the following two identified subjects have voiced intent to harm/maim or kill a former Narcotics Division member now a fellow staff member here (Sgt. Bannon).

Discussion:

Staff need to study the attached photos, copy of which, without comment or identifiers, will be placed on the bulletin board facing the receptionist's desk.

Recommendation:

Be aware.

Attachments

Copy:
Capt. Welch Rm#400

Politics, Pot, and Police – A "deadly" combination

MY CHAMBER FIFTEEN

"DEA – Double Agent"

About two months later, I received a call again on my home phone. It was the captain of the Police Narcotics Division.

"Joe, can you meet me in the chief's office tomorrow morning at nine?" he asked.

"Sure Captain," I said. "What's it about?"

"I'll brief you tomorrow morning, Joe," he said and hung up.

As I slowly hung up the phone, I somehow knew that my police career was about to take yet another radical turn.

I arrived at police headquarters shortly before 9:00 A.M. the next morning and was ushered into the chief's conference room a few minutes later. There were several officials already seated around the long table, including the chief, deputy chief, my captain, and three men dressed in suits and ties.

The chief introduced me to these men, who turned out to be high-ranking officials of the U.S. Drug Enforcement Administration (DEA). One of them was originally from Alabama, one from Washington DC, and the other from California. The latter was the special agent in charge of the DEA Office for the Bay Area and Northern California.

"Sergeant Bannon, your chief tells us that you've conducted an outstanding investigation into the Cannabis Buyers Club," the Alabama agent said in a thick southern drawl.

"We tried to put a case together against those people two years ago. But it didn't meet our guidelines and we were told that it was a local political issue," he added.

"Joe, these gentlemen would like to see some of the video footage that you shot inside the Club," the chief said. "I've taken the liberty of bringing along your tapes. Would you mind running the video for us?"

"Sure, Chief," I said, suddenly excited that the narcotics case I'd worked so hard on was back on the front burner.

A TV set and a VCR had already been set up in the conference room and for the next half-hour we watched people smoking, buying, and selling marijuana. There were scenes of juveniles standing around getting stoned, and women holding infants as they made their drug buys, subjecting the infants to second-hand marijuana smoke.

"Stop the film!" one of the agents suddenly shouted. "Go back to the part where that woman is holding that little child."

I replayed the scene, then showed them several more instances in which young children had been present in the Club as marijuana was being purchased and smoked.

"I felt stoned after being inside and breathing second-hand smoke for just ten minutes, and I'm 6'2," 200 pounds," I said. "Imagine how stoned these young children get after being in there for a while."

"This is an outrage," said one of the DEA officials. "This cannot be tolerated. Politics or not, this must be stopped."

"I've heard that many of these people are homosexuals, many of them suffering from AIDS," the agent from the Bay Area said. "Is that true, Sergeant Bannon?"

"A percentage of them are sir," I replied.

Then the chief interjected: "I know two of you guys are new to San Francisco and you may not be used to the diversity that we have here. We even have some openly gay police officers who are outstanding examples of great cops."

"I see," said one of the agents, followed by a silence in the room.

"Chief," the lead agent in charge of the Bay Area office finally said. "We understand that you need our help to prosecute this criminal organization because it's such a political hot potato here in San Francisco."

"Yes, we do," said the chief. "Our district attorney doesn't want to take it on because the involvement of AIDS patients and other sick people makes it such a sensitive issue."

"Well Chief, we've seen enough on that film and in Sergeant Bannon's case file to make us interested in pursuing the people behind the Club. All we have to do is convince the United States Attorney to prosecute the case. I will also brief the director of the DEA in Washington DC."

The next day the chief ordered me to give a preliminary presentation to a group of special agents at DEA headquarters in the Federal Building. My presentation lasted for two hours and was followed by a barrage of questions. The meeting went very well, and I left satisfied that the feds were very much in favor of doing the right thing. The next day three federal agents and I gave the same presentation to the chief prosecutor of the Federal Organized Crime Drug Task Force.

Following this second presentation, the U.S. Attorney's Office decided to take the case. I was confidentially assigned to the DEA as the police case agent on the investigation. The only persons who were knowledgeable of my "double agent status" were the chief of police and the captain of the narcotics division. This was to be a top-secret San Francisco Police joint investigation to avoid local politics, sympathizers, and possible security leaks. This decision was made to circumvent the San Francisco District Attorney and pursue the case federally. This decision put me, the chief of police, and the narcotics division captain in direct violation of the San Francisco Board of Supervisor's Medical Marijuana Resolution. But we all agreed that we had to do what was right.

I took the oath of office and was officially sworn into the United States Department of Justice, Drug Enforcement Administration as a federal agent who was acting as a double agent against my own city government. Great place to be for the advancement of my police career – yikes!

The task force was to consist of ten federal agents and myself. A DEA agent and I would share the responsibility of leading the team. I was given my own desk at DEA headquarters and told that I would be given any assistance I needed during the ongoing investigation. The guys on my team treated me very well, and I soon learned that they were all very professional and dedicated to their jobs. The next day my new team initiated a major surveillance operation on the Cannabis Buyers Club. We were primarily interested in two people; the guy who moved the money and the guy who moved the marijuana. That night, two members of the San Francisco Board of Supervisors received a call from Dennis Peron, the head of the Club. Peron complained that he was being followed and wanted to know why, especially after the mayor and the police chief had agreed publicly that the prosecution of "medicinal marijuana" cases would be the lowest on their priority list. Peron told the board members that he was concerned that the cops might raid his Club and beat up sick people.

Politics, as I'd feared, reared its ugly head, and Peron was assured that the police would not intervene in his Club's operations. I was now "kited" as a lone operator as they would say in the intelligence community. I was operating covertly behind the backs of all city officials including the mayor, board of supervisors, and the district attorney. I felt like I was sitting on the end of a long tree branch, and someone was slowly sawing the branch off from behind me. I had to wonder if anyone would have my back when I hit the ground, or if I would be the sole object of "plausible deniability?" At this point I really didn't care. I was in a battle between right and wrong and I would leave my fate up to God.

The next day the Club was temporarily closed. "Damn," I thought to myself, they've burned our surveillance already! I got hold of one of the fliers that the Cannabis Buyers Club staff members were handing out and brought it back to the DEA office. It said: "Club closed temporarily. Call for an updated message."

"We got a problem fellas," I said to my DEA Team. We all agreed that it didn't make sense for the Cannabis Club to close just because Dennis Peron thought that he was being followed. I had this eerie gut-level feeling that there was more to it than just that. My suspicion was confirmed two days later. A confidential informant of mine handed me a flier. I got a very queasy feeling in my stomach as I read the boldly printed words on the flier: "Cannabis Club temporarily closed due to federal harassment. Protest at the Federal Building, 1:00 P.M. on April 10th, to fight for our right to use medicinal marijuana."

So much for our 'confidential' investigation. There was no doubt in my mind that there was a security leak. But did it come from the DEA's side? The United States Attorney's side? Someone in Washington D.C.? Or the San Francisco Political side? I felt very disheartened that someone involved in this investigation may be giving information to the opposition. I also began to wonder whether someone was on the take or betraying the investigation because they didn't want to see the case prosecuted. The involvement of the DEA had changed the rules and increased the stakes. It was obvious that the investigation had stepped on some sensitive political toes and rattled a few cages somewhere.

I recalled a scripture from the Bible, from the letter of Paul to the Ephesians, the sixth chapter:

"For we wrestle not against flesh and blood, but against principalities, against powers, against the rulers of the darkness of this world, against spiritual wickedness in high places."

It seemed that wherever I went in life, I found some form of government corruption, and began to wonder if I would soon have yet another contract put out on my life; maybe from corrupt politicians? For the moment, all I could do was find a phone and notify the DEA and my captain of the San Francisco Police Narcotics Division. I drove to the DEA office to make copies of the flyer my informant had given me. The following Monday, at least five hundred protesters showed up at the Federal Building with signs saying, "Make Marijuana Legal." As they marched in a circle, the crowd chanted, "*Hey, Hey, DEA, the Cannabis Club is Here to Stay*!"

I was there to observe this protest and managed to make my way into the middle of the crowd wearing a green bandanna, sunglasses, earrings, and a paste-on beard. I fit in well. When the protesters had worked themselves into a frenzy, Dennis Peron got up to make a speech. He reminded me of a cult leader as he told the crowd that if he died, they'd all die and if he gets arrested, they'd all get arrested. People got up on stage to praise Peron and swear that marijuana had saved their lives, and they couldn't live without the drug. Watching all this, it suddenly struck me that I was dealing with much more than a sophisticated drug operation disguised as a haven for sick people. I was facing a *13,000* – member cult and political movement with Dennis Peron as it's leader.

What made my investigation even more complicated and convoluted, was that Dennis Peron had become a candidate for California State Governor. This created yet another protective layer of insulation for him that I had to find a way to legally penetrate through. Investigating a political candidate now came with a completely different set of rules and restrictions.

Dennis Peron was no dummy, or at least his legal advisor wasn't, which in all likelihood was Terence Hallinan who was a well-known defense attorney for drug dealers. Peron and Hallinan went back many years together as friends. What a great friend for Peron to have, and what an increased precarious position for me and my investigation to be in.

I became more determined than ever to take down this deceptive wolf in sheep's clothing. And if I could include any corrupt politicians who were working with Peron, all the better.

MY CHAMBER SIXTEEN

"Penetrating The Emerald Triangle"

During the course of the weeks that followed, our investigative efforts were intensified. Federal teletypes were sent to other DEA field offices across the country and our investigation started to expand beyond California. We redirected our strategy to circumvent the local politics in San Francisco and began to focus our efforts on the Club's source of marijuana supply high up in the mountains of Northern California. Our objective was to locate a financial nexus between the Cannabis Buyers Club and the organized crime syndicate of The Emerald Triangle.

The Emerald Triangle was an area in Northern California whose nucleus was centered around Humboldt, Trinity, and Mendocino Counties. This is where multimillion-dollar marijuana gardens grew and were run by the heavily armed marijuana drug cartels and their hired "protectors of the crops." They were known for their human trafficking, migrant labor groups, and murder.

I was co-assigned to a very specialized team of military narcotics operators who went by the code name: "Team Delta." This team's sole purpose was to eradicate drugs and drug-related organized crime both in Northern California and South America (*as in Operation Snowcap in the late 1980s*). Also assigned to this operation were some state narcotics agents who specialized in marijuana investigations and eradication. The members of both teams were highly trained and experienced in narcotics enforcement in extremely dangerous environments such as the treacherous high mountain terrain that we were now operating in. We had become a combined task force who brought many diverse resources to the investigation. This greatly increased our chances of gathering valuable evidence and ultimately, a successful criminal prosecution of the Cannabis Buyers Club.

We used clandestine aircraft that were equipped with thermal radiation detection devices and specialized enhanced optics that could detect the presence of marijuana fields and large indoor marijuana cultivation grows within The Emerald Triangle. This specific type of aircraft could fly at altitudes that were unsuspicious and untraceable from the ground.

We "low-crawled" through the foliage of The Emerald Triangle at night to get a close-up look at some of these locations. We wore camouflage clothing and face paint while using night vision scopes, coded communications, helicopter insertions, and each of us was armed with machine guns in case of enemy contact. We also had a long-range sniper with us during our covert operations. If we couldn't isolate and take the Club down locally, then we would attempt to take it down through its connection with the organized crime syndicate that was supplying the Club with huge amounts of marijuana each week. "*Operation Emerald Triangle*," as it was now called.

We attempted to gather as much evidence as possible and connect it to the criminal enterprise of the Cannabis Buyers Club. Our main goal was to locate the financial assets of the enterprise and present a money-laundering case to the United States Attorney. We even sent an undercover DEA agent into the Club posing as a business entrepreneur anxious to establish a partnership with Peron and to learn how he laundered the untraceable mega amounts of cash that the Club took in. My team and I would frequently sit around a conference table devising strategies to further our investigation. At this point our confidence was high that we could get past the local politics and carry out a successful investigation and prosecution of the drug dealers and growers that were supplying and profiting from the Club. Within this process, our hope was also to develop informants who could supply us with damning evidence and information against Dennis Peron and the Club.

During this period, the San Francisco Police Department had little idea exactly what I was doing. The chief of police knew that I was assigned to the DEA as a task force agent, but he hadn't been apprised of my specific duties on this other team. I just kept getting more deeply involved in our mission. The "plausible deniability" was probably a good thing for both the chief and my captain, but for me? I was being 'kited out' farther and farther as a lone operator. The DEA and Team Delta had their own agenda, which was in direct opposition to the political machine of San Francisco, with me operating somewhere in the middle. Now, as a federal agent, I was prohibited to brief my police department superiors on certain elements of this case that I was now heavily involved with. Great place to be for career advancement!

The more we dug into the case, the bigger and more complicated it became. It was not only a criminal enterprise making a great deal of money; it was also a high-powered political movement to legalize marijuana, backed by some very powerful public figures. I was getting myself involved very deeply in what could very well pan out to be a case of extreme political corruption. A case that had the potential to get me fired or killed. But I was doing my best to "*find the money*" as I had been tasked to do by both the San Francisco District Attorney and the United States Attorney in charge of organized narcotics crimes. To me, it was worth the risk.

This case was much bigger than just the owner of the Club, Dennis Peron. This was a case of high-level politics and criminal enterprises. At this point I was entrenched as deep as a double agent cop could get. I constantly had to decide who my allegiance was to. The DEA, Team Delta, or the San Francisco Police Department? "God, please help me make the right decisions, but I'm willing to do the right thing despite my San Francisco Police career," I prayed.

The federal government sent me to clandestine laboratory school, urban raid, machine gun, SWAT, and airborne helicopter assault schools. These certification schools had made me more valuable to my team and to our mission.

The U.S. Attorney still denied our request for a search warrant for the Cannabis Buyers Club Case. He said that he needed more evidence of money-laundering or a structured criminal enterprise before he would grant a warrant. I told him that I could produce the evidence that he required if he would give me a search warrant, but he declined, insisting he needed the evidence first.

It seemed all backward to me. Normally, a search warrant is granted if you have probable cause; the search then produces more evidence. I had more probable cause for a search warrant than most cops could ever dream of. I could only assume that the politics surrounding the case had made even the Federal U.S. Attorney nervous. "Medicinal Marijuana" was a hot issue in San Francisco and apparently in Washington D.C. as well. I could only hope that my work in Northern California would produce the evidence that he required, specifically a money trail leading back to the Cannabis Buyers Club. I had to find a way to connect the Club to the money.

Unfortunately, as the investigation wore laboriously on, more and more people started to lose faith that the case would ever be prosecuted because of the incredible restrictions that the U.S. Attorney had placed on my team. To make matters worse, the IRS couldn't follow nor determine the money trail and were pulled off the case. I knew that the marijuana club was a scam and I remained determined to take the operation down, no matter what the odds against me were. This was my mission, and I was not about to fail or come up short.

I was considered a "rogue operator" by all definitions of the term. The chief of police had a lawsuit filed against him on an unrelated matter and was pretty much preoccupied with the lawsuit and out of the loop of my investigation. My captain of the police narcotics division had an idea what I was doing but told me he didn't need to be constantly briefed on all the specifics. That's good, because if he had been, he would have probably pulled me off the investigation. He was a very smart man and knew what questions not to ask me. So, to protect both he and my investigation, I briefed him on as much as I could, but not more than he needed to know. I respected my captain very much and each day I had to reevaluate my "code of silence" relative to him. Do I brief my command staff and violate DEA protocol? Or do I not fully brief them and stay within DEA and Team Delta's protocol? That was the decision that I had to make every day. I was doing my best to protect both sides of the investigation. I was 'stuck between a rock and a hard place' to say the least. Only the government and I knew exactly what I was doing up in The Emerald Triangle. "Career wise," I was in the worst position imaginable.

The summer was now ending, and the fall marijuana harvest was drawing near. By this time some of the marijuana plants had grown up to ten feet tall and the gardens were worth millions. Scores of illegal aliens are hired at this time to bring in the crop for the drug lords. The labor was cheap, which yielded higher profits, and the illegals didn't dare go to the police for fear of being arrested and deported (*at least back then*).

At 7:00 A.M. on a Monday morning, I sat in on an operational briefing with my airborne reconnaissance and eradication team. The first order of business was a pointed reminder about the officer who'd been shot by local American Indians a while back. Northern California has some Native American reservations, and a lot of these Native American people do not like police or government agents nosing around their lands. The rumor mill had it that some of the Native American Indian tribes had threatened to kill police officers if they caught them trespassing on their land. As the agent in charge was going over the tactics the Indians used, I sat there thinking to myself that American Indian attacks were supposed to be confined to history. Before I'd joined the task force, I'd never dreamt I'd have to worry about American Indians on the warpath in the mid-1990s.

The next topic for discussion was booby traps. A lot of the marijuana gardens, as well as the mountain trails that lead to the plots, were protected by camouflaged booby traps. These devices are set to dissuade both law enforcement officials and marijuana poachers who often attempt to steal marijuana crops when the growers are away. Some of the booby traps the growers used were pretty nasty. Fishhooks were strung at face level from thin filament lines, making them all but invisible in the brush. Sharpened punji sticks or vertical spikes common in Vietnam, were set along trails, as were trip wires attached to explosives. But the booby trap that really gave me the creeps was the camouflaged pit filled with pissed-off rattle snakes. Some of the growers were Vietnam Veterans and they were very skilled at this art. As if the booby traps weren't dangerous enough, the growers also occasionally used snipers with hunting rifles equipped with high-powered scopes to pick off anyone who came near their precious crops.

We not only had to be aware of American Indians, booby traps, and snipers, but we faced natural hazards as well: poison ivy, poison oak, fire ants, poisonous snakes, bears, mountain lions, ticks, brain-broiling sun, rockslides, and exhaustion from trekking through rough terrain were just some of the dangers – and I thought leaving the Caribbean and returning to San Francisco would be a walk in the park.

The growers usually grew their crops in very high, secluded areas of the mountains which made our job of getting to them very difficult. The upside of it all was that we got to have a lot of fun by putting a severe hurt on the drug lords when we captured their gardens. Sometimes we'd leave a taunting sign behind saying, "*The Police were here but you were not – so we left and took your pot.*" A twisted form of humor.

Each morning before we went out into the mountains to raid the fields, we held a briefing during which we studied maps, the latitude and longitude coordinates of our target areas, and helicopter evacuation procedures in case one of us was shot, bitten by a snake, or seriously injured during the operation. We were all certified in helicopter air assault tactics and when we had successfully attacked and eradicated the target of the day, we'd fly reconnaissance missions to find new ones. As we flew above the tree lines looking for the marijuana gardens, we always kept one eye open for any snipers who might try to shoot us down. Pretty hard to see them in the brush though. The only thing that would become visible would be the muzzle flash from a rifle, but by then it could be too late. A lot of people up there in the mountains were military veterans who had surplus military weapons, including .50 caliber rifles, and other deadly firepower. We really had to watch our asses.

We were very fortunate to have an expert helicopter pilot flying us around. Dave had been a helicopter scout in Vietnam and was shot down on more than one occasion and almost captured by the Viet Cong. Dave told us that if our helicopter were ever disabled by sniper or rocket fire, he would do his best to crash-land us as safely as possible, or at least what would be left of us.

Sometimes we employed a hair-raising tactic called "*STABO LINEING*" in which we hung from either a 100 or 150-foot cable attached to the bottom of the helicopter. We used this maneuver whenever we had to descend into dense trees or brush where the helicopter couldn't land. As soon as our feet touched the ground, we would disconnect the cable from a harness and complete our mission. We'd later radio the helicopter to return, hook up to the cable that Dave would send down, and we would be extracted. We had to move very fast when we were using this tactic because hanging on the end of a cable in mid-air made us a sitting duck for snipers.

Whenever we had the option, we'd do a land reconnaissance to find a safe landing zone for the helicopter. Often, though, we'd have no choice but to descend on the end of the cable to a steep mountain slope or a heavily forested area because the helicopter couldn't get any closer to our target.

If we were ever shot down or the helicopter became disabled while we were hanging on the end of the STABO line, the procedure was that the pilot would try his best to put us at least 20 feet from the ground. We were then to cut ourselves off the cable and fall to the ground. We would get hurt but probably not killed. We were to then wait for the helicopter to crash and then rescue the pilot. None of us looked forward to this, but if it ever happened, at least we had a plan.

Normally, when we were on a STABO Mission (*Short Term Airborne Operations*), we were one to two thousand feet up in the air and moving fast. This made us harder to hit with a projectile from the ground. Despite the danger, I really liked STABO lining because I got a tremendous adrenaline rush from hanging at the end of the cable several thousand feet up in the air. Admittedly, STABO was an extreme tactic, but one that was frequently necessary for us to infiltrate the often-inaccessible terrain where the growers hid their marijuana gardens.

One very hot afternoon we were eradicating a large marijuana plot that had over one thousand mature marijuana plants in it. Suddenly, one of my team members uprooted a large wasp's nest and hundreds of angry wasps started to attack us. We had to radio for the helicopter to hover over us and force the wasps to the ground with the wind from the rotor blades before we could finish our job and leave. We popped some smoke grenades which discouraged them from sticking around as well.

Sometimes we flew recon at a high altitude in an unmarked helicopter using a pair of gyroscopic binoculars to spy on the garden below and the workers maintaining it. We would then radio the plot's location to a ground team, who would assault the garden and arrest the workers. If a ground team wasn't close enough, we would have to raid the garden ourselves from the air. Usually, by the time we STABO'd or repelled in, or found a sufficient landing zone, the workers had fled, leaving all their belongings behind.

Most of the gardens that we had encountered were encircled by a metal fence or chicken wire. This was to keep the wild animals in the area from eating the marijuana leaves. Rat traps were also usually spread around on the ground to keep rodents from destroying the valuable plants. On moonless nights we would sometimes infiltrate a known marijuana garden and secretly place camouflaged video cameras in the nearby trees to capture footage of the growers as they worked in their gardens. This evidence was then used in future court cases. Some of the more sophisticated gardens were equipped with silent alarm systems to warn the enemy of our approach. This was a real danger for us because it gave away our location without us knowing it and could have prompted a surprise enemy attack.

Remaining alert at all times was our best defense. Many times, the gardens were so well camouflaged that we could not spot them from the air and we'd have to conduct a covert search of the suspected area on foot. A lot of times while getting to these areas, we had to cross open fields and trek through waist-high brush not being able to see anything from the waist down. Our team had to move quickly, not only to avoid being spotted but also targeted by our enemy with a high-powered rifle. In addition to this, there was nothing more nerve-wracking than to be rushing through this waist-high brush and hearing the sound of rattlesnakes in close proximity knowing that there could also be potential booby traps strategically placed along our path. This was nothing compared to the tunnel rats in Vietnam but scary, nonetheless.

Reconning from the helicopter one day, we spotted a marijuana plot sporadically stretching over one-half mile along the banks of a river. The pilot had to do what was called a "toe-in landing," a maneuver necessary when there was not enough flat ground to land the skids. The pilot would nose carefully up to the top of a cliff and while the helicopter hovered there, he'd push the skids against the rock wall with the force of the rotor blades, thus creating a bridge for us to exit the helicopter. We'd then "tight rope" walk along the skids to the top of the cliff. This was a very dangerous tactic because if we slipped it was a long drop straight down. Another hazard was weight transfer. We had to perfectly time our exit off of the skids. If one of us jumped off too quickly, the sudden weight change could cause the helicopter to pitch drastically. If the pilot couldn't compensate with the rotors fast enough, the helicopter would suddenly slant up and probably crash. The rotors themselves could also do you in. They move so fast that they're invisible to the eye. If you walked into one of them, it would chop you up like a Cuisinart. I heard that this had happened to an agent a few years back and that it wasn't a pretty sight.

On this one day, we did our toe-in landing and descended to the river. We began collecting samples of marijuana plants, jumping from one rock to the next trying to keep our balance and avoid falling into the water. We each had a large bundle of plants to carry with us and the bundles got larger and heavier as we went along. The helicopter landing zone was about one half mile north of us and we had a long way to go. This area was a high-danger zone for snakes, wild animals, and as always – snipers. We began to make our way out along the bottom of a ravine with high ground on both sides of us, a perfect sniper setup. Aware of the danger, we moved as fast as we could. Meanwhile, our helicopter flew recon above us on the lookout for snipers and other hazards. As I passed through some heavy brush, I heard something make an 'animal' noise; something that sounded very big and unfriendly. Not wanting to find out what it was, I started jumping along the river rocks as if I were doing an Irish River Dance.

After one 12-hour day of extremely strenuous work, the special operations commander invited me out for dinner. Earlier that day, he and I had been hanging on the end of a STABO line together with our legs wrapped around each other to keep from banging into each other or getting twisted in the cables from high wind oscillation. The commander and I established an instant rapport, and at the end of the day, I flew back to headquarters with him in the helicopter while the others drove back in ground vehicles. It was good to know people in 'high' places. God had always shown me His favor in my life with the people who I came in contact with.

One day, I was dangling from a STABO line about 500 feet up while ascending in the air with my partner, when the metal carabiner that held me to the lifeline slipped and all my body weight was suddenly concentrated on the weakest part of the shackle that held me to the cable. I couldn't correct the problem in mid-air because my body weight had frozen the carabiner in place. If it broke open, I could have fallen 500 feet if my partner couldn't have supported my body weight. I radioed the pilot, and we made an emergency landing on the closest flat terrain. I then quickly corrected the problem, and we were back in the air in minutes. Thank God for small favors. As it says in Psalm 91, "He gives His angels charge over us." Or He works through His helicopter pilots. I was grateful for either one.

On our way back to the airport that night, we encountered dangerously high winds. The helicopter was pushed every which way by the wind, especially when we flew over a canyon. I began to wonder just how much stress those rotors could take. Sometimes my faith in God was the only comfort I could find in F'd up situations like this. I was scared all right, anyone would be, but I also knew that I was in God's hands and was willing to accept my fate – as I always had been in the past.

I worked on these missions in Northern California approximately three to four days out of the week. I stayed in a hotel under the guise of a traveling businessman. I had to be cautious because a lot of drug dealers who traveled up to make buys, stayed at these hotels as well. I often wondered if the guy in the room next door might be a dealer intending to purchase the very marijuana crop that I was going to confiscate that day.

Northern California was inundated with high-scale marijuana smugglers and corrupt politicians. In some areas, a large part of the local economy was tied into the marijuana industry. The last thing that a lot of these people wanted to see up there was someone like me messing with their local cash crop. I would have been in considerable danger if the wrong people had found out that I was an agent for the DEA, so I kept an extremely low profile when I was staying in one of those small towns up in the Emerald Triangle – seriously outnumbered by the Marijuana Drug Cartels. My life was not the only thing in danger here if I was found out by the cartel. My job would also be in danger if the San Francisco Police Department had any idea exactly what I was doing on my "special assignment." Working as a double agent was a crap sandwich at best, but to me, the greater good of exposing the truth about the Cannabis Buyers Club was worth it.

I usually got up before the sun rose, loaded my machine gun into a tennis bag, traveled to remote mountainous areas to complete my mission, and then returned to the hotel after dark. I trusted no one, spoke only when spoken to, and stayed in my room at night with the "do not disturb" sign on my door. I registered under a fictitious name and gave a phony company as my employer. A falsified undercover driver's license and credit cards completed my cover story. On the nightstand next to my bed was a bible and a machine gun. I used the first to bolster my faith to fight the devil, and the latter, to increase my security to fight the drug lords. God doesn't do "everything" for me. "Faith without works (*machine gun*) is dead." **James 2:17**

Members of my Covert Low Crawl Spy Team

STABO Lining – AKA "Sniper Bait"

Raiding the Multi-Million Dollar Marijuana Gardens

High Up in the Mountains of the Emerald Triangle

"Stood Down by the White House" – After several months of extremely hard work and obtaining overwhelming amounts of evidence against the Cannabis Buyers Club, we were finally granted a search warrant by the United States Attorney's Office. We were only forty-eight hours away from serving search warrants on several locations that we had identified during our investigation.

My team was suddenly called into the Special Agent in Charges' Office of the DEA. He told us that he had just been notified by the Director of the DEA in Washington, D.C., that we were to stand down and not serve any search warrants. We were also ordered to close our investigation against the Cannabis Buyers Club unless we could get an indictment against the Club by a grand jury. The director also commanded that the DEA was not to be the lead investigative agency on this case any longer because of the politically heated nature of the case.

More intensely restrictive hoops to jump through. There were obviously some very heavy players working against us. We were told that the Director of the DEA stated that our investigation had made it to the desks of President Clinton, United States Attorney General Janet Reno, Health Secretary Donna Shalala, and "Drug Czar" General Barry McCaffrey. At that point, it was basically decided at the highest level of the United States Government that we were not to touch the Cannabis Buyers Club of San Francisco.

"Could Dennis Peron possibly be that connected and insulated?" I thought to myself.

This monster was bigger than all of us. Who knew who was really behind the Cannabis Buyers Club? How high did it really go? We all had many unanswered questions, suspicions, and theories. Nevertheless, the case was over, and I cleaned out my desk at the DEA office and turned in my machine gun, federal identification, and other equipment to my supervisor. But before I left, I did something extremely unconventional and unprecedented.

I was able to locate the fax number to President Clinton, U.S. Attorney General Janet Reno, and Drug Czar General Barry McCaffery. I faxed all three of them a four-page letter explaining the highlights of the Cannabis Buyers Club Investigation in an effort to get them to reconsider their decision. I could have gotten fired or brought up on administrative charges for doing this. But I still believed that all of the evidence that we had collected, including allegations and circumstantial evidence against Dennis Peron of having sex with young boys while supplying them with marijuana, should not be overlooked. I included the address of the San Francisco Police Headquarters as my return address in case they wanted to get back to me. Which to my amazement, two out of the three had. (*See return letters on the following pages*).

I know this sounds presumptuous, but I now knew way too much to turn my head and look the other way before exhausting all my options and resources. It seemed that I had in fact, made this my "*personal war*" that the then lieutenant, now captain of the narcotics division, had warned me not to do years prior. But he was now my captain and in this war with me. How ironic.

I then went back to the San Francisco Police Department with my tail between my legs to brief both the chief and the captain that the case had been shut down by the powers that be in Washington D.C. and that the DEA was out of the game.

UNITED STATES DEPARTMENT OF JUSTICE DRUG ENFORCEMENT ADMINISTRATION CASE FILE CLOSED

UNITED STATES DEPARTMENT OF JUSTICE
DRUG ENFORCEMENT ADMINISTRATION
450 GOLDEN GATE AVENUE, BOX 36035
SAN FRANCISCO, CA 94102

September 5, 1996

Mr. Fred Lau
Chief of Police
San Francisco Police Department
Hall of Justice, Room 525
850 Bryant Street
San Francisco, CA 94103

Dear Chief Lau:

Re: **Commendation of Officer Joseph F. Bannon, Star #431**

Although the investigation of the Cannabis Buyers' Club may provoke discussion between the opposing camps, the efforts of SFPD Officer Joseph F. Bannon, Star #431 in this particular investigation, must be mutually viewed as exceptional.

As you may be aware, for several months Officer Bannon worked very closely and diligently with Special Agents of this office in developing a prosecutable case against the Cannabis Buyers' Club and its proprietors. During that lengthy time, Officer Bannon exhibited all the traits of an expert investigator. His representation of the San Francisco Police Department was oustanding. Over that period, I came to know and appreciate Joe Bannon, and admired him for his competence; his commitment to public service; his dedication to duty; and his allegiance to the investigation.

It is my opinion that Joe Bannon possesses all those qualities that we, as managers, hope to find in all of our subordinates. I commend him to you and your police organization. You can be very proud that he wears a badge of the esteemed San Francisco Police Department.

Sincerely yours,

William J. Mitchell
Special Agent in Charge

THE WHITE HOUSE
WASHINGTON

May 14, 1997

Mr. Joseph Bannon
San Francisco Police Department
Narcotics Division
850 Bryant Street
San Francisco, California 94103

Dear Officer Bannon:

Thank you for writing to me regarding the use of marijuana for medical purposes. I appreciate knowing your views. My Administration has worked very hard to ensure that Americans have access to safe and effective medicine.

My Administration strongly opposes the California and Arizona drug legalization measures because they contradict our federal law and our national drug control strategy. They disregard the medical and scientific process by which our nation evaluates and approves safe and effective medicines. And, most important, they send the wrong message to our children -- undermining the efforts of parents, educators, elected leaders, and countless others who are working to ensure a healthy, drug-free society.

However, in response to anecdotal claims about marijuana's medical benefits, the Office of National Drug Control Policy is funding a comprehensive research review by the National Academy of Science's Institute of Medicine. The purpose of this study is to ensure that good science remains the basis of our drug control policy.

As we work to protect the health of children and our nation, I appreciate your interest in this issue.

Sincerely,

Bill Clinton

I Was a Bit Confused by President Clinton's Words to Me

U.S. Department of Justice

Drug Enforcement Administration

Washington, D.C. 20537

MAR 6 1997

Officer Joseph F. Bannon
Narcotics Division
San Francisco Police Department
850 Bryant Street
San Francisco, California 94103

Dear Officer Bannon:

Your letter of January 13, 1997, to President Clinton was forwarded to the Drug Enforcement Administration by Attorney General Reno.

On behalf of Administrator Thomas A. Constantine, I would like to thank you for your efforts to elucidate the true nature of the San Francisco Cannabis Buyer's Club and to enforce the Controlled Substances Act. The citizens of this country are well served by individuals like you and the many others who are dedicated to upholding and enforcing the laws of this country. I am confident that through your efforts, the truth about marijuana and those who wish to perpetuate this serious problem will be recognized and denounced.

Please rest assured that the Drug Enforcement Administration will continue to aggressively enforce the drug laws of this nation. Once again, thank you for taking the time to share your concerns with us.

Sincerely,

Donald E. Joseph, Chief
Information Services

Really? Did I Miss Something Here? – "Politics at its Finest"

DRUG
ENFORCEMENT
ADMINISTRATION
UNITED STATES
DEPARTMENT OF JUSTICE
PRESENTS THIS
CERTIFICATE OF
APPRECIATION
TO Officer Joseph Bannon
-San Francisco Police Department-
FOR
OUTSTANDING CONTRIBUTIONS
IN THE FIELD OF DRUG
LAW ENFORCEMENT

Michele Leonhart
Special Agent in Charge
San Francisco Field Division

Gearing Up for an Air Insertion Mission
"Into The Emerald Triangle"

On Patrol Two Miles from Our Helicopter Landing Zone
"While Scouting for Snipers, Booby Traps, Snakes, Bears, or Whatever Else"

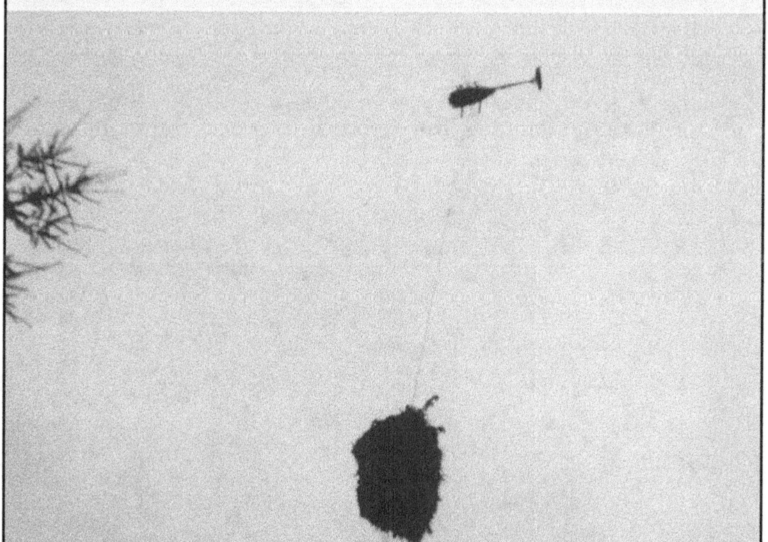

Airlifting Out Another Haul of Weed

I'm Sure This Pissed Off Some Drug Lord

Where All the Weed Ended Up
'The Cannabis Buyers Club'

Air Assault Team Three
"The Green Team"

MY CHAMBER SEVENTEEN

"The Resurrection of Lazarus"

Now when He had said these things, He cried with a loud voice, "Lazarus, (Cannabis Club Investigation) come forth!"

John 11:43

After a meeting between my captain, myself, DEA officials, and representatives from another law enforcement agency, the Cannabis Buyers Club Case and all the evidence we had collected was transferred to the California State Bureau of Narcotic Enforcement (*BNE*) under California State Attorney General Daniel Lungren.

Side note: This agency was eventually led by the now Vice President Kamala Harris when she was the Attorney General of the State of California.

I was transferred to this other agency (*BNE*), and the case was eventually accepted for prosecution by California State Attorney General Daniel Lungren's Office – Department of Justice.

By the time this all took place, San Francisco had a new mayor, police chief, and district attorney who could not be trusted to keep this case confidential. Recently appointed District Attorney

Terrance Hallinan was a former defense attorney for drug dealers and a long-time personal friend of the owner of the Cannabis Buyers Club – Dennis Peron. I had always suspected that Hallinan was Peron's legal advisor before he had been elected as the city's district attorney. Another "win" for Dennis Peron, the Club, and the marijuana legalization movement. District Attorney Hallinan believed that both marijuana and prostitution should be legal. Great!

I was told by this new state agency (*BNE*) that the San Francisco Mayor or District Attorney could not be briefed on this investigation. My captain of the Police Narcotics Division felt obligated to brief the new chief of police. However, the details of my involvement were again downplayed. The new chief of police stated that he understood the need for "case confidentiality" and my necessary "administrative" role in the investigation. However, he also stated that at some point he would be obligated to advise both the mayor and district attorney of this new agency's investigation into the Club including my involvement in it. I knew we had to move fast before the chief advised them both which would have been suicide for our investigation.

I was now sitting on the end of that tree branch again that was slowly being sawed off from the trunk, and it was going to be a long and hard fall when it broke off. The only person holding the tail of my kite in the San Francisco Police Department that knew the specific details about my status with this new agency, was my captain. We both knew what our eventual fate would be but we were too far into the game to back out. This was political suicide for both of us, and we knew it. But in my heart, I knew it was the right thing to do in the eyes of God, and to uphold the oath of office that I swore to when I became a police officer. My captain also believed that this was the right thing to do and was willing to fall on the sword for what he believed in as well.

Special agents from every field office throughout the State of California Department of Justice were brought into San Francisco to work the case. I presented a mass briefing to more than one hundred narcotics agents at the Presidio Army Base relative to the history behind the case, and the evidence collected over the past almost two years between the San Francisco Police Department and the DEA. I also described the political sensitivity of the case. When I stated that the San Francisco Mayor, Board of Supervisors, Police Commission, and the new District Attorney were unaware of this investigation and my active participation in it – we all knew what my eventual fate would be when they found out. *My career as a San Francisco Police Officer would be over.* I received a standing ovation for my courage and integrity to do the right thing and not give up over the past two years.

We conducted more surveillance operations and set up clandestine cameras in locations that could capture activity in both the front and back of the Club to freshen up the case to this new agency's standards. I was also able to acquire a confidential informant who worked inside of the Club that was loaned to me through the FBI. His/her information was invaluable.

"When I went to work for the Club, I believed in the cause. But when I saw how corrupt Dennis Peron and his operation really was, I lost my faith in the movement. Peron gave marijuana to young boys in exchange for sex, and sold drugs other than just marijuana," stated my confidential informant.

I spoke with some of these boys who confirmed what my informant had told me but none of them were willing to come forward and testify against Peron.

At the conclusion of the case, we had to put my confidential informant into a Witness Protection Program to keep him/her alive from the death threats that he/she had received. Another damn security leak that would have gotten my informant killed if we had not relocated him/her.

Right before search warrants were served at the Cannabis Club and several other locations. I was sat down at a long conference table. Seated at the table were every high-ranking official of the California Attorney General's Office and the Department of Justice (*DOJ*). The Bureau Chief in Charge asked me if I was sure that I wanted my name on the search warrant as the affiant. I was told that my career would be over once the affidavit with my name on it went public. I was given the opportunity to have another agent's name put on the search warrant to insulate me. I looked each man sitting at the conference table in the eyes one at a time and said, "I started this, and I will finish it. That is the vow I took before man and God when I was sworn in as a police officer."

"That's admirable Joe," replied Chief Doane of the Department of Justice, "But you cannot even brief your captain of the time and day of the raid. Do you agree?"

I hesitated for a minute at this request based on my loyalty and allegiance to my captain, but I also knew that this would protect him to a certain degree when he would eventually be asked by the San Francisco Chief of Police if he had been appraised of the raid date. I finally said, "*I agree*." After the meeting, I called my captain out of respect and told him what I had agreed to. He told me that he understood their position and he was okay with it.

"I'll call you after the raid begins Captain, but you will not be hearing from me until that happens." The captain again agreed.

"You know Joe, after the raid, you and I will be sweeping floors at the Hall of Justice for a living," said my captain as we both laughed.

"Yes sir, we probably will," I replied.

On the morning of the raid, I sat in the command post at the DOJ Headquarters Building listening to the police radio as the many teams of special narcotics agents were about to crash through the doors simultaneously at several locations. As soon as the teams reported that they had secured each location, I called my captain at home at 7:00 AM on a Sunday morning.

"It's all over Captain, it happened."

"Ok Joe, I'll call the police chief and brief him. Expect a phone call from him," stated the captain.

"I can't wait," I replied sarcastically.

Dennis Peron was arrested, and the Cannabis Buyers Club was officially shut down. I had the great pleasure of driving to Peron's house and breaking open his bedroom walls with a fire axe in an effort to, "*find the money.*" The money, however, was hidden in a room behind a covert spring-loaded bookcase at the Cannabis Club itself. But unfortunately, the bulk of it had been moved out before the raid. Damn the bad luck.

When the case went public, It was discovered by several news agencies and activist groups that I was the case agent who started this investigation and the affiant whose name appeared on the search warrant. My captain and I were dragged through a media circus who twisted the truth of the investigation for the drama effects, and to create havoc in the City. The "Fake News" that we are all well aware of these days, was very prevalent even back in the late 1990s.

Many people viewed me as a traitor and a murderer of AIDS and suffering patients. Cartoons in newspapers were drawn of me attacking a little old lady in a wheelchair. San Francisco Mayor Willie Brown, District Attorney Terence Hallinan, and the City Board of Supervisors spoke out against me on the six o'clock news. My picture was plastered on the front pages of newspapers. I was thrown out of and refused service in some of my favorite restaurants. There were protests in the streets. As I was being torn apart in the media, pictures of me were burned in effigy, and posted on buildings and bus stops with the words "traitor" and "murderer" written across my face. In response to this, the chief of police offered me police protection at my residence. "Oh, hell no, not again," I sarcastically laughed to myself.

I lost several friends who believed the twisted, one-sided reporting by the evil, biased media. I became a superstar overnight, but not in a positive light. This case was by far, one of the most newsworthy and politically hot drug cases in the City's history.

The captain of the police narcotics division called me at home and said, "Hey Joe. Remember when I said after the raid that you and I would be sweeping floors at the Hall of Justice?"

"Yes sir," I replied.

"Well, I just received a call from the chief of police. Grab your broom buddy, you and I are the new janitors at The Hall of Justice."

My captain was busted down to lieutenant and reassigned to a patrol station. I lost any potential of retaining permanent civil service status of my rank of sergeant, and my future career prospects as a San Francisco Police Officer had permanently ended. But this was no surprise to me. I knew that this would happen halfway through the investigation.

I was ordered by the new chief of police not to give any statements to the media who were all calling me on my home phone. I was also told to stay at my desk over at the Bureau of Narcotic Enforcement and just do paperwork in preparation for the upcoming court trail.

"Joe, under no circumstance are you allowed to do any police work," quote the chief.

I had become a hero to law enforcement agencies across the country, and a public enemy to the unaware sympathetic public, the San Francisco Mayor, District Attorney, and many others. No matter what they accused me of, I could not tell them the truth about what I had discovered over the past two years. I was to say nothing until the case went to court and the evidence against the Club was made public. Including finding District Attorney Terrance Hallinan's business card with his home phone number written on it that was confiscated at Dennis Peron's home. Just as I had suspected all along.

I had other evidence against Hallinan, but I couldn't convince the State Attorney General to file charges against him. I guess that was too political even for him.

I isolated and kept as much of a low profile as I could. This "gag order" to say nothing cost me my reputation and my friends. And yes, more death threats. My San Francisco Police career that I had travelled across the country for was now over.

Sneak attack on San Francisco

Sunday, August 4, was a day that will live in infamy in San Francisco.

This is a city that has a well-earned international reputation for being famously Democratic, and tolerant to the point of being, well, loose.

Sunday, August 4, was the day that the right-wing faction in the Republican party pulled off a sneak attack and took over — at least for a well-publicized moment — the machinery of law enforcement in San Francisco.

That day, the politically ambitious California attorney general Dan Lungren sent 100 agents, along with some high-profile San Francisco cops, to bust a comfy living-room-type cannabis club that took care, mostly, of middle-aged HIV-infected people who wanted to smoke some dope to ease their pain.

It is the official policy of this city that giving people pot for medicinal purposes is okay and the cops here have been told to leave them alone.

But suddenly the Republican, Lungren, who is angling for the veep spot on the national ticket, invades San Francisco a fortnight before the Republican convention in San Diego, using San Francisco cops to his political advantage, and none of the Democrat chief law-enforcement officials in this city knows about it until after it happens?

Democratic Mayor Willie Brown, a very much hands-on manager, didn't know the Republicans were coming because Police Chief Fred Lau didn't tell him.

Chief Lau didn't tell the mayor because, he says, he didn't know 100 state agents armed with guns and riot gear were coming into the city.

Democratic District Attorney Terence Hallinan was likewise uninformed about the Republicans.

Thus the question becomes, who in the Police Department did know — and, if they knew, why didn't they tell the mayor about an obviously politically inspired Republican assault on San Francisco civic policy? (Excuse me, does anyone believe that Saturday was the first day Lungren heard about Democratic San Francisco's tolerance policy toward marijuana and of his own narcotics bureau's long-term investigation into the cannabis club — and that the timing of his

See HINCKLE, page 7

SAN FRANCISCO'S NEIGHBORHOOD NEWSPAPER

THE INDEPENDENT

NOE/HAIGHT/CENTRAL EDITION — TUESDAY, AUGUST 6, 1996

Sneak Attack: "*A Day That Will Live In Infamy in San Francisco*"

State of California

Office of the Attorney General

Daniel E. Lungren

Attorney General

September 4, 1996

Mr. William Lau
Chief of Police
San Francisco Police Department
850 Bryant Street, Room 525
San Francisco, CA 94103

RE: Officer Joseph Bannon

Dear Chief Lau:

As you know, Officer Bannon has worked closely with this Department in connection with the Cannabis Buyers' Club investigation. Indeed, if it had not been for the dedication and sacrifice of Officer Bannon, the case would not have been pursued. This Department is proud to have been able to work with Joe to curb the drug distribution activities that were happening at Cannabis Buyers' Club.

There are divergent views with respect to the action which has been taken relative to Cannabis Buyers' Club. Those who have disagreed with what has been done will, I believe, have a very different opinion as the facts become known to them. These persons will appreciate what Joe Bannon learned early on, that the Cannabis Buyers' Club wasn't about persons who were ill, rather it used ill persons in a calculated way to achieve the real purpose of drug profiteering. Joe knew and convinced us that the Cannabis Buyers' Club had become a source of drugs for minors. Most important, Joe was motivated by his knowledge that young children were being exposed to the second-hand smoke with its potent effects.

What Joe Bannon has done is in the very best tradition of outstanding police work; he found a serious criminal problem and, without regard to his own interests, did whatever he had to do to focus sufficient resources on the problem. It is this mindset that allows the best of police officers to act unselfishly and unhesitatingly to do what is right without regard to what may be best for their career or what might be most politic.

1300 I Street • Suite 1740 • Sacramento, California 95814
(916) 324-5437

Page One of Two

Mr. William Lau
Page 2

The Department of Justice commends Officer Joe Bannon for his courage and for his integrity. He is truly one of your City's and this State's finest police officers. As Chief Law Officer of this State, it is a matter of considerable pride to know that Joe Bannon has chosen to serve the citizens of this State who reside in your City as an officer of the law.

Please know that Officer Bannon is held in the highest esteem by the men and women of the Attorney General's Office and the Department of Justice who have worked with him.

Sincerely,

DANIEL E. LUNGREN
Attorney General

Page Two of Two

State of California

Department of Justice
Bureau of Narcotic Enforcement

Memorandum

To: Officer Joseph Bannon
San Francisco Police Department

Date: May 12, 1997

Telephone: ATS

FACSIMILE

From: Robert S. Elsberg
Sr. Special Agent in Charge

Timothy J. Bobitt
Special Agent in Charge

Subject: Letter of Commendation

Cannabis Buyer's Club Investigation - SF96-0130

In May 1996, at the direction of the California Attorney General, the Bureau of Narcotic Enforcement, San Francisco regional office became involved in the Cannabis Buyer's Club (CBC) Investigation which you had initiated in November 1994. Our first step in working on this investigation involved our evaluation of your previous investigative activity. It quickly became apparent that you had approached this case with a great deal of tenacity, dedication, and sincerity. Although our office assumed the responsibility for completing the final phase of this investigation, your daily input as a co-case agent remained invaluable. This case could not have been completed in the successful manner it was without your insight and expertise.

We were particularly impressed with your performance in completing the tedious task of evaluating and preparing for court all the evidence generated by the many members of your agency, along with agents of the Drug Enforcement Administration, over the past two years. This attention to detail clearly demonstrates your commitment to the success of this case.

In addition to your investigative accomplishments, I have been informed by many members of our office of the pleasure it has been in working side-by-side with you. You should be proud of your efforts. We congratulate you for your work on this case.

nt

The Captain of Narcotics and Me Receiving an Award from The Department of Justice Right Before Being Busted in Rank by the "New" San Francisco Police Chief

"My Resignation from the Police Department" – I was personally invited by the California State Attorney General and the Chief of the Department of Justice to become a special agent within their Bureau of Narcotic Enforcement. After much thought, I accepted their offer under one condition – that I be allowed to attend the Special Agent Academy at Beale Air Force Base, so I didn't appear to any of my future partners as a "charity case" or a "juice boy." I attended the academy for four months and was assigned to the Los Angeles Field Office upon graduation. I was presented the Department of Justice "Most Inspirational Award" at my academy graduation ceremony. I also missed the academy "Top Gun" shooting award by one bullet. I was beaten by a former Marine.

I had left the police department and the city that I loved and moved to Los Angeles to start my life and my career over. But God had a greater plan for my life during all of this. Note: I was starting to get burned out by, "*God's greater plans for my life.*" But, I guess

I owed Him for all of the stupid things I had done in my earlier years.

> *"But as for you, you meant evil against me; but God meant it for good, in order to bring it about as it is this day, to save many people alive."*
>
> **Genesis 50:20**

After graduating from the academy and being sworn in as a special agent with the Bureau of Narcotic Enforcement, it was week-long surveillances in cars, planes, and helicopters, across state lines and to the Mexican Border. Undercover narcotics buys from the ruthless Mexican Drug Cartels. Infiltrating dirty cops involved in drug trafficking. Sting operations and penetrating criminal organizations.

Spying on serious threats to our nation that had planted themselves here on domestic soil and working within a network of high-level intelligence agencies from around the world. This was my new mission in life..... 'Again.'

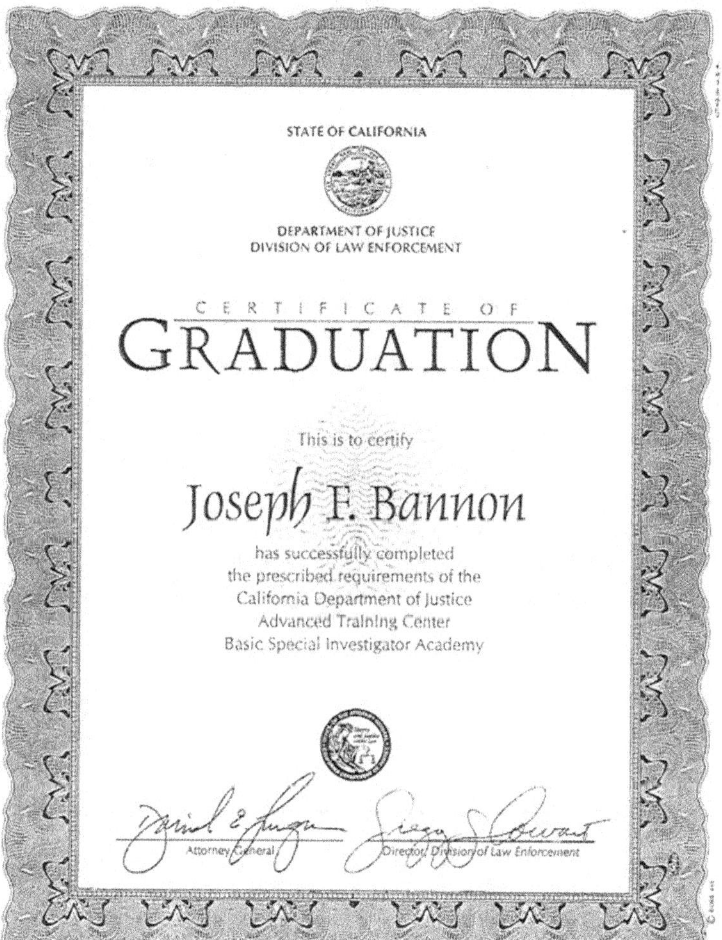

STATE OF CALIFORNIA

DEPARTMENT OF JUSTICE
DIVISION OF LAW ENFORCEMENT

CERTIFICATE OF

GRADUATION

This is to certify

Joseph F. Bannon

has successfully completed
the prescribed requirements of the
California Department of Justice
Advanced Training Center
Basic Special Investigator Academy

Attorney General | Director, Division of Law Enforcement

State of California
Office of the Attorney General
Daniel E. Lungren
Attorney General

October 21, 1998

Special Agent Joseph F. Bannon
Bureau of Narcotic Enforcement
Division of Law Enforcement
Department of Justice

Dear Agent Bannon:

Congratulations on your successful completion of the California Department of Justice Basic Special Investigator Academy.

As a Special Agent with the California Department of Justice, you will play a vital role in ensuring the safety of millions of Californians. In addition, your efforts will assist local law enforcement in their struggle to protect the public and to reduce crime. Without the dedication and talents of people like you, this would be an impossible task.

Please accept my sincere best wishes for success in your career with the California Department of Justice. I am confident you will find it an exciting and rewarding experience.

Sincerely,

DANIEL E. LUNGREN
Attorney General

I got to attend just about every type of specialized training school that any law enforcement officer could ever dream of. During this time as a special agent, I had also been sworn in (*cross-deputized*) as a Special Deputy United States Marshal on "America's Most Wanted" Violent Fugitive Apprehension Team, also known as, "The Equal Justice Task Force." What an incredible adrenaline rush it was to be a hunter and predator of other armed and dangerous men. Sitting with your team in the back of a van getting ready to burst out and kick a criminal's door down. Or while assigned to different spec-ops teams throughout my career, hearing the "30 seconds out" warning from the crew chief of a helicopter air assault unit right before you either landed skids down or repelled down a rope had become my new adrenaline rush. Being a '*predator of shoplifters*' as a prior store detective at Macy's was kindergarten compared to being a '*hunter of men*' as a United States Marshal. "Adrenaline rushes on steroids."

One day, while I was on vacation, my former team went out to serve an arrest warrant on a wanted fugitive. As they approached the front door they shouted, "United States Marshals, open the door." Suddenly the fugitive shot through the door and hit one of my partners. While my partner was being extracted and medevac'd to the hospital, the rest of my team finished their mission. When I heard about this, I thought of my ex-partner Jim Guelff from the San Francisco Police Department who was shot and killed on my birthday while I was out celebrating. Again, my "survivor guilt" kicked in and my mind went to places that it shouldn't have.

I eventually just stuffed it down into my emotional ass bag with the rest of my mental trash and moved on. At least this time, my partner lived to fight another day, unlike Officer Jim Guelff.

I was appointed to the Violence Suppression Unit (*SWAT Team*) where we served very high-risk search and arrest warrants that were too dangerous for certain local police departments to facilitate because they lacked the necessary resources. The housing projects at *'Nickerson Gardens'* and *'The Jungle'* in South Central, Los Angeles were always on our menu. I had also been appointed the chief defensive tactics instructor for all the Department of Justice Special Agents in Southern California.

I was asked to design and implement the 55-special agent and sheriff's protection detail for the California Attorney General during the Democratic National Convention in Los Angeles. The detail was so successful, that I was awarded, the Attorney General's – "*Exemplary Service Award.*" God's favor had obviously followed me to Los Angeles.

Immediately after the terrorist attack against our country on September 11, 2001, I was reassigned to the Criminal Intelligence Bureau of the Department of Justice and worked alongside the FBI Joint Terrorism Task Force (*JTTF*) as a counter-terrorist agent. More schools, more training, and more skillsets. Our office was located in a business complex identified only by a street address number. On the outside, it looked like any other office building. On the inside, just about every type of government clandestine operation one could imagine was being conducted.

My team surveilled suspected terrorist organizations and gathered intelligence information on them. We stole their garbage at four o'clock in the morning that was either in their backyards or placed out on the curb and were able to come up with documents and other helpful intelligence information to build a case against them. I was able to infiltrate certain suspected foreign-based terrorist organizations as an undercover special agent operative posing as a sympathizer and marched in Middle Eastern anti-war protests while holding anti-American signs and shouting pro Middle Eastern and contra-American chants. I would secretly meet with the Central Intelligence Agency (*CIA*), Defense Intelligence Agency (*DIA*), and other intelligence agencies in secluded areas and exchange information with them on my findings. This was "deep cover" at its finest.

During one of my investigations, I was assigned to interview a top military general directly under the president of a Middle Eastern country who spilled his guts about locations, people, and how that specific country would torture their own citizens in graphic detail. He gave me a location in the Middle East that contained very valuable intelligence information. I turned this information over to the appropriate government agency, and the general was immediately put into a witness protection program.

My Former Counter Terrorism Intelligence Unit – (2001)

I was involved in two more very nasty shootings while serving search warrants in the Los Angeles high crime district known as "South Central LA," that really took their toll on me emotionally. It was these final two shooting incidents in my career that put me over the edge. And they were both identical in nature and almost exactly one year apart.

We crashed through the door of a house while serving an arrest warrant on a wanted criminal. As the breacher rammed the front door open, I was the first agent in the eight-man stack to make entry into the house. I was immediately met by a vicious pit bull who was about to castrate me. I had no other choice but to shoot the dog. Once we had located and taken our "tango" (*target suspect*) into custody, I was approached by a little boy about five years old. He looked at me with tears in his eyes and said, "Mr. Policeman, why did you kill my doggie?"

I felt terrible inside and was at a loss for words on how to respond to him. With tears in my own eyes, I got down on my knee, put my hand on his shoulder, and said, "I'm so sorry little boy." I then got up and left the house just to be alone for a while until my partners eventually came and checked up on me. What do you say to a little boy who asks you such a painful and innocent question? "Because your father is a scum bag and that's why we are here?" I don't think he would have quite understood that. I often wonder how that little boy grew up. Was he successful? Was he a criminal like his father? Did he hate cops for the rest of his life because of me? To this day, I have no clue.

About a year later, I was involved in an identical scenario. We were again in South Central Los Angeles serving a search warrant at a wanted criminal's residence. The breacher smashed the front door open with a battering ram and another agent tossed a flash bang grenade inside as we flowed in to clear the house and locate our "tango" (*target suspect*). Out of a back room, a German Shepard came straight for me and the breacher who was still holding the battering ram in his hands. I waited until the last second trying to give the dog a chance to run out the front door. The dog chose to come after me and my partner instead. In my head, I could hear myself saying, "No, no dog – don't do it, not again, please."

I had no other option than to shoot the dog with my M-4 Machine Gun.

Once the house had been cleared and declared "Code 4" (*safe*), a uniformed police officer (*idiot*) walked two young children through the front door and said that the children needed to use the bathroom. Both children saw their pet dog dead on the floor with its tongue hanging out of its mouth to one side. They both looked up at me while I was standing next to the dog with my machine gun. One of them said crying, "Why did you shoot my doggie?"

I couldn't believe that I was experiencing the same exact scenario again. I felt terrible and said the same thing to them that I did to the other little boy a year earlier. "I'm so sorry." I then walked out of the house and sat in the car. I almost felt like putting a bullet through my own head because I felt so terrible that had I brought such horrific pain to innocent children.

"I'm Done. No More Killing" – I vowed to myself. I was a very strong-spirited man, but I felt myself coming unglued at this point. This was my last shooting incident of many throughout my law enforcement and paramilitary career. But these last two were the straw that broke the camel's back for me. I had no problem killing bad people when necessary, but hurting innocent little kids? That was not within my nature. I chose never to carry my gun when I was off duty. I looked at a gun as an instrument of evil. I would have used it again in a heartbeat while on duty if needed, but when off duty, my gun stayed locked in a safe in my bedroom.

For the next several weeks when I went to bed at night, all I could hear in my head was, "Mr. Policeman, why did you kill my doggie? Why did you kill my doggie? Why did you kill my doggie?" The children's voices played nonstop in my mind. I was frequently awakened by loud gunshots and from nightmares that I was being attacked by a vicious dog. I even dreamt several times that I missed the dog and accidently shot the child instead. I violently woke up and was relieved to know that it was only a bad dream.

I feared going back to sleep because it would just play out in my dreams all over again. When I was awakened by these nightmares, my heart would be pounding out of my chest, I was sweating, my teeth and fists were strongly clenched, and my body was rigid. Every morning when I first woke up, for the first minute, I relived flashbacks of almost every shooting and critical incident that I had been involved in throughout my career. It was like a video film playing in fast-forward mode. I had to take strong narcotic medication just to be able to sleep at night. That went on for several years to follow. Many of my teeth had to be replaced because I ground them so hard in my sleep that they fractured. My dentist made me a heavy plastic mouthguard to wear when I slept.

I eventually retired on a medical disability. Not from PTSD, but from an injury to my back from jumping out of a helicopter.

After a long hard career in law enforcement; surviving multiple armed confrontations, as well as murder contracts on my life, and seeing life at its absolute worst on a daily basis – my mental and physical combat tour was finally over. I had survived the fire and brimstones of hell. I was now officially a square peg in a round hole. No more adrenaline rushes, shootings, screams over a police radio, or dangerous missions. What a letdown and time of withdrawal it was for me. My retirement party only made it seem more final. It was difficult retiring because I didn't want to abandon my partners who were still left behind and who may have needed me. But I knew that it was time.

I was now, "Retired Special Agent Joseph Bannon – Department of Justice, Office of the Attorney General, Criminal Intelligence Bureau."

'The Grim Reapers' – If You Were on Our List, We Would Find You

"Team Los Angeles"
Special Agent Academy – Beale Air Force Base

The Real "Men in Black"
My Former Bureau of Narcotics Enforcement Raid Team

What I Miss the Most in Retirement is the Team Comradery
My Blood, Sweat, and Tears, Remain with Them
"Always"

The Arena

He steps into the arena every day of his life. He fights every kind of animal on earth. Sometimes he wins and sometimes he loses.

It may be just a broken body, a torn piece of flesh or death. Death is his only escape. Bones heal, flesh mends and then he can fight again.

The years go by, and he gets a little older and he gets a little slower. The bones don't mend as fast and the flesh tears easier.

One day he is too old, and he no longer must face the arena. He has survived years of combat. But his soul stays in the arena, also beaten and torn.

A Gladiator?

No, My Brother (*Sister*-added), You the Street Cop.

Sgt. Jack Richards (Retired) – S.J.P.D.

MY CHAMBER EIGHTEEN

"Taking my 'Mark of the Urn' of the Temple of Life"

I had finally completed and barely survived the first seventeen chambers of my life's path. Many failures, many accomplishments, and many successes. Many great memories, and many horrible nightmares. But I had certainly lived out my childhood dream of becoming a police officer to the fullest with absolutely no regrets. I am very grateful to God for my amazing career.

At my retirement party, I was presented multiple awards and accolades by senators, congressmen, government officials, the attorney general himself, and the different agencies that I had worked for over the years. I was awarded a proclamation from Mayor, now 'Governor' Gavin Newsom memorializing my retirement day as, "Joe Bannon Day" in the historical archives of San Francisco for my years of public service. I guess I was back in good graces with the mayor's office since Mayor Willie Brown had moved on. It was a bittersweet combination of relief and sadness as I was handed my retirement badge and credentials (*my metaphorical 'hot urn' of the Shaolin Temple*). Not quite burned into my forearms, but affixed inside of a wallet.

Since retirement, I have been inducted into three martial arts halls of fame, as well as the American Police Hall of Fame for, "Long and Honorable Service."

I was nominated for the "J. Edgar Hoover National Gold Medal and Law Enforcement Officer of the Year Award" by the Veterans of Foreign Wars (*VFW*) Commission. I came in number one in the State of California, but the award was given to another worthy nominee in a different part of the United States. Congratulations whoever you are.

Now What? I sat in the recliner in my living room and gazed at all my awards that were hanging on my wall. They were nice to look at but what was I going to do now – open a flower stand or a Jamba Juice store? Hell, I don't know. I was still a warrior at heart but no longer had any wars to fight.

The first year of my retirement was very difficult. I had lost my identity, my purpose, and my validation in life. Brief thoughts of "checking out" passed through my mind on occasion. My doctor had put me on very strong pain meds for the excruciating pain in my back and neuropathy in my legs from my helicopter injury. I just sat in my black leather recliner all day long, motionless, while staring at the remnants of my life that were now simply hanging on my wall as memories. Many times, I would go onto the internet and replay battle scenes, listening to mayday calls, and cops calling for help over their radios with the dispatcher interacting with them. I did this repeatedly. This gave me an adrenaline rush and temporarily got me out of my funk. These internet film clips had become my new stimulant drug of choice.

I knew that drinking alcohol was not an option for me, so I got even more heavily involved in "dating sites" (*sex hookups*) and pornography just to get a rush from my own brain chemistry (*Dopamine*). I isolated and couldn't stand being around people. I began to fear my own anger and temper and what I could do to another human being if provoked; so I stayed inside and away from the public and ignorant people as often as I could.

I continued to study martial arts at my Chinese Taoist Kung Fu Temple. Between the fighting arts and the healing arts that were taught at this temple, I was able to find relative peace inside. The temple was my place of solace. Going to the temple, church occasionally, getting lost on the internet, and weightlifting, became some of my forms of escape from the PTSD and pain of my past.

I found great satisfaction and reward in teaching my fighting skills to the other disciples at the temple. I figured if I couldn't fight as a mortal combat warrior anymore, then I would teach other warriors and martial artists how to fight and efficiently destroy their opponents and enemies. I began to develop quite a following. I formed my own training corporation and taught at military bases, police academies, and accredited private schools. I was eventually awarded my tenth-degree black belt (*see following photo*) and taught my own system of mortal combat. For some strange reason, I found peace, self-worth, and satisfaction while teaching violence. Mostly to soldiers that were going to, or coming back from Afghanistan, Iraq, or some other place in the world. My programs made them much more efficient and lethal to successfully facilitate their missions. I turned human brains and bodies into lethal killing machines. This had become my new passion in life which gave purpose back to me – ***"Teaching Others How to Kill."***

Being Awarded my 10th Degree Black Belt at the USMAA Hall of Fame by Supreme Grand Master / Founder, William Rankin

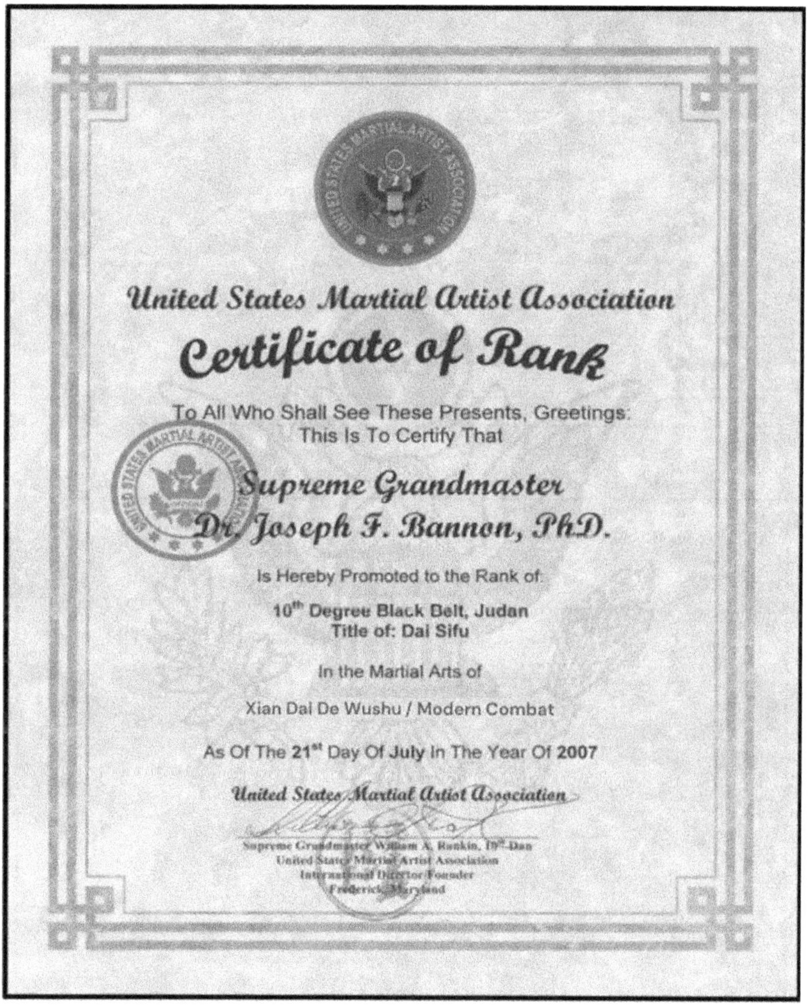

United States Martial Artist Association

Certificate of Rank

To All Who Shall See These Presents, Greetings:
This Is To Certify That

Supreme Grandmaster
Dr. Joseph F. Bannon, PhD.

Is Hereby Promoted to the Rank of:

10th Degree Black Belt, Judan
Title of: Dai Sifu

In the Martial Arts of

Xian Dai De Wushu / Modern Combat

As Of The **21st** Day Of **July** In The Year Of **2007**

United States Martial Artist Association

Supreme Grandmaster William A. Rankin, 19th Dan
United States Martial Artist Association
International Director Founder
Frederick, Maryland

American Police Hall of Fame

LONG AND HONORABLE SERVICE

THIS WILL CERTIFY THAT

Joseph Franc Bannon

has honorably and faithfully served in Law Enforcement for a period of 25 years. The above-named individual is issued this certificate in recognition of their fidelity, integrity and honor in serving their nation, state and community.

Issued by the National Board of Trustees upon the recommendation of the Awards Committee this 21st day of February, 2007

PRESIDENT

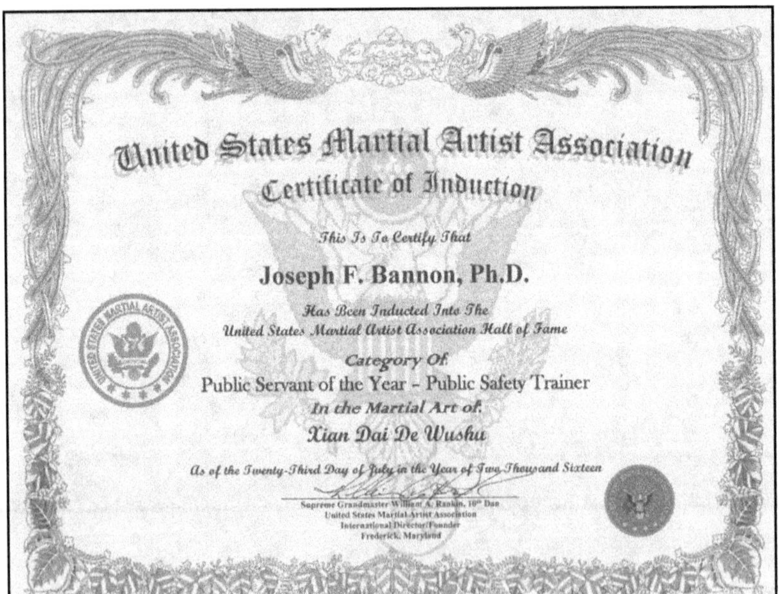

United States Martial Artist Association

Certificate of Induction

This Is To Certify That

Joseph F. Bannon, Ph.D.

Has Been Inducted Into The United States Martial Artist Association Hall of Fame

Category Of:

Public Servant of the Year - Public Safety Trainer

In the Martial Art of:

Xian Dai De Wushu

As of the Twenty-Third Day of July in the Year of Two Thousand Sixteen

Supreme Grandmaster William A. Rankin, 10th Dan
United States Martial Artist Association
International Director/Founder
Frederick, Maryland

Passing on my Sword of the 18th Chamber

"Bringing My Skillsets to Hollywood"

A former police partner of mine and 'brother from another mother' named Paul Lozada had become a Hollywood movie technical advisor. He imparted his skillsets and character traits to Denzel Washington in the movie "Training Day." Through Paul I met and had become friends with Hollywood Director Antoine Fuqua in 2001 during the filming of "*Tears of the Sun*," starring Bruce Willis. I assisted in the jungle combat technical advising on the set with Harry Humphries who had served with Richard Marcinko as a Navy Seal in Vietnam. I got to hang out with both Humphries and Willis for several days on and off the set. We had a great time together. I had a student at my Kung Fu Temple named Mike Humphries. Come to find out that he was the son of Harry Humphries.

In 2013 I was honored to be brought in as the Secret Service Technical Advisor and 'personal character study' for Gerard Butler in the movie, "*Olympus Has Fallen.*" What a great guy to work with. They even used a version of my last name for his character, "Mike *Banning.*" I was able to teach him many gun, knife, and Secret Service tactics that he demonstrated in the movie. I also worked with Navy SEAL Keith Woulard setting up the main battle scene on the front lawn of the White House and many of the interactive tactical scenes that followed. Woulard had an amazing resume of films he had worked on. Fuqua, Butler, and I went out for dinner every night after filming and had a fantastic time hanging out together. It was fun getting to know Gerard Butler on a personal level. I was also able to make some edits on the original screenplay to make the movie appear more realistic.

Student and teacher: Butler was taught the tricks of the trade in security from Dr Joe Bannon, right, who has protected two presidents and their first ladies, lawmakers and even the Pope

Me with Gerard Butler (*Mike Banning*) on the Movie Set
"Olympus Has Fallen"

Ten Years Later – 2023
This Movie Almost Seems Like a Plausible but Sad Reality

Mockup Strategy of the Ambush Scene on the White House Front Lawn
"Olympus Has Fallen"

"Shooter" – again, working with Director Fuqua, I had a few words to say on the movie "*Shooter*," starring Mark Wahlberg. Being a former sniper myself, certainly made my input valuable to the project.

"Dexter" – lastly, I had become the personal advisor and friend to Jim Manos – creator of the TV serial killer drama, "*Dexter*." Mr. Manos also wrote an episode of "*The Sopranos*" that won him an Emmy Award. Additionally, he was the Consulting Producer on the TV police show, "*The Shield*."

Passing on my Sword of the 18th Chamber

"My Transition from Combat Operator to Combat Instructor"

I received a call from the owner of Executive Security International (ESI), Bob Duggan after he had seen me on a TV show. Mr. Duggan remembered me from when I graduated from ESI's Executive Protection Program back in 1990 after my assignment in the Caribbean. He was kind enough to remind me of how my partner and I rolled one of his cars during our High-Speed Vehicle Escape and Evasion Course. He asked me if I would come back and teach as a senior instructor at ESI. I was extremely honored to receive this invitation from such a world-renowned man and school.

Many warriors have walked their own paths through their 18th Chamber of trials, tribulations, triumphs, and accomplishments in life. I was about to be given the great opportunity to become a senior combat and covert operations instructor to many of these warriors for the next several years to come. The men and women that I was about to pass on my sword to consisted of about every 18th Chamber one could imagine. Marine Force Recon Personnel, Army Delta and

Special Forces, Navy Seals, Presidential Bodyguards from other countries, Intelligence Officers, Special Operators, and SWAT officers from all over the world. Private Military Contractors from Africa, Europe, Asia, Afghanistan, and Iraq. And a host of other positions and MOS' from Lance Corporals to Lieutenant Colonels.

I filled out all of the required paperwork and became a certified senior instructor for ESI under the State of Colorado Board of Education, and the Colorado Office of Veteran's Education and Training (*COVET*).

ESI had several intelligence-based security and protection programs running throughout the year. I began teaching the arts of Sting Operations, Surveillance, Counter Surveillance, Covert and Undercover Operations, Covert Protection, and How to Survive if Ever Interrogated by a Drug Lord. All subjects that I had become an expert in during my former life. I would fly in and out of Colorado from Los Angeles throughout the year.

I was eventually appointed to the cadre of firearms instructors. ESI probably had one of the finest tactical combat shooting courses in the world. We shot from every conceivable position. Shooting through windshields, out of moving vehicles, upside down, individual as well as within small teams. High-stress reloading, and many other tightly timed and severe stress "*fight for your life*" combat firearm drills.

I also taught defensive tactics, knife fighting, knife and gun takeaways, as well as hand-to-hand combat. We taught the students to not just know how to protect himself in just about any imaginable situation, but to protect and evacuate the person he / she was assigned to as their bodyguard (*Executive Protection Specialist*). After all, that is the ultimate objective of being a protective agent – Save the Client. "Because dead clients don't pay." (*a slang saying in the industry*).

I looked forward to these classes throughout the year. They allowed me to still keep one foot in the game while passing on my sword to the younger generation of warriors while polishing the old. A game where my identity as a man and as a warrior found their validation again. My students all referred to me as 'Master Joe,' or 'Doctor Death,' (*a title I took a twisted form of pride in*).

I taught classes on how the human brain functioned during Mortal Combat. As well as the potential Fight, Flight, or Freeze phases of battle, and how to condition the brain to push through the "Fog of War." I also taught on how to create an undefeatable warrior brain during the heat of battle and to take out an assassin as quickly and efficiently as possible out on the gun range.

At ESI we also taught Private Military Contractor (*PMC*) Courses as well as Special Operations (*Spec-Ops*) Courses to mostly military veterans who had already, "been there – done that." Our training was in line with the Department of State Regulations for "Worldwide Protective Services" (*WPS*) which certified the student in motorcade operations, ambush response, escape and evasion driving, movement security, tactical medicine, specialized emergency services, hostage rescue, and other protective services while operating in hostile, high threat areas around the world.

There was just one small issue though. Each class consisted of about forty students. Most of them were fresh out of Afghanistan, Iraq, or some other combat zone in the world. That meant that some of them dealt with various levels of PTSD, and this had to be taken very seriously. Especially when each one of them is running around a combat scenario-based firing range with a fully loaded high-powered rifle and pistol.

Most of them (*us*) chewed tobacco and drank Monster energy drinks, Red Bulls, and coffee in insane amounts all day long. I did too, so I was just as ramped up teaching them, as they were learning from me. The only thing forbidden was alcohol. Add adrenaline dumps, the element of surprise, extremely violent scenarios, screaming and yelling at the top of our lungs, caffeine, and a touch of PTSD; and you have the makings for a serious fun time.

PTSD flashbacks were always a potential concern that we as instructors always had to look for. I got to the point where I could read it in their eyes before they actually acted out. Once they got that 'glazed over' look in their eyes while holding a loaded firearm, I had to be extremely delicate as to how I approached them. Their jacked-up brains could view me as the enemy in a nanosecond. And yes, I did have that happen to me at training venues other than ESI. Luckily, I was able to contain the situation without further incident.

On a few occasions at various training locations, I found myself on the ground wrestling combat veteran Marines who thought that I was the enemy. Thank God that the issue was quickly managed and resolved. But I must tell you, wrestling one of your students who is having a flashback and thinks you are the Taliban, is a FUBAR of a situation. One of those times was in the back of a moving pickup truck on a freeway.

Teaching at ESI was one of the most rewarding and proud eras of my life. I had met some of the most 'bad-ass' warriors from all over the world. The entire training cadre was world-class. I not only taught my students the arts of war, but they also taught me a thing or two from their worlds.

ESI, Bob Duggan, Fonda Gomez, Rich Kluck, Clay Owens, Tony Pagni, Todd Haller, Joel Hodges (*all better shooters than myself who I had learned much from*), my fellow Training Cadre, and my students, will always be an irreplaceable life experience and a deep part of my heart. Thank you for having me. It probably saved me from spiraling down a very dark rabbit hole. God knows what we need when we need it.

Executive Security Int'l Ltd.

Certificate of Training

Certified Special Operations Instructor

Joseph F. Bannon

This certificate validates the completion of 150 hours in Firearms Proficiency, Course of Fire, Range Safety & Protocol, Diagnostics & Correction, and Principals of Firearms Instruction, State Department Qualification, Motorcade Ambush Response

President — Range Master — 5/14/07 Date

Executive Security International Academy

Instructor Contribution Acknowledgment

ESI

Certificate of Appreciation

ESI extends its appreciation to Range Master

Joe Bannon

For 1000 hours of Sting Operations, Counter Surveillance, and Advances and Escorts in
ESI's Executive Protection Program

May 14, 2012

Robert Duggan
President and Founder
ESI Ltd., Grand Junction, CO.

Fonda Delcamp
Vice President
ESI Ltd., Grand Junction, CO

Executive Security International Academy

Instructor Contribution Acknowledgment

Certificate of Appreciation

ESI extends its appreciation to Range Master

Joe Bannon

For 850 hours of Development and Professional instruction in
ESI's Executive Protection Defensive Shooting Program

May 14, 2012

Robert Duggan
President and Founder
ESI Ltd., Grand Junction, CO.

Fonda Delcamp
Vice President
ESI Ltd., Grand Junction, CO

Force on Force Range

"The Kill House"

For the first few days at the ESI gun range, all the range masters rotated through different ranges that were set up to teach many skill sets with several different pre-staged scenarios and objectives. Then after about the third day, we all took over our primary ranges that we had been assigned by the lead range master Tony Pagni, who had been my shooting instructor back in 1990 when I was a student at ESI.

My primary range was the "Kill House," also known as "Force on Force" for the more politically correct folks. But when you entered my range, you either got killed (*simulated*) or you survived, period! So, I will refer to it as "The Kill House" where many of my students "got killed" (*simulated*) until they became proficient at the tactics that I had taught them. I was very familiar with this type of training as I had previously trained and received my certification at the Military Operation Urban Terrain (*MOUT*) Training Facility at Fort Ord, Army Base while still a government agent as well as a former sniper.

The Kill House was a wooden building that had several rooms and obstacles contained within it. The objective of the student was to successfully clear this house under high levels of stress. At any given time, an aggressor with an electric-powered pellet gun, or a 900-volt training knife (*both which hurt like hell*) could pop out from any one of many hiding places and aggress the student. We started off slow at first, then worked up to a level of violent aggression.

Sometimes I hid some of my assistant instructors in the house playing the role of a bad guy, or we had other props such as, booby traps, "shoot – don't shoot" paper targets, Improvised Explosive Devices (IEDs), and many other creative surprises for the student to make instantaneous decisions and work through. Communication and teamwork were the main tactics necessary to survive "The Kill House." Over the years while teaching at several training facilities, I believe I have seen every potential human reaction, FUBAR, success, and failure that a combat and tactical instructor could possibly witness. Including real life PTSD Fight, Flight, Freeze, and Flashbacks.

It was an incredibly fun range for me to lead, but an instant learning experience (*ILE*) for most of the students. But the tactical lessons learned, were lifesaving, to say the least. Many of my students would take these lessons back to the Middle East or other parts of the world and apply what they had learned in real life or death scenarios. The greatest compliments that I had ever received were from some of my former students who called me from halfway around the world:

"Master Joe, I just wanted to call and tell you that my team and I were in 'Bum Fk Egypt' clearing a building and we began to receive enemy rifle fire. Without hesitation, I recalled some of the skills that you taught me at ESI, and they saved not only my life but the lives of my team members."

To me, there were no better types of calls to receive than these. Then there were those calls to inform me that one of my students had been killed in a foreign country. Not so great of a call. These calls kept me up at night asking myself what I could have done better in my teaching that may have changed the outcome of my student's life. Sun Tzu wrote in his book, *The Art of War*, "that if a student fails, the teacher must first examine himself to see if the failure was first within his teaching method before judging the student's actions." I took Sun Tzu's words to heart every time and put my brain through a strainer until my imagination ran out of options. Once I had come to a place of peace within myself, I released the outcome to fate. But I definitely used the information to enhance my training for the next class of students.

Above the open-air Kill House was a catwalk which gave me an aerial view where I could observe the student's movements from 360 degrees. After the students got the hang of what I was trying to teach them, I jacked up both the stakes and the stress level. I had my electrically fed fully automatic pellet rifle and waited for a student to make a tactically stupid mistake. I usually didn't have to wait too long. If they exposed one of their body parts (*arm, leg, hand etc.*) through a doorway into an unsecured room, I would light that body part up with automatic pellet fire. These pellets were extremely painful, but pain is one of the best tactical teachers on the planet. After this baptism of 'pellet hellfire,' they usually never repeated the same mistake twice. No live guns, knives, or other weapons were allowed in The Kill House, and for very good reason. One PTSD flashback or battle stress breakdown, and several of us could have gotten seriously hurt or killed. And many flashbacks did occur inside The Kill House, but they were managed successfully.

Me on the Catwalk Waiting to Open Fire on a Student

We used very real look-alike props and targets. One day my student Paul was clearing the rooms and he came across a paper target with the picture of a Taliban soldier pointing an AK-47 rifle in the fire position. As Paul turned the corner he froze like a snowman. "Paul, are you having a flashback?" I asked. I knew he was, but I had to be very skillfully thoughtful to help him out of his brain freeze. I came down from the catwalk and very gently had him holster his firearm (*pellet gun*) while speaking to him very calmly and respectfully to not demoralize him in front of his team. I also didn't want to further shock his already shocked brain. I spent some time with him and then immediately had him repeat the drill.

I found that in training if a student falls off a horse (*metaphorically speaking*), the best thing he can do is get back up on the saddle as quickly as possible. Beating a man down for failure is not always productive. Allowing him a second chance to achieve success, is extremely productive. On Paul's second attempt, he aced the drill. He looked into my eyes with a deep gratitude and hugged me, and neither one of us spoke a word. But many nonverbal words had been spoken between us in just a few seconds. Paul was back in the saddle. I spent some time with Paul after class to help him manage his battle stress.

Then there was Glen, a SWAT Cop from Chicago. He was a highly decorated police officer who had been in several shooting incidents throughout his career. But this day, his brain got clogged up in The Kill House. His entry was perfect. His nonverbal communication skills were textbook. His "slow is smooth – smooth is fast" movements resembled a Shaolin Monk walking on air. His muzzle discipline was excellent. As he continued to advance through the house, he came up to a door that led to an unknown room. His approach to this room was tactically superior. But as he entered the room, he immediately shot a silhouette target of a man pointing a pistol at him. He shouted, "Suspect down" and walked out of the room with seemingly great pride. Great pride that is until I told him to go back into the room and reexamine the target that he had just killed. A look of bewilderment came upon his face as he complied with my directions.

"OHH CRAP," he screamed as he observed that the target that he had just killed was a uniformed police officer with big letters on his chest that said, "POLICE." Glen got tunnel vision and just saw the gun pointing at him. All students were briefed before each drill that there may be friendlies (*good guys*) in the house as well as bad guys. One of the lessons taught in The Kill House was "target confirmation." A lesson that Glen learned the hard way that day. Coming from his world, and almost shooting a fellow officer one night in my own life described in my (*Chamber Nine*), I shared his pain. Glen fell to his knees in anguish, "I just shot a fellow officer."

I experienced his pain so intensely that my own eyes began to tear. "Glen, let's "hot wash" (*debrief*) your actions."

Glen was experiencing extreme PTSD, depression, fear, and eventually anger at himself. My job now wasn't to throw salt in his wound, but to re-moralize him and get him back up on the horse's saddle. It took a while, but I was finally able to pull his head out of his ass. As an instructor, I could be severely aggressive and brutal on my students when necessary. But as a PTSD Debriefer, I had to know when to ramp up and ramp down. This was a time to ramp down. Glen got back on the saddle and passed his final test in The Kill House, but he was over-cautious and looked like he was walking on eggshells. The Kill House could either make or break a student no matter how much real life experience he or she brought to the table.

I could tell many stories like this, but this was the main function of The Kill House. "*Better to sweat in training, than to bleed in battle*." Meaning, "better to get killed in a training scenario and deal with a bit of humiliation, than to die in real life in some third-world foreign country."

The Art of Hunting and Killing

"Armed and Dangerous Men"

"Born to fight, Trained to kill, Prepared to die, Never will, Keep low, Move fast, Kill first, Die last, One shot, One *kill, No luck, Pure skill."*

Following are my opening words that I presented to an elite anti-terrorist task force at a nondisclosed government training facility several years ago:

"Good morning gentlemen. My name is Retired Special Agent Joe Bannon, and I will be your chief combat and covert operations instructor for the next two weeks. First let me start out by saying it is a great honor for me to be in a room filled with great warriors such as yourselves. I'm very humbled to be standing up here in front of you all. At least until I can figure out who the 'brain surgeons' are who make a rock look like a precision instrument (*sarcastic term for deficient operators*). Then I will work extra hard with them by creating a 'special ed' class for spies and special operators."

"Laughter from entire class."

"How many of you are here to learn how to become more efficient hunters and killers when the need presents itself to you on your missions?" I asked.

The entire room replied in the affirmative.

"Hunting and killing begin in the heart of a man. If you struggle with either one in your heart, then you will struggle with both in acting upon them when needed. We must first be killers in our heart before we are killers with a rifle, a knife, or our hands. Combat tactics are useless with a double minded heart that can't drive them forward to their endpoint under severe battle stress. If there is anything clogging up our war brains, we need to deal with it here and now. Our mind is our greatest weapon, and it must be cleaner, more sighted in, and function more smoothly than your rifle or any other piece of equipment that your life might depend on.

I have been tasked to teach all of you how to hunt, track, trap, and capture, your Tangos (*targets, people of interest, or enemy assets*) and extract intelligence information from them. I will present to you some of the tracking and capture tactics that we used when I was a member of the U.S. Marshal's – America's Most Wanted Team and others.

We've used 'Honeypots' (*beautiful undercover female operators*) to get close to men and emotionally weaken them, so that these men will spill their guts to her thinking that they're eventually gonna get some. She in turn gives us the information that we need to further our investigation. This is how Delilah got Sampson to give her the secret of his great strength, as was written in the Bible. We've also appealed to the greed and desire of men who are enticed by the material things of this world. We lured them out of hiding by sending letters to their mail drop locations. The letters stated that they had won a prize and to come to a certain 'mock storefront' location that we had set up ahead of time to claim it. When they showed up to collect their big screen TV or other fabulous 'bunk' prize, they were greeted by a SWAT team who took them into custody. These are only a few of the baited traps that we would set to capture our prey. Most of the tactics that we used were based on the capitalization of human greed, desire, lust, curiosity, and basal instinct. Like baiting a hook while fishing, or in this case, '*hunting.*' The same tactics the devil himself uses against us.

The American Indians used both taught and natural instinctive tracking skills to hunt their animal or human prey. They masked their body scent with the smell of smoke (*camouflage*) as to not alert the animal. They also used tactics called the 'buffalo jump' or the 'buffalo impound.' They either corralled and trapped their prey or ran them off a cliff. Either way, they got their buffalo. Other tactics were to look for signs of human movement and behavior such as footprints, human waste, broken twigs, or other disruption to the natural environment. Deception is our greatest tool. The military uses tactics called channeling and choke points to accomplish this as you well know.

You will learn to become sensitive to your natural predatory and survival instincts during this training. I will evoke them within you by blindfolding you in a dark room, then sneaking up barefooted towards you while holding a knife. Your goal is to tell me when I am within six feet from you and where I am in the room. Yes, you all can accomplish this when you quiet the chatter and voices inside of your heads. This is a great skill to have if someone is sneaking up behind you to slit your throat. I will also teach you how to defeat this same skill within your enemy so that they won't hear or sense you sneak up behind them to slit their throat. Kind of like playing '*Hide and Seek*' when you were a kid.

Each year technology gets better and better and markets all of these "bells and whistles" to add on to our rifles that you feel you just can't live without. Some of you have so much high-tech crap on your guns, I'm surprised that you can still find the trigger. But we must first learn to operate without technology because when technology fails, as it tends to do; you will have natural, instinctive skills to fall back on. Plan A without a Plan B is suicide – Oorah?"

"Oorah," shouted my students.

Almost every one of you in this room have killed men before. That's good because that means I don't have many virgins in the class. But virgin or not, my job is to teach you how to become even more efficient killers than you already are.

As a doctor who has majored in the study of human anatomy, psychophysiology, and combat psychology, I will teach you the so called 'forbidden arts' of black medicine and mortal combat. You will be taught to dehumanize and objectify your enemy while focusing your attack on the most vulnerable and ideal anatomical points on the human body. You will learn exactly where to place a bullet, a knife, or an impact weapon, to get the best results in taking down your enemy. One bullet, knife, or impact wound in the right place will do the job. If the ideal scenario for that does not present itself to you, then many bullet holes, knife, or impact wounds will work. The objective here is to cause as much bleeding, mental disruption, or trauma to your adversary as quickly and efficiently as the combat scenario allows for. The only rule in mortal combat is to win and stay alive at all costs – period! If it comes right down to it, you will learn to chew the side of a man's face off with your canine teeth, while growling like an animal and gouging his eye out at the same time in your effort to stay alive. This is one of the nastiest martial arts you could ever practice called, Kino Mutai, and I have spent many years teaching it to operatives such as yourselves. I will also teach you how to kill a man with an apple, a pen, or a bar of soap.

As an intelligence officer, my directive is to teach you the covert arts of spying, surveillance, counter-surveillance, hunting armed and dangerous men, interrogation, undercover operations, and the gathering of useful enemy intelligence information. During our training exercises when you are out and about in the metropolitan area, you will be covertly hunted and tracked by my assistant instructors whom you haven't met. Their job is to gather intelligence information on you to develop an attack plan to kill you (*simulated*). Your job is to identify them and gather intelligence information relative to them and their terrorist cell group. Once you gather sufficient information about them, you will then be required to devise a plan to take the entire terrorist cell down. After this training, not even Jason Bourne will have anything on you men.

You will also become conditioned to control your own thoughts, feelings, and emotions during this process. I am a former sniper, and the only feeling that I allowed myself to entertain at the time, was the feeling of my finger smoothly pressing the trigger of my rifle while controlling my emotions and breathing. Nothing is more irritating than to see your own exaggerated heartbeat or respiration at the muzzle end of your rifle while trying to hold a steady sight picture of someone's head in your rifle sights.

Please forgive me if I am being overly graphic and insensitive, but if you were expecting Mother Theresa to stand up here in front of this classroom, then you are in the wrong 'fkn' place. She has her mission in life, and I have mine. She can pray while you spray. If you bring me a warrior's heart, then I will give you warrior skills in exchange. I can give you skills, but I cannot give you heart. That is something that you are required to bring to this party. Is that understood gentlemen?"

"Yes sir," responded my class in one accord.

"Some of you are Marines, Navy SEALs, and Special Forces Commandos. Others of you are Government Special Operators and Spooks. Many of you have spent time in Afghanistan, Iraq, Somalia, and several other equally beautiful vacation crap-holes of the world. You are masters of your craft – but you will leave here with superior skills than those you currently possess. Your training and skillsets must be greater than those of your enemy's. There is no political correctness here and the word 'sympathy' can only be found in Webster's Dictionary between the words, 'shit' and 'syphilis.' I'm not here to bandage anyone's butt hurt, emotional boo boos. Agreed?"

"Yes sir!"

"Gentlemen, I have spent the last thirty years of my life as a research professor of mortal combat and have discovered some of the most effective and economical ways to kill another human being. Any residual weakness, double-mindedness, and displaced sympathy must be purged out of you. The enemy will look for weakness. Keep it off their radar. The best way to do this is to be unconditionally committed to your mission without hesitation. The Bible states that, "A double minded man is unstable in all his ways." Don't be double minded. I will present to you the psychological tactics and necessary brain conditioning needed for successful mortal combat. You must see yourselves as dead men walking and the last man standing. If you are already dead, then you cannot be killed. Fight until your soul leaves your body. And as your soul leaves your body, pray for those left behind to avenge you.

Having said that, I will stuff as much training into your brains as they can possibly hold. Some of you will have greater capacities to understand new information than others. That is obvious to me by the extremely clueless looks some of you have on your faces. If it's true that fish is good brain food, then some of you look like you need to eat a freakin whale."

"Laughter from entire class."

"There will be no humane, nor ineffective, pretty and pathetic bullcrap tactics taught here. If it doesn't work on the street or on a battlefield, then it's worthless. I greatly respect all martial arts, but combat sports fighting, and mortal combat are not necessarily always the same thing. We fight to kill lest we be killed, not to win a pretty trophy or a title. Our only trophy is to come home and live to fight another day.

Israeli Defense Force Major Avi Nardia said it best. "It is better to be a student of reality, rather than a master of illusion" (*this also pertains to your mental and spiritual beliefs*). I couldn't agree with him more. In other words, what seems to work in a controlled environment, does not always transfer into life-and-death combat on the battlefield or on a city street. Learning in an overly sterile, safe, or controlled environment with excessive rules and watered-down fighting techniques can lead to a false confidence. A false confidence which could prove severely detrimental and get you killed. It's like taking your car on a road trip thinking you have a full tank of gas, only to find out that the gas gauge was broken and lying to you. You are now unexpectedly stuck in the middle of nowhere in a snow blizzard with an empty gas tank. Just like a broken gas gauge can present untrue information, an untested combat technique or mindset is a lie until proven true under severe pressure. And I will call out every lie that I see you pulling out of your butts during our combat scenarios. Like I said, the 'false confidence' that can get you killed.

Going back many centuries to the Shaolin Temple in China as well as other cultures; martial arts were originally intended as 'arts of war' that were meant to kill, maim, cripple, and destroy their opponents. War is war and sports are sports. Do not confuse the two. I've never seen an opponent in a sports competition armed with a machine gun or an RPG whose sole mission was to kill you. That crap only happens in our world. Even the Roman Gladiators fought blood-thirsty lions with no judges to call a time-out. If you lost, you became lunch. Enough said.

But in all sincerity men, I am honored to be your instructor and I look forward to our joint training mission together for the next two weeks. I will always be available to you if you need me for anything – including talking about your faith or lack of faith in God. And believe me, sometimes it gets down to just Him and us, and that's not a bad thing. Some of you may have anger issues with God because of what you have had to endure in combat including the loss of your partners. Or observing how the Taliban or other tribal groups rape little innocent girls. I get it. I have gotten extremely angry at God for these and other human atrocities that I have seen as well. But sometimes we need to put those feelings aside because when the crap is hitting the fan, it's better to have God in the foxhole with us than not. We can get pissed off at Him later after the bullets stop flying. And yes, we will speak about our belief or lack of belief in God as it relates to combat. We can't leave any stones unturned that could hinder your decision-making process of taking a man's life when warranted. Remember, the accurate translation of one of the Ten Commandments is, "Thou shalt not *murder*." It does not translate to, "Thou shalt not *kill*." That is a big difference in the intent of our heart and actions, even though the endpoint is the same.

This was my usual opening presentation to my students, and they loved me for it because I kept it real, and many times, even entertaining.

"Death Touch" – I had intensely studied the work of Dr. Po in Australia for several years. Dr. Po was probably one of the most lethal men on this planet who could kill you and heal you at the same time. He was a Kung Fu Grand Master, an Acupuncturist, and a Doctor of Chinese Medicine. This man taught one of the most lethal traditional martial arts in the world at his academy. This lethal art was known as Dim Mak, or in some circles, "Death

Touch." I found this "duality" of both killing and healing very intriguing. After years of reading his and other master's published works and research manuals, I was given the opportunity to fly to Australia and train under Dr. Po personally. This was a once-in-a-lifetime opportunity and before I could say the word "bloke," I was on a seventeen-hour Qantas Airlines flight to meet Grand Master (*Dai Sifu*) Po in person.

I found it respectfully amusing to listen to a Chinese Kung Fu Master speaking English with an Australian accent. I studied this art of Dim Mak in both his martial arts school as well as at his acupuncture clinic. I have studied martial arts for most of my life under several masters, but this man was the tip of the spear. From him, I learned some extremely lethal concepts. The "*36 Shaolin Death Points*," as well as the "*72 Shaolin Knockout Points*." The breaking of bones and disrupting brain function in an opponent. Restricting blood to the brain and oxygen to the lungs. Attacking the vital energy flow (*chi*) in the mind and body. Ripping and tearing of flesh, ligaments, and tendons. Very brutal but effective tactics.

He also taught me a great deal about energy (*chi*) and Chinese Medicine. The killing as well as the healing arts all under the same roof you could say. He eventually entrusted me with his family's herbal formula for Dit Da Jow, which is an herbal remedy for bruised body parts.

I had the great honor of being one of his only two international students who had ever received a dinner invitation to his private home. The other was a fellow student who was a kick boxing champion in Germany named Dietrich. Dietrich and I later got together in Los Angeles where he and his brother filmed a documentary that I had played a role in. God has always shown me His favor in my life's experiences.

When I returned home to Los Angeles, I became very sick and almost died in the hospital. I'd developed a severe respiratory infection. I had stopped breathing during a bronchoscopy examination and was rushed into ICU. I was diagnosed with a very rare form of pneumonia. Because I had been out of the country for a while, my doctors suspected it was either SARS or the Bird Flu. My private doctor told me to get my affairs in order because I was probably not going to leave the hospital. I had lost forty pounds and had never been that sick before in my life.

One night while lying in the hospital bed on high concentrations of oxygen with tubes sticking out of me, I felt an inner peace tell me, "You will not die but live." I believe to this day that it was the 'still small voice of God' speaking to me.

Because "Faith without works is dead," I fought with everything I had to get out of that bed and walk. I had a stationary bike brought to my room, and an extension tube for my oxygen mask. I pushed hard to get my strength back every day. It was during this hospital stay that I wrote out and formalized my own fighting and healing system. I called it, "The Surgical Strike System of Shaolin Dim Mak." I based my lethal fighting and holistic healing system partially on what I had learned in Australia known as the "*Two Dragons of Dim Mak*." When writing my curriculum, I referred to the chapters and lessons as "chambers" to parallel the legend of the 18 learning and testing chambers of the Shaolin Temple. The same concept that I used to write this book. My "system" as I called it was eventually sanctioned by the United States Martial Artist Association (*USMAA*) as a traditionally based martial art.

For many years to follow, I had been offering my training to military, paramilitary, government special operators, protection agents, private military contractors, and law enforcement personnel. My mission was to teach them extremely efficient combative and covert skillsets to help increase their chances of survival on their deployment missions. Teaching them what I had learned in Australia was very intriguing to them, as they had never seen combat techniques quite like these.

After training these elite operators from all over the world, I could not overlook the many incidents of Post Traumatic Stress Disorder (*PTSD*) that these "lethal warriors" had brought back with them from the battlefield. This new battlefield and theater of operation had relocated itself inside of their minds, as it did in mine during my professional career.

I observed a common pattern in many of my post-battle students. After I had trained them to successfully meet the occasion of mortal combat, some came back severely altered and reprogrammed by the combat experience. I now identified my mission objective as not only to train them how to kill, but to teach them how to heal and live life after combat. This was my version and approach to the "*Two Dragons of Dim Mak*" that I had studied in Australia.

I needed to create a path to help them debrief from their combat missions and teach them how to heal from the killing and severe violent lifestyles that they had just experienced. This is where being a former combatant myself, a PTSD debriefer, and a chaplain all came into play. I then formed "*Bannon Institute of The Arts*," where I taught both the martial and healing arts.

"On a Different Note" – I had the opportunity to train a group of special operators who were gearing up to go to Africa on a mission to rescue a group of girls from the sex slave trade. Their mission was to rescue the girls, take no prisoners, and transport the girls to a safe place where they could receive the help that they needed – then get the hell out of Africa as quickly and undetected as possible. This mission reminded me of a movie that came out back in 2011 named, "Machine Gun Preacher" starring Gerard Butler. It was based on the true story of Sam Childers, a former gang biker turned preacher, and his attempts to protect the children of South Sudan from the atrocities of Joseph Kony. Kony was one of Africa's most notorious warlords who abducted children to become child soldiers and sex slaves. God bless the men and women who volunteer for these types of rescue missions. These children are conditioned at a very young age to be both killers and prostitutes. These type of "unfair scenarios" still challenge my faith in God's love and sovereignty to this day.

T.R.I.A.D.

"My Last Hoorah in the Killing Arts"

A good friend of mine, Grand Master Rich Kluck and I had been teaching the combat, special operations, and executive protection arts together for several years. Grand Master Rich had founded the Mortal Combat Art of T.R.I.A.D. I had founded the Mortal Combat Art known as the Surgical Strike System. Master Rich and I morphed our arts together and called it, "T.R.I.A.D. – Surgical Strike System." Eventually, we just referred to the art as strictly **T.R.I.A.D.** "**T**raining **R**egime **I**ncorporating **A**ggressive **D**isciplines."

T.R.I.A.D. is a progressive training program for like-minded and trained individuals seeking a multi-dimensional and serious approach to gun and knife fighting and other combative tactics. The T.R.I.A.D. training and proficiency drills are extremely unconventional and far exceed what is taught in most military and police training schools. As a matter of fact, our training concepts would not be allowed in most other training venues. We push our training envelope as far as we can while still adhering to safety principles. T.R.I.A.D. was sanctioned as a lineage-based martial art in 2008 by the United States Martial Artist Association under Supreme

Grand Master William Rankin – a Vietnam Combat Veteran and international martial arts champion.

Being that most of our students had both a military and special operations background, we did not use a traditional colored belt ranking system. We used a government tier-ranking system. Tier five being equivalent to a traditional white belt, and tier one being equivalent to a brown belt. Our senior instructors (*senseis*) were 1st degree black belts and above. Every member of T.R.I.A.D. earns their rank with blood, sweat, pain, and tears.

Candidates are taken to their absolute breaking points. T.R.I.A.D. is not open to the public and a potential member must first be vetted by a current member to be considered for tryout/ membership into our organization. They are observed during their initial training and then either voted in or out by the current membership counsel and board of elders appointed by Grand Master Rich and me. T.R.I.A.D has members all over the world.

As a result of my research and combat training program development over the years, I discovered something that revolutionized my teaching of the combat martial arts. I called this discovery, "*Brain Fighting.*" Brain Fighting, or "*Mind Scripting*" acted as a double-edged sword. The objective was to cause the enemy's brain to quickly fail, while our student's brains took on almost supernatural qualities through the application of neuropsychology and psychophysiology. Subjects that I had previously studied in college. These techniques that I had developed conditioned our student's brains to become fearless killing machines. This concept developed for T.R.I.A.D. training had placed me, my research, T.R.I.A.D., and Grand Master Rich within the archives of the United States Martial Artist Hall of Fame under the category of, "Pioneer of the Year" in July of 2009. I taught these concepts to the highest levels of the intelligence and mortal combat communities.

This is where my knowledge in the healing arts, led me to create and teach extremely lethal curriculums within the deadly martial arts of mortal combat. However as previously stated, this type of mortal combat training and lethal mindset as a lifestyle, or as a profession over a protracted period of time, does not come without its downside.

I realized one day that I had become mentally, physically, and spiritually what I had taught – **A Killer of Men**.

It went from "what I did and taught as a profession," to "who I had become as a man." I had crossed an invisible line where I had become more passionate about killing than I had about healing. I struggled to believe that this was God's will for me any longer. I knew inside that I had to quickly find a balance, or I could progress too far into the dark side.

As stated in the Book of Ecclesiastes, chapter three as written by King Solomon, son of King David: "A time to kill and a time to heal." Now, was the "time to heal." Not only for my students – but for me as well.

Earlier, I had referred to the Chinese Shaolin Temple where the warrior monks trained as a lifestyle as opposed to three days a week like a gym membership. The Shaolin Temple offered much more than just learning lethal martial arts skills and passing through the 18 testing chambers. There was a spiritual element that brought a peaceful balance to their lethal fighting tactics. It is this peaceful balance that I had been striving to achieve most of my life, and for a good part of my life, it eluded me – until I experienced the **19th Chamber** of the temple (*next chapter*).

It has been a time to kill and or achieve accolades for many of us during our missions within our own personal eighteen chambers. It's now time to heal and take back our full power and become not only lethal warriors, but 'balanced' warriors. "Train to become the most lethal warrior on the planet, but live in such a peaceful way, that fighting or killing becomes a last resort." However – '*balance*' for me, was to leave the killing arts altogether.

In the study of "The Art of War," we find an incredible amount of "battle wisdom" written within its pages. In summary:

"Know when to fight and when not to fight. Avoid what is strong and strike at what is weak. Know how to deceive the enemy. Appear weak when you are strong, and strong when you are weak. Know your strengths and weaknesses. If you ***know the enemy*** and ***know yourself*****,** you need not fear the result of a hundred battles."

The major takeaway in this quote for me was to now '*know my true enemy*' and '*to know my true self.*' My experience within the 19th Chamber proved to me that I knew neither one. I only thought I did. I did know one thing though for sure – that it was time for me to make a major change in my life. It was time for me to leave the killing arts altogether before I progressed to a very dark place of no return. Nevertheless, I had left a legacy behind in the warrior world that many still speak of to this day.

The year was 2014. I held on as long as I could, but my time had finally come to retire from physical warfare and training men to violently kill their external physical enemies. There is obviously a time and place for that, but no longer in my own life.

God now had other plans for my life to use me in a different way. My season of killing was now over, and my season of healing was about to begin. But now on to the reason I have written this book. Not to teach death, but to teach life, and life at a more abundant level. Life after combat and trauma so to speak. This was my first lesson within the 19th Chamber. But it took me almost a lifetime to get there.

Yes, I will miss the training and the lifestyle, but more importantly, I will miss the comradery and Brotherhood of like-minded warriors...... **Nintai!**

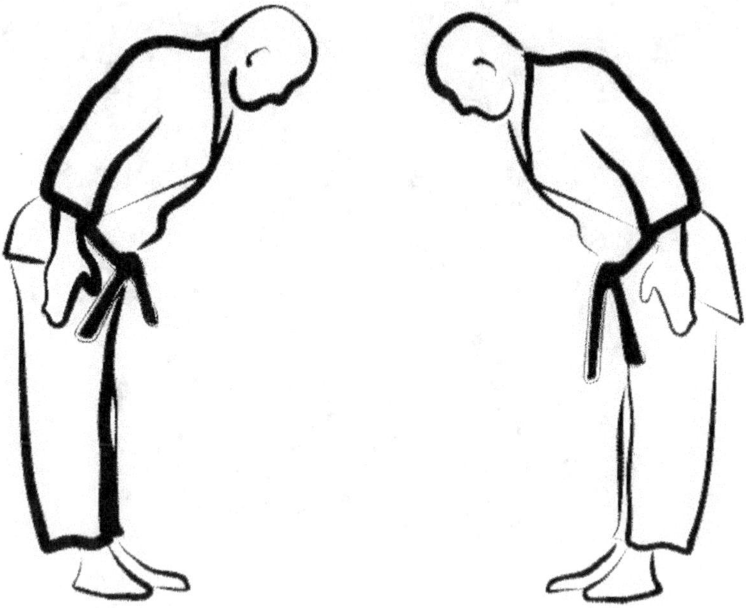

Killer **Healer**

United States Martial Artist Association

Certificate of Induction

To All Who Shall See These Presents, Greetings:
This Is To Certify That

SGM Joseph F. Bannon

Has Been Inducted Into The
United States Martial Artist Association Hall of Fame

Category Of
Pioneer of the Year
In the Martial Art of:
T.R.I.A.D.

As of the 18th Day of July in the Year of 2009

Supreme Grandmaster William A. Rankin, 10th Dan
United States Martial Artist Association
International Director Founder
Frederick, Maryland

Me (left) – SGM Rankin (middle) – Grand Master Rich (right)

United States Martial Artist Association
Certificate of Induction

This Is to Certify That

SGM Joseph F. Bannon, PhD.

(Certificate Number 2005-01-0267-CA)

Has Been Inducted into The

United States Martial Artist Association Hall of Fame

Category Of:

Diamond Life Achievement

In the Martial Art of:

Xian Dai De Wushu

As of the Fifteenth Day of July

In the Year of Two Thousand Twenty-Three

Supreme Grandmaster William A. Rankin, 10th Dan

United States Martial Artist Association

International Director/Founder

Palm Coast, Florida

'Diamond Life Achievement Award' for 60 Years in the Martial Arts

The Legendary Dan Inosanto and Bruce Lee

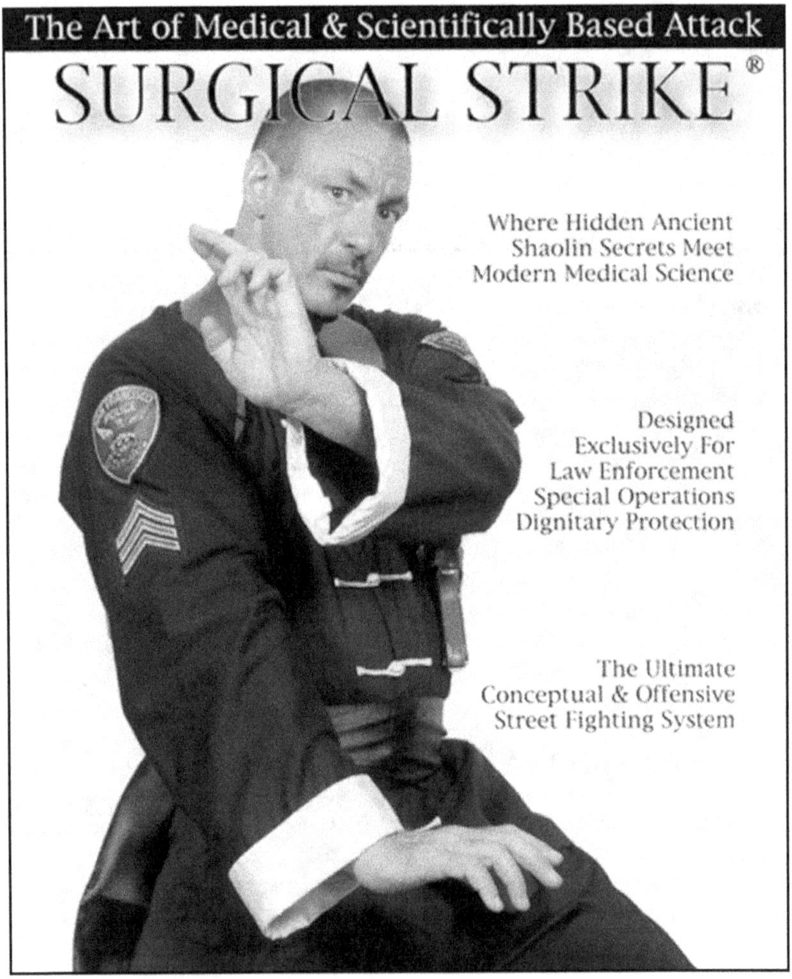

'Killing a Man is Easy'
Forgiving a Man, Healing from the Past, or Forgiving Ourselves
Is the Real Challenge Now

The 19th Chamber of the Shaolin Temple

"A Metaphorical Spiritual Journey"

2 Corinthians 12:1-6 – "It is doubtless not profitable for me to boast. I will come to visions and revelations of the Lord: I know a man in Christ who fourteen years ago – whether in the body I do not know, or whether out of the body I do not know, God knows – such a one was caught up to the third heaven. And I know such a man – whether in the body or out of the body I do not know, God knows – how he was caught up into Paradise and heard inexpressible words, which it is not lawful for a man to utter. Of such a one I will boast; yet of myself I will not boast, except in my infirmities. For though I might desire to boast, I will not be a fool; for I will speak the truth. But I refrain, lest anyone should think of me above what he sees me to be or hears from me."

My Inspirational Vision … I don't want to infer that what I am about to present to you is even similar to the above vision spoken of by the Apostle Paul but nevertheless, it was incredibly spiritual and convicting, to say the least. God had to use severe life circumstances to humble me over a period of forty years while sparing me from the death of combat, addictions, and the insanity from PTSD on countless occasions. I boast of God's greatness over my weakness as you are about to experience in the following words.

Interpret my 19th Chamber experience in any way you like – even if it was just a dream, or an enlightening metaphor. It really doesn't matter what I call it, as the meaning of it and the challenge behind it were extremely powerful to me. So powerful, that the challenge of it eventually changed my life. It taught me the gut-level truth between the virtues of the inner warrior versus the skills of the outer warrior. A soldier, a first responder, a martial artist, the inner Christian versus the outer Christian, or anyone else for that matter. It applies to people from *all walks of life* in the same manner. Rich or poor. Great or small. Young or old. It really doesn't matter.

As you probably have learned by now, I had spent most of my life developing my outer warrior skills and mindset within my chosen professions. Severe mortal combat training, full contact martial arts, gun fighting, knife fighting, and many years of perfecting and teaching the overt and covert killing arts. Yes, I was the epitome of what my students and partners had nicknamed me – "*Doctor Death*;" and at the time, I was very proud of it.

One day several years after my promotion to the martial art rank of 'grand master,' I was driving to my kung fu temple to train and meditate. As I was driving, I was listening to a sermon spoken by Billy Graham. He spoke of a scripture written by the Apostle Paul in the Book of Romans 2:16 – *"The day will surely come when at God's command Jesus Christ will judge the secret lives of everyone, their innermost thoughts and motives; this is all of God's great plan which I proclaim."*

Mr. Graham went on to say that "we all do things that are wrong; we hide all kinds of problems, habits, and failures within the dark inner areas of our lives. That when we judge others, we need to judge ourselves in the same measure because most of the time when we judge others, we are guilty of the same things that we accuse others of. We need to conduct an honest moral inventory of ourselves before we start pointing our fingers at anyone else." These words had penetrated me very deeply. It was almost as if he was speaking directly to me.

As I parked in front of the temple, I turned off the radio, but those words kept playing over and over in my mind. I couldn't get them out of my head. They almost began to haunt me. Nevertheless, I entered the outer temple courtyard, bowed in respect, and sat next to the temple garden and Bonsai Trees. It was a beautiful spring day. The gentle wind was blowing through the 25-foot bamboo trees that surrounded the courtyard. The sound of a waterfall combined with Tai Chi music and windchimes playing in the background acted like a sedative.

Breathing in the scent of traditional Jasmine temple incense only added to the peaceful experience. The temple cat that we had named "Xiao-Mei," was sleeping next to me. This was my retreat from the chaos of life and my work. This is where I would connect to my source of chi (*Life Force*) and Higher Power, whom I choose to call God. I looked down at both of my forearms that had a dragon tattooed on one, and a tiger on the other. They represented the duality and striving balance between Yin and Yang Energy in the Chinese Culture, and the practice of Taoism which was the core spiritual path taught and practiced at this temple.

While meditating, I drifted into a deep, almost hypnotic state of thought. I saw myself walking down a long narrow, barely lit hallway with old-fashioned lanterns glowing onto the rustic stone walls that they were hanging from. I sensed that I had just walked out of the final 18th Testing Chamber of what appeared to be the Shaolin Temple in China. I looked down at the symbols of the tiger and dragon that had been burned into my forearms from carrying a hot charcoal filled urn. I felt very proud that I had successfully made it through all eighteen chambers of combat, life challenges, and achievements alive. I had "*graduated.*"

I felt that there was no sense of age or time within this temple. Yesterday, today, and tomorrow all blended together as if I was standing in a time warp. It felt a bit overwhelming, but it all seemed somewhat familiar to me as I felt a weird sense of peace about the experience.

Then it happened.

Still standing in this dreary but quaint hallway with its entrance behind me; I saw to my right what looked like the doorway to any one of the other eighteen chambers that I had just successfully passed through. I stopped to look inside and saw some very strange-looking people or creatures, or whatever they were, just standing there looking at me.

Most of them were very ugly but some were very beautiful. Some appeared bigger and stronger than some of the others, but I could sense that they were all very strong and capable opponents. Some male and some female. But whatever they were, I sensed that they certainly didn't like me and wanted a piece of my soul and flesh.

They appeared to be ageless and in existence since the beginning of time. Behind them on a brick wall hung thousands of pictures of people on the earth, whom they had defeated in one way or another. Sickness, addictions, suicide, child abuse, and the like. They all seemed to take great pride in this "wall of fame" for lack of a better term. The greater the person was in human history, the greater pride these beings seemed to take in their defeat of them. In this "dream," I just seemed to have the ability to know these things instinctively. This chamber or room was eerie and very evil and felt similar to I guess what hell would feel like. I began to head back towards the entrance that had brought me here in the first place, but the entrance had disappeared. I had no clue where it had gone to. I was searching frantically for a way out of this place. I felt trapped inside of this dungeon. I started to get a bit concerned, as I basically expected Satan himself to show up at this point to welcome me. I began to walk farther away from this room that contained these creatures. They were so dark and ugly that I didn't want to look at them. I did my best to distance myself from them, but then I heard a voice.

"Wait, you are not finished," said a voice from inside of that room. I somehow knew that these words were directed at me, and I slowly walked back to the entrance of that room to see who had spoken them.

As I stood in the doorway to this chamber room, a figure appeared before me. It appeared to be an older Asian Man dressed like a Shaolin Priest or Abbot. He was fairly thin, had a long grey beard, and piercing fiery eyes like I had never seen before in my life. Somehow, I knew that it was him who had just spoken to me.

"Congratulations Si Tai Gung," he stated, which refers to a martial arts grand master in Chinese. "You have trained yourself very well in each of the eighteen chambers and have passed all your tests very successfully. You have no fear to fight any person who threatens you, and you have defended many innocent people in life who could not defend themselves – well done, this is very good," he added. He then stared down at the marks of the tiger and dragon on my inner forearms and the 10th degree black belt wrapped around my waist. "What do those mean Si Tai Gung?" he asked.

"They represent my graduation from the eighteen training and testing chambers of the temple of life. I have proven myself to be capable of fighting violent opponents with weapons, bare-handed, or even more than one opponent at a time. I have also mastered several weapons both ancient and modern," I responded with a sense of pride.

"Impressive," said the Shaolin Priest. "What else? Please tell me more about yourself, if may I ask?"

"I am a grand master, teacher, and practitioner of my art. I teach many others how to fight to the death and survive in the violent world that I come from," pointing toward the entrance at the end of the hallway which had earlier vanished from my sight. "I have memorized all eight virtues of the Samurai Code of the Bushido and have taught my students to do the same." I added.

"Hmmm, Bushido, sounds Japanese," responded the priest.

"It is. I have also survived countless violent physical confrontations – some even against all odds. My body is conditioned to withstand a brutal attack. I have even rid myself of alcohol, drugs, and other addictive things of the earthly world through the virtues of my spiritual beliefs and the martial art warrior lifestyle."

"I see," said the priest. "That sounds very impressive. But which virtue of this Samurai Bushido Code does sexual addiction, promiscuity, pornography, cursing, anger, and lusting after woman come under?"

"Umm, I'm still working on those," I answered.

"Working on them or willfully practicing them? There is a big difference grand master. It sounds more like to me, that you are playing with and submitting to these opponents instead of conquering them like you have your physical opponents that you seem to be so very proud of. May I continue?"

"Sure," I responded in somewhat of a dejected tone.

"Have you ever considered you may be abusing God's Love, Grace, Mercy, and Forgiveness, while using them as a license to cover and excuse your sinful behavior?" he asked. "By misusing these gifts from God, you are taking His forgiveness and turning it into His judgement. You are turning medicine into poison by your behavior."

"Sinful behavior? Judgement? Medicine into poison?" I asked.

"Grand master, those sins and sex acts are going to pile up on you like a mountain of burning coals someday. A day that may come unexpectedly like a thief in the night. Sex is a gift from God to be used within its proper context – not a toy to be played with or a drug to make you feel better when you are anxious or depressed. You cannot preach an external philosophy to people and not live by it inwardly yourself. That is hypocrisy. You were given the gift of salvation when you were nineteen years old. Do you remember that?"

"Of course I do."

"Then why did you jump back into the world of sin? No need to answer that question. We both know the answer. It's because you focused much more on your external accomplishments rather than your internal spiritual growth. You thought that if you build and develop a strong and successful exterior with all the titles, accolades, and accomplishments, that you could hide your inner spiritual weakness, pain, character defects, and deficiencies."

"Yeah but."

"No buts grand master, just honest moral accountability. It is better to deal with these issues now while you still have the chance, than to be judged for them later. Consider these words I speak very strongly and carefully. Remember many years ago when you were on life support in a hospital and couldn't even breathe on your own?"

"Yes."

"Then in that case, you literally owe God the very air that you breathe today. Many people say this as a formality, but with you, it is your literal reality," said the priest.

"But I've done a lot of good in the world and I believe that I was serving God in the process. I have protected presidents, the pope, and other high-echelon dignitaries. I retired from a very successful career as a law enforcement and paramilitary intelligence officer with the government. Before I retired from law enforcement, I was on the top of my game. People looked to me as a national role model. I've been on national television several times. I am known throughout my profession as a world-class trainer and instructor. I am highly decorated with trophies, awards, fourteen Hall of Fame inductions, titles, and medals of valor. I hold a certified 10th Degree Black Belt in the martial arts under the United States Martial Artist Association.

I have helped many people in my life. I believe in God and am a member of a church. I study the Bible, read spiritual books, meditate, and pray almost every day now. I have survived life against all odds – even an abusive, unfair, and violent childhood. I am finally the person that I want to be and have accomplished everything that I have ever set my mind to do. That is what those marks on my forearms signify to me – graduation, overcoming, beating the odds, and becoming the best damn warrior any man on this planet possibly could be," I proudly boasted.

"Commendable," he replied. "But what does any of that have to do with what I have just spoken to you about? Never mind, we'll get back to that later. But I'm curious. Now that you are retired, what will you do with the rest of your life?"

"I'm still trying to figure that out. To be quite honest with you, I feel that I had lost my purpose in life a bit after I had retired."

"Maybe you have lost a bit of yourself as well as your purpose," he said with a gentle smile on his face. "Maybe a good part of your personal identity was tied up in your profession and accolades?" he added. "You seem to have a big, strong, muscular body, especially for your age," he said as I again felt pride rising up inside of me.

"Thank you," I responded.

"You're very welcome."

"I work out very hard at the gym every day," flexing my bicep to show him.

"Very impressive grand master. I also see that you hit the steroids a bit," he said as he lovingly looked into my eyes without a hint of judgement. This man, angel, spirit, priest, or whoever he was had such an incredible amount of peace and kindness about him. It penetrated to the core of my being.

"Do any of those five hernias, slipped discs in your back, or torn rotor cuffs that you acquired during your many years of weightlifting still give you trouble?" he asked.

"How do you know about all of that?" I asked in amazement.

Again, with that penetrating smile he said, "Nothing is hidden here Joey, all things are exposed within the light of the 19th Chamber."

"Joey? 19th Chamber? There is no 19th Chamber. There are only eighteen and I have mastered them all, and how did you know my nickname was Joey? I haven't been called that since I was a kid back in New York," I stated abruptly.

"I beg to differ with you Joey," he stated.

"Enough with the Joey," how do you know all these things about me?" I asked. Still in amazement.

"Like I said earlier, nothing can be hidden in the light of the 19th Chamber. There are no secrets here," he said.

"Light?" I questioned. "The only light I see in this crap hole is coming from those stanky ass lanterns hanging on the wall. This is a dark, dreary freakin place."

"Not at all grand master, The 19th Chamber is pure light. The darkness you see and feel is a reflection of you, your inner being. You brought it here with you."

"The hell I did," I responded angrily. "That crap was here when I got here."

Again, this priest, abbot, temple keeper, or whoever he was looked gently at me and asked, "Would you care to show me some of your martial art skills that you are so very proud of? The ones that got you these fourteen Hall of Fame inductions that you boast of?"

"Now you're talking pops, let's do this," I said with an extreme prideful passion as I could sense a challenge here. "What do you want me to show you? Break some wood, shoot a gun, cut the crap out of something with a blade, or how about my impact weapon skills?" I asked.

"Let's start with something very simple," he suggested. "Please step into the circle with me grand master," he directed.

"What circle?" I asked.

"That one," he stated as he pointed to the floor next to us when suddenly a ring of light appeared on the floor.

"Oh, a magician I see," I responded still trying to be cool-headed and not show the bewilderment and fear that was rising up within me.

"No, not a magician, just a master of time and space," he responded.

"Please, after you grand master," he invited as he pointed again to the circle of light on the floor.

"Let's start with some sticky hands and tai chi," he said.

"Sticky hands, tai chi?" I repeated. "That is for pussies, let's rumble," I demanded.

"Ok, but please first oblige me in some sticky hands (*Chi Sao*)," he asked. "I want to get a feel for your sensitivity training."

"Ok, what the hell, it's your turf old man, but then we get to rumble, right?" I asked with confidence, knowing that this was my strong point.

"Yes, grand master, as soon as you oblige me, we can 'rumble' as you say."

"Good, let's do this pussy crap and move on," I agreed.

We stood within this circle and he presented the first drill, 'Pak Sao.' This is where we stood in a bladed fighting stance and gently touched the back of each other's hand. The fastest one to backhand the other's face wins the match. The only way to succeed in a drill like this is to be in touch with the sensitivity of oneself and that of his opponent.

"Begin," he said.

As we set up in the Pak Sao position, 'BAM,' I saw nothing but felt like I just got punched in the face by Mike Tyson.

"Again," he said. Again, and again we did this, and I kept losing worse and worse, never getting any better. He kept suggesting similar drills and I continued to fail miserably at them. My face was throbbing with pain.

"Had enough grand master?" he asked.

"No way old man," I retorted. "I never give up. I have never given up, not once in my life and I'm not gonna start with you. In all the hundreds of street fights I've been in as a cop in the nastiest hell holes on earth, I've never once been beaten, not once in all the years of my law enforcement profession," I answered. "My animal name given to me by my grandmaster, Sijo Raynaud Lozada was

'Mongoose' because he observed how fast my hands were. Now let's get to the rumbling that you promised me earlier," I demanded.

"As you wish, Mongoose," he replied, "as you wish."

"Make the first move," he challenged.

I threw a straight Wing Chun punch at his face from my center-line. He smoothly evaded it. Again and again, and again, he evaded every technique that I presented to him.

"Is that all you have, Mongoose?" he asked.

"Hell no," I shouted in a rage, as I unleashed everything I had on him until I completely gassed out of energy. I stood there in my own pathetic defeat.

"Screw this, give me a gun, a knife, or a club, and I'll show you how to fight old man," I said out of desperation.

"But you are a grand master, why would you request such things?" he asked.

"Because obviously you have the hometown advantage and I can't beat you at your own game. Come onto my turf and it will be a whole different ballgame," I challenged as I threw a cheap shot at him. As he evaded my blind-side punch, he gently touched me on my forehead which caused me to fall powerlessly onto the ground.

"What are you feeling right now grand master?" he asked.

"Anger, a whole lot of freakin anger," I shouted with tears of fury in my eyes.

"Well, if it's any consolation to you grand master, you're a very good external fighter, but your internal arts are weak. Your survival instincts are highly developed, and your tenacity is impressive, I surely will give you that. But what about the spiritual values that you touted earlier? The Virtues of the Bushido? Honor, Respect, Self-Control – what were the rest?" He asked.

"I can't think right now, but I told you, I live by them and demand that all of my students live by them as well. I make them memorize each one," I responded.

"Memorize you say, grand master. Does memorize and internalize mean the same thing to you?" he asked.

"Yes, it's the same thing. I told you, I live by those virtues and I pride myself in being able to quote those virtues on demand. Go ahead test me," I challenged him.

"I see. You mean like you were able to quote them earlier when I had asked you when you were filled with rage and couldn't remember them? So, you "PRIDE" yourself on memorizing and allegedly "LIVING" by those virtues?" he asked.

"Yes, I do and you're not going to take them from me by making me look like an idiot," I stated.

"Take them, grand master? How can I take from you what you don't possess?" he asked. "Where are your virtues of the Bushido, the tenants of Taoism, Buddhism, and Christianity that you have so diligently studied over the years and preached to so many people in your seminars, lectures, and teachings?" he requested.

"They are always there, every day," I answered.

"Always there? Every day? In every situation?" he asked. "Hmmm, what about that time when a homeless person asked you for some money at the store a few months ago and you rudely dismissed him? That man already has a very low self-esteem and you disrespectfully shunned him only hurting him even more by making him feel worse about himself."

"But I didn't say anything to him; I just made a face."

"This is true," the priest of the temple (*as I will now refer to him as*) answered. "But I believe within your inner dialogue you referred to him as a 'worthless piece of shit,' and an 'air burglar."

"So what, he never knew that. I doubt he is a mind reader like you seem to be," I stated.

"No, he is not, but he sensed it by your demeanor," the priest answered.

"But he's a parasite and useless to society," I responded angrily.

"He is a disabled Vietnam Veteran. He doesn't claim that because he has severe PTSD and wants to forget his pain in his alcoholism and drug addiction. His family disowned him when he came back from the war, calling him a murderer and a monster. They told him that a murderer and a crazy person with PTSD is not welcome in their family," he responded.

"That 'crazy, murderer' as they accused him of being, saw half of his platoon blown up by mortar fire. He ran into incoming gunfire to try and save whoever was still alive. And that was only after he pulled a punji stick out of his own foot. He received a medal of valor for his actions, but he will never tell you that because he wants to distance himself as far away from identifying with his military past as possible to avoid those memories. But you called it right grand master; he is a 'parasite,' a 'worthless piece of shit' and an 'air burglar,' right?" asked the priest.

"No, no, God no," I shouted. He is a freakin hero. Damn, if I knew that, I would have helped him any way I could have. If he only had a sign or said he was a disabled veteran," I added.

"If, if, if, always if," said the priest.

"If you lived by the unconditional love, respect, and tolerance that you preach to others, you wouldn't need conditions or back stories; you would treat all people fairly because 'everybody' has their own unique back story. You probably would have a different attitude and had been willing to help many more of these 'parasites' and 'air burglars' as you call them if you only knew their backstories and struggles in life. Many of which are not uncommon to you and your own life. But you fail to stop and ponder that because you are quick to judge and you're always in a hurry, missing many opportunities that are on your path right in front of you," he added.

"You have walked the Christian path for many years, haven't you?" He asked.

"Yes, I accepted Jesus as my Lord and Savior when I was nineteen years old, right after I got out of an alcoholic rehabilitation center in New Jersey," I answered.

"What did Jesus say about judging others or offering a drink of water to a thirsty man?" He asked.

"Umm, He said, 'judge not lest ye be judged,' and 'if you give a drink of water to even the least of these, you have done it unto me," I answered.

"Have you been living by that example?" He asked.

"I guess not," I responded, feeling ashamed.

"Do you remember the Bible scripture where Jesus referred to the Ten Commandments given to Moses, specifically the one that states, "Thou shalt not kill?" He asked.

"Of course, everyone knows that," I replied.

"Yes, I'm sure they do. Then why do you kill innocent people?" He asked.

"Innocent? I've never killed an innocent man in my life. If I killed someone it was in the line of duty. Besides, I've been cleared by every shooting review board that I have ever appeared before," I said angrily. "Now you're going to judge me for taking a man's life righteously?" I asked.

"No, grand master, I would not judge you for a righteous and justified shooting in the line of duty. Just the unrighteous murders that you have committed," he answered.

"Unrighteous murders? You old bastard. They had it coming. What was I supposed to do just stand there and take one for the team?" I responded angrily.

"Do you remember when Jesus referred to the Law of Moses regarding the commandment, 'thou shall not kill'? he asked.

"Yes dammit, how many freakin times are you going to ask me that?" I shouted, feeling my own PTSD welling up inside of me. "Besides, the correct translation is, 'thou shall not murder,' I added.

"Ohh, a biblical scholar I see," said the priest. "But yes, you are correct in your translation."

"Then what is the problem?" I asked.

"The problem is that you are forgetting what Jesus added to that scripture. Jesus stated that if you have anger in your heart towards your brother, then you have in like manner murdered him," answered the priest. "You see grand master, the law of Moses dealt with a person's outward behavior. Jesus addressed the inward, hidden behavior within a man's heart. It is easy for a man to give a public appearance that he is righteous, but God is interested in the vileness in a man's inner heart. That's why He came to earth to die and take away a man's hidden, inner vileness. That was His 'mission' on earth. This only describes the hypocrisy within you grand master.

You put on this outward appearance that you have it all together, but inside, you hate, you are bitter and filled with rage and unforgiveness against people who have wronged you. What makes you any different from an atheist? Outwardly, you appear very strong and successful. An achieved martial artist within your own right. But inside you are a hypocrite and spiritually immature. Ohh yes, you have all the awards, diplomas, ranks, and degrees of a very successful and achieved man, but inside you are hiding a lot of pain, anger, and misery. Why don't you get honest with yourself for once?" He asked.

I stood there silently without words, feeling a deep sense of conviction, and then I became ragefully defensive.

"I have every right to be angry. If you grew up in my freakin abusive childhood with all of its insanity, you would be angry too. Many times, I wish I was never born," I screamed.

I then went down a long list of the things I was forced to endure throughout my life. I finished ranting, almost out of breath while feeling a great amount of rage, anger, and bitterness. I was half exhausted from expressing that intense tirade of emotions.

The priest had tears in his eyes and with an extremely sad, compassionate look on his face said, "I am so sorry Joey, it breaks my heart to know these things. No one on this planet should have gone through what you had to endure as a child, but let's get real for a minute. Look back at all the people who showed up in your life at your lowest possible times. All of those so-called coincidences. In hindsight, you are very grateful to the countless people that you so generously credit for helping you; your Jewish neighbors, who took you into their homes when your mother attempted suicide. Surviving the armed confrontations as a paramilitary commando and police officer. The high-speed vehicle pursuits through city streets and highways that could have gotten you killed. The death threats on your life that were unsuccessful, and many other near misses. But you fail to see that this was the Hand of God's protection orchestrating all of this behind the scenes. Your anger at God and the hardness inside that being a police and paramilitary officer has created in you have blinded you to His goodness towards you. As difficult as it was, God showed up on time, every time. You would not have made it to the 18th Chamber if He had not.

You are a grand master and tenth-degree black belt in your external combat skills, that's a given. Of course, you have a great deal of goodness in you as a person, but on a stretch, I would give you a green belt at most on your inner skills, and level of internalized spirituality," stated the priest.

"A green belt?" I responded in humiliation.

"And that's pushing it," he said. "Haven't you studied many religions along your life's journey?" He asked.

"Yes Sir I have. I even graduated from a seminary college where I studied Christian Theology and the healing arts. But I can see that I gave my education more lip service than actual practice and application," I said remorsefully.

"You are a psychologist and a well achieved mortal combat instructor, and you have helped many, many, soldiers and law enforcement officers with their PTSD while training them tenaciously for their combat missions. Very well done sir, but have you ever fully addressed your own PTSD and brokenness inside? Or just enough to remain sane and hide it from people who admire and look up to you? Or are you still treating and self-medicating your inner wounds and PTSD with your addictions to worldly achievements, sleeping pills, promiscuous sex, inner secrets, and pornography? How about the fear that you have inside that if people such as your students should ever find out that behind your mercenary approach to killing, is a very loving, compassionate but extremely angry and fearful man? Not afraid to kill mind you, you're very good at that art, but afraid to love and be loved?" He added.

I just stood there silently with a heavy chest and tears in my eyes.

With a very gentle look on his face, he stared down at the tattoo marks on my forearms and my 10th degree black belt. Before my own eyes, the marks on my forearms disappeared, and my black belt turned into a green belt.

"What are you doing? – Where did they go?" I shouted with a great feeling of violation and humiliation.

He looked at me again with that same very loving, gentle, and compassionate stare, while placing his hand on my shoulder and said, "You haven't truly earned them yet. You are not a true grand master until you have defeated them," pointing at the creatures that I saw earlier in the last room at the end of the hallway.

"Who are they?" I asked.

"They are what still live inside of you," he responded. "Opponents you have not yet defeated," he added.

"Opponents? Where inside of me?" I asked with an anger-tainted confusion.

"Within the 19th Chamber," he answered.

"The 19th Chamber? I keep telling you that there is no 19th Chamber. There are only eighteen chambers and I have already passed through and graduated from all of them," I reminded him.

"You have not yet defeated the opponents nor passed the tests contained within the 19th Chamber. You cannot be a true grand master until you do," he added.

"Where is this damn 19th Chamber?" I asked in a challenging tone ready to do battle.

"The 19th Chamber is in the realm of your soul," he answered.

"My soul?" I questioned.

"Yes, and the opponents that you still have not yet defeated and the tests that you still have not yet successfully passed only operate within this realm – or "chamber" as you may better understand it," he stated.

"Who are these opponents?" I asked.

The priest pointed inside the room where I was standing at its doorway and said, "This is the 19th Chamber and those are your opponents."

I looked closely at them as they stood inside of the room taunting and challenging me to come in and fight them. I noticed that there was a name printed across each one of their chests – **"Anger," "Pride," "Prejudice," Impatience," "Hatred," "Unforgiveness," "Vengefulness," "Resentment," "Lust,"** and several others.

"Crap," I shouted. "How do I fight them?" I asked the priest.

"You don't," he said as he smiled gently. "You let them go and don't give into them when they come to challenge you. Release them and allow love and forgiveness to take their place. That is the true 'Wushin – No Mind' and Chi that you teach, but have not yet mastered yourself," he answered. "This is where you must lean on God and allow Him to empower you to fight your inner battles. Just like He delivered you from alcohol and drugs so many years ago, allow Him to deliver you from these negative emotional wounds as well."

"Ok, I'm up for this challenge, but what weapons or techniques work against them?" I asked.

The priest looked at me and again put his hand on my shoulder. "None of the ones that you have become a grand master of within the previous eighteen combat chambers," he answered.

"Then which ones do?" I asked in sincerity. "Teach me – show me?"

"The sword of the spirit," he replied.

"Which is?" I asked.

"The virtues of Godliness: *Love – Kindness – Mercy – Forgiveness – Patience – Charity – Peace – Respect – Humility, and the Words of God as written in the Bible,"* he answered.

"But I already have these virtues," I responded in bewilderment. I know about them and I even teach them to my students back at my temple in Los Angeles," I said.

"Yes, you know them, you teach them, but you don't live by them. They are not burned into your heart as those tattoos were burned into your forearms. You only give them lip service. Your life is certainly not driven by them. What you teach and how you live are not the same. You live by a double-edged sword; a sword that will swing back and also judge you one day. Actually, it already has. That is why you are here in the 19th Chamber with me as your teacher. A teacher, like you have never had before. You're a hypocrite, my friend. You are a good person Joseph; may I call you Joseph, or would you prefer 'Doctor Death' as your students call you?" he asked.

"Yeah, yeah, call me whatever the hell you want," I responded.

"See what I mean Joseph, you are still a very angry man inside," he replied.

"Who are you teacher?" I asked.

"I am the Supreme Grand Master of the 19th Chamber, the High Priest. I am the one to whom you have prayed and meditated to for the last 60 years of your life. You have searched for me up in the galaxies and outer reaches of the universe when actually the martial arts concept of 'economy of effort' would suggest that you have reached too far. Yes, I am there – but I also reside in your very spirit, soul, and conscience. I speak to you and answer you but you have not always heard me. Your focus sometimes is on the external things of this world which blinds you to the much greater world within. Yes, it is true, you have accomplished the impossible, but certainly not without my help," he stated.

"If you really helped me then why did I suffer so much? Why do so many people still suffer in the world if you really are there to 'help' them?" I asked somewhat angrily.

"As difficult as it will be for you to understand what I am about to say to you, I will say it anyway – man has free will and I am bound by my own word and code of honor not to violate that free will. I don't want a bunch of preprogrammed robots to follow me or my path. I prefer people to choose to follow me by their own free will. But nevertheless, I help as much as people will allow me to. Mabey not the way you think I should nor in your timeframe or expectations. Not even in the way that you say that you would, 'if you were me.' But rest assured Joseph, there will be a final judgement of all people who have ever lived from the beginning of time. They will be judged for the good that they have done, the obstacles that they have overcome, as well as the evil that they have committed. No one escapes the final evaluation. Learning about the 19th Chamber is the last opportunity that I give to people to allow me to help them prepare for this final spiritual evaluation. Like the opportunity that I am giving you right now. There are many biblical scriptures that address this," he answered.

"Where do I find these virtues that you say I lack?" I asked.

"They are inside of you – they were placed within your spirit when you became a Christian. They are referred to as the "Fruit of the Spirit" which are love, joy, peace, patience, kindness, goodness, faithfulness, gentleness, and self-control. You have just misplaced them and allowed life to make you insensitive towards them," he answered. "You certainly understand the meaning between the external and internal martial arts. Well, for the sake of this conversation, let's call everything that has to do with the physical body and strength as the 'external arts,' and everything that has to do with the soul realm, as the 'internal arts.' You are a master of the external arts – this is true. But your physical skills are meaningless and completely ineffective inside of the 19th Chamber. My challenge to you is to become a master of the internal arts of the soul. This will require that you put on a white belt and start all over again."

"Oh, now it's a white belt? Another demotion from green belt? You took away my 10th degree, my dragon and tiger. I worked so hard for them. I paid for them with years of hard study and practice. I paid for them with my blood, sweat and tears, torn flesh, broken bones, and incredible pain. This isn't fair." I shouted.

"Not fair you say. Were your blood, sweat and tears, torn flesh, broken bones, and incredible pain greater than that of Jesus? The God who saved you from a fate worse than death when you were nineteen years old and thrown out of an alcohol rehabilitation center as a hopeless case?" asked the Priest.

"No Sir, not even close," I replied feeling ashamed of my selfish attitude.

"Remember when you were a guest teacher at another martial art master's school and the entire class consisted of black belts, and you asked them all to take off their black belts and put on a white belt? You asked them to humble themselves and to 'empty their cup,' as Bruce Lee had stated."

"Yes," I answered.

After a long pause the priest asked me, “What are you feeling inside right now?”

“Pride, anger, and sadness,” I responded.

“Well then – it appears that your first three opponents of the 19th Chamber have just challenged you. Do you accept?” he asked.

I paused in deep thought. “Well, he said – do you, or don’t you? You have never turned down a challenge in your life, why do you hesitate now?”

“This is gonna be hard. Especially if I can’t kick it, punch it, shoot it, or stab it,” I stated.

“I didn’t say it would be easy,” he responded. “As a matter of fact, it will be harder than any grueling training that you have previously endured, or any life and death battle that you have already fought, or any test that you have already passed within the first eighteen chambers of your life.”

“Yeah, yeah – I’m ready, I can do this. Bring them on,” I said angrily as I started to enter the room where the creatures were ready to do battle with me.

“Oh no Joseph, not in here – out there,” he said as he pointed to the end of the hallway where I began to see and hear the images of everyday city life. The same entrance that brought me here in the first place.

“They will meet you and challenge you in some of the most unexpected and deceptive ways. They have the ability to change their image and form at will. Sometimes they will confront you in a man’s body, sometimes in a woman’s, maybe even a child’s. On a freeway, a phone call from someone who needs help when you are in a hurry, or an endless list of everyday life situations. They are masters at what they do and know just where your weak points are and how to push your buttons. They very rarely telegraph their movements, so you never really see them coming. They are excellent in their use of the element of surprise. They cannot be punched, kicked, or choked out, and they do not respond to conventional weapons, intimidation, or other military combat-type tactics. They will be more challenging to you than anyone you have ever fought before."

"I need a coach, a training manual, or someone who can train me to get ready for this fight," I said.

"You already have them at your disposal," he responded. "You have studied the words and lessons of various religions, philosophies, spirituality, and the masters who have come before you. The sixth chapter of the Book of Ephesians in the Bible teaches about 'spiritual warfare,' not 'physical warfare.' You may want to study this concept and apply it more seriously than you ever have before. Put on the whole armor of God and prepare for spiritual warfare. This is the ultimate form of combat.

Take the spiritual teachings that you have studied and live by them on a daily basis no matter what the challenge or circumstance may be. But please know this: *not all of these philosophies, spiritual paths, and religions that you have studied in the past are equal,*" he said.

"Many of these teachings contain good morals and spiritual virtues but they lack the presence of an eternal God behind them. Good morals alone without a relationship with God are good, but not good enough to satisfy God's expectations of man. Besides, your spiritual enemies do not fear good morals, but they do fear God."

"I have known some of these teachings since I was a kid," I responded.

"Yes, you have, but you have allowed them to weaken in your pursuit of the physical skills and mortal achievements of the eighteen chambers of the earthly temple. Use the same determination and tenacity here and you will also be a champion of the 19th Chamber of the Spiritual Temple. You are a doctor – use your skills to heal people. When someone challenges you with violence; respond to them with positive energy and a gentle kind word."

"But what if they try to hurt me physically?" I asked.

"There is a time and a place on the earth for physical combat – but not as a first option. Avoid it as often as possible and use your internal skills to calm, make peace, and heal whenever you can. This is the only way to defeat the opponents of the 19th Chamber. The longer you avoid physical combat in a confrontation, the greater your physical skills will become if your opponent is persistent and leaves you no other option. Universal Law will see that you have attempted to use peaceful options for as long as you possibly could and were given no other choice but to use physical combat as a last resort. Your physical skills will be much greater in this case because the righteousness of the universe (*God*) will assist you in your efforts because you chose the way of peace first but were given no other choice but physical counterforce by your violent opponent. But peace and mercy can exist even in the midst of violence."

"But I can't teach this concept to soldiers on a battlefield. They will be annihilated. They need to kill first and ask questions later." I responded.

"True, but I am not speaking about them right now. They are still fulfilling their current missions on the earth. I am speaking to you and your inner spiritual life. You are retired and no longer on a battlefield nor teaching the arts of war and killing, so what's your point?" He asked.

"I guess I don't have one," I answered.

"With expanded lethal knowledge Joe, such as your extensive study of Dim Mak better known as "Death Touch" or "Black Medicine," comes the need for more patience, mercy, and love. To study Dim Mak, one must also do his best never to use it. Again – the great mystery behind the balance of Yin and Yang. Train to kill but strive for peace."

The priest then looked at one of the creatures in the room and lifted one finger and the creature fell to the ground completely weakened, petrified, and defeated.

"Good God," I stated. "How the hell did you do that? Please sir – teach me this technique?" I asked.

"This 'technique' as you call it that you have just witnessed makes all of the techniques that you have learned over the past 60 years inferior. Only a true Supreme Grand Master knows how to perform what you just saw. First you must learn to love, have mercy, and demonstrate patience towards all people – only then can you be trusted with this type of power," he explained.

I just hung my head in amazement.

"This is an example of the lessons within the 19th Chamber," stated the priest. "This is exactly why Jesus came to earth because the Jewish Law could not save a man, as no man could live up to its requirements. Jesus came to fulfill the requirements of that law and paid the penalty Himself so you wouldn't have to. But He expects you to embrace this concept and grow in it, and not just look at Him as a license to stay in your sinful, judgmental state."

I had nothing to say at this point.

"You see Joseph – it is not just your outwardly expressed behavior that I am talking about here. Many people are disciplined enough to not act out their feelings through words and actions. This is no great feat at all. They suppress their feelings and bite their tongue so to speak; then they go home and yell at their spouse or children because even feelings are clusters of energy that will always find a way to express themselves somehow. The true mastery is in the releasing of this negative energy and the ability to prevent it from creeping back in. Some refer to these negative feelings as, "character defects" and character defects need to be spiritually managed. But once you release the negative thoughts and energy, they must be replaced with positive thoughts and energy. This comes through conscious choice, surrendering your will, prayer, meditation, understanding God's Word, and having fellowship with likeminded people.

I would strongly advise that you read Philippians chapter 4 verse 8 in the Bible which states, "Finally brethren, whatever things are true, whatever things are noble, whatever things are just, whatever things are pure, whatever things are lovely, whatever things are of good report, if there is any virtue and if there is anything praiseworthy – meditate on these things." This will also help you with your inner turmoil and PTSD. Controlling your thoughts have a direct effect on what you experience in your emotions, but it will take discipline on your part. This is a great management tool for people dealing with PTSD and wandering thoughts. As soon as you feel yourself going down that rabbit hole of negative thinking or rehearsing past events, read this scripture that I just gave you.

You will also find that the more positive energy that you put out into the world – the less negative energy you will attract towards yourself. Strike hard and strike effectively using the secret art of Chinese Dim Mak, yes – but only when needed and as a last resort whenever possible. Train your body daily in physical combat skills but live in a way that you will never need to use them. Isn't this the philosophy that you teach your students?

As I stated earlier, this is the great mystical law of Yin and Yang. When there is a balance of both, peace forms in the middle of the two. There is even a higher art of Dim Mak that you are not yet aware of that does not require your physical body to defeat a violent opponent, but that will only come as you practice these higher spiritual principles. Can you grasp this concept Grand Master Joe Bannon?" he asked.

I held my head down slightly and looked back into his eyes – "I am not a grand master sir. I have only completed half of my training. I have not mastered some of the greater and higher skills of the martial arts. I have not yet successfully passed the spiritual tests of the 19th Chamber."

"Well spoken," he said.

"Sir, I see my picture hanging on the wall behind my opponents with all of those other pictures of people," I stated.

"Yes, and it will stay there until you graduate from the 19th Chamber," he responded.

"When will I graduate?" I asked.

"You will know," answered the priest.

"How will I know?" I asked almost childishly.

"You will know when the tactics that you will need in the 19th Chamber have developed to the same intuitive and spontaneous level that you have developed your physical skills. When they come so naturally that you will not have to think about them. When your kind thoughts, actions, feelings, responses, and words move as fast as your lethal Mongoose-like hands – then you will know that you have become a master of the 19th Chamber, and only then may you wear your black belt and symbols on your forearms again."

"I understand sir," I said as I bowed to the priest.

"May I suggest that you choose a definite spiritual path and live by it before you leave here?" he asked.

"What are my options?

"Well, you have studied Buddhism, Taoism, the Japanese Bushido, and Christianity, to name a few," he reminded me.

After careful thought, "I will choose Christianity," I answered.

"Why is that?" asked the priest.

"Well, it's the only path that helped me get sober from alcohol when I was nineteen. Christianity is the only path that claims its founder rose from the dead and still lives today. And besides, me and Jesus used to be pretty tight before I compromised and went back into the world of glamor, glitter, and physical achievements," I responded.

"Yes, we were very tight, and we can be tight again if you so choose," answered the priest.

"We?" I asked.

"Yes, we. Well then, if this is your choice, then give your entire self to this spiritual path of Christianity and don't compromise anymore. Being 'lukewarm' is no longer an option for you. Go and share your testimony about the prior eighteen chambers of your life and what you have learned here today with whomsoever will listen. Teach the concepts of **spiritual warfare** rather than only the concepts of **physical warfare**," he commanded.

"One more thing before you leave Joseph. Just like your promotions through the ranks of the physical martial arts over the years were dependent on your performance and determined by a board of high-ranking judges – so shall your eternal promotion be based on your spiritual performance in your daily life and determined by the ultimate judge of the universe – God. Go forth and use your healing skills more than your martial skills. Become a healer of men before a killer of men whenever possible."

He then bowed to me and pointed to the end of the hallway where the view of everyday city life was occurring. The same door or vortex I had walked through to get here in the first place that had vanished earlier. He then handed me a scroll and told me to read it when I arrived back in my home city. He suggested that I say the words that were written on the scroll as a prayer each morning when I awaken – I agreed.

I walked to the end of the hallway and was immediately back in the middle of city life. The door to the temple had vanished behind me. I knew now that this was not the end, but only the beginning for me.

It had finally become obvious to me that I had just experienced the Spiritual 19th Inner Chamber of the temple– which unbeknown to me all this time, was just beyond the physical 18th external chamber. A chamber that I had believed for many years had represented the completion of my life's achievements. I thought that I had "arrived" and achieved the ultimate level of being a warrior, but I couldn't have been more incorrect.

I was now standing on a city sidewalk and began to read the scroll in the midst of people hurrying by me and the loud noise of traffic jams in the street. This is what was written on the scroll:

> "My Creator – I am now willing that you should have all of me – good and bad, I pray that you now remove from me, every single defect of character that stands in the way of my usefulness to you and to my fellow man. Grant me the strength as I go out from here to do your bidding by contributing to the health, happiness, and betterment of this world. To teach and practice peace, love, and healing first, and combat, violence, and killing second. Help me to not speak negative, hateful words and even more importantly, to not have the negative, hateful roots of these words in my heart. That all creatures on this planet great and small are all representatives of You and when I disrespect or unjustifiably hurt one of these creatures – I in turn disrespect and hurt You. Help me to remember this on a daily basis ~Amen."

Just as I had finished reading the scroll, a person rudely bumped into me and told me to get out of his "fkng" way. I clenched my jaw and right fist instinctively while I started to give him a dirty look and began formulating my verbal response. All of this had occurred within me in a split nanosecond. I suddenly saw the priest's face in my head. I caught myself and bit my lower lip as I remembered my conversation with the Supreme Grand Master of the 19th Chamber. I refrained from saying anything to this rude person, but in my heart and mind I was murdering him.

The 'Supreme Grand Master,' or 'The Priest,' as I had known him in this 'dream,' was none other than Jesus Christ Himself, coming to me in a way that I could understand and not deny.

Obviously, the preceding scenario is metaphorical in nature, but I believe it was Divinely inspired. It is very challenging and increases the awareness of anyone who has the ears to hear this message and is willing to take on the challenge of the 19th Chamber. One does not have to be a martial artist to take this challenge. The challenge is there for anyone of any walk of life or achievement level to take.

The 19th Chamber is obviously a chamber of growth, knowledge, and challenge that really sets apart the children from the adults. Or the black belts from the white belts in my case. It is not necessarily what a man says or doesn't say with his mouth or does or doesn't do with his hands that makes him a good, bad, or a spiritually evolved person – but what lives in his innermost being, in his heart, in his soul, in his thoughts. This can only be accomplished in a committed relationship with Jesus Christ and His Written Word – The Bible.

Also known in a spiritual warrior's world as – **The Sword of The 19th Chamber.**

> *"Would not God search this out? For He knows the secrets of the heart."*
>
> **Psalm 44:21**

Midnight Confessions

"Killer by Day – Healer by Night"

I began my transition out of the combat arts and into the healing arts as the High Priest of the 19th Chamber had told me to even though I still taught at ESI. "Who needs healing more than soldiers and cops dealing with PTSD?" I thought to myself. This was the beginning of my healing ministry. Helping others with PTSD, physical sickness, emotional wounds, trauma, and addictions.

I still carried a gun and taught others how to use one because this was my job and what I was paid to do. But it was no longer my drive nor passion. I also had a new message and attitude in my heart since my experience within The 19th Chamber. I wondered how this new me was going to look and be perceived by my students.

I wasn't quite ready or comfortable to open the first day of my class with a sermon on spiritual warfare out of the Biblical Book of Ephesians. But here and there I came across students who were able to grasp the concept. They understood that there were spiritual forces behind mankind's wars that were much bigger and stronger than mere men alone. I believed that this was a great place to start.

The first day of a new class at ESI usually consisted of a room full of very experienced warriors who weren't easily impressed with verbal bullcrap. I usually bonded with my students on day one. I didn't need to read a long resume of my life experience. They could see it in my eyes and hear it in my voice. This is what I call "*The Silent Resume of a Warrior*." It's a strange phenomenon but we can intuitively recognize each other.

I told them that each day will become increasingly more challenging and stressful. But graduating from these courses will not only make them better warriors, but also increase their chances of receiving promotions and being appointed to the specialized teams that they had their hearts set on. That the effort would be worth it on graduation day. ESI was the school that paved the way for me to be assigned as a bodyguard to the Mayor of San Francisco, and eventually to the United States Secret Service – Presidential Protection Detail.

Many if not all my students were combat veterans. They were either enhancing skills that they already possessed or learning new skills to apply to their current or transitionary missions, either in the military or as private military contractors. I told them that I would be their combat drill instructor during the day, and their chaplain and psychological counsellor at night. And if they needed someone to talk to about PTSD, the spiritual aspects of combat, or any other issue, that they were welcome to meet me after class to discuss any life challenges that they might be facing.

Many of them took me up on my offer and showed up to my room at night. They shared many very deep emotions with me because I had earned their trust and respect. Their emotional and physical symptoms were not uncommon for what many of them had been through. I gave them the best advice I could. We spoke about the emotions and physical symptoms of PTSD and what may improve them. We even spoke about God, spirituality, and the virtues of a warrior including the Bushido Code of the Japanese Samurai, the Military Code of Conduct, and to those who were open to it – Jesus Christ and Christianity. I had to start where they were at and not shove religion or heavy doses of spirituality down their throats if they weren't ready for it. Surprisingly enough, many of them were ready for it.

I developed a group therapy session each night after dinner. I set up a circle of chairs where my students would all face each other. Many times my training partner Rich would join us and share valuable input with the group. Approximately four to twelve students showed up each night. I told them that the only rules were not to bring a firearm or a knife with them, no acting out or physical contact, and no cross talking or giving advice to other students during this group session. I told them to try and think about the combat experience that made them the angriest or most fearful; the one that still plagues them the most. They all agreed and for the most part, behaved very well. A few hiccups here and there but all in all, well contained.

"Ok gentlemen let's get started. We will start to my left and work around the circle clockwise. Please do not refer to me as 'Sir.' 'Doctor Joe' or just 'Joe' is fine. You can say anything you want to and express any emotion that you are feeling. There will be no recordings, note-taking, nor any judgement or reporting up the chain. The only mandatory reporting would be if I feel that you are a danger to yourselves, to someone else, or if you are planning to commit child abuse, spousal abuse, or a serious felony. Understood gentlemen?"

"Understood Sir!" they unanimously replied.

"Doctor Joe" or "Joe" fellas. I want to keep rank, chain of command, and administrative bullcrap out of this group. Rich over there is a Lt. Colonel in the Marine Corp. But in this group he is just "Rich"..... Oorah?" (*a Marine Corp term of acknowledgement*).

"Oorah," they all retorted.

"Ok Randy let's start with you. Just state your name and agency that you have previously or are currently working for along with the greatest form of PTSD that you are presently dealing with."

"I'm Randy and I am currently an active-duty US Marine. I have served three combat tours in Afghanistan and am about to be discharged into civilian life. I'm not sure I am ready to be a civilian. I only feel comfortable around other like-minded Marines. My wife and kids said that I have changed, and they are very afraid of my bouts of explosive anger. They say I am no longer the husband and dad that I used to be before I began my combat tours. I have never put my hands on them, but they are petrified that at some point I will. I am scared to return to civilian life with this rage inside of me. It was my fuel in combat, but it is poison outside of combat. I am really perplexed about this."

"Thank you for sharing, Randy. PTSD definitely can involve our entire family, not just us. And you are by far not the only one who experiences this type of anger that you spoke of," I responded. "We will discuss some options on how to deal with these types of issues later in the group."

"Alex," I motioned.

"My name is Alex. I am an Army Special Forces Green Beret. I have served in combat in many locations around the world. I grew up in a Christian home and had a strong belief in God before I joined the Army. But after all the shit I've seen – like little kids getting blown up and missing body parts. Young teenage and even younger girls being gang raped by the Taliban and then having their faces burned with acid. Dragging my wounded or dead partner back to our Humvee. I have one thing to say. Fuck you God! Fuck your disgusting world and all the hell that you allow to take place. Where was your so-called, 'all-powerful loving ass' when those little girls were being raped and tortured? I lost all respect for God, and the only time I would ever walk into a church again would be to urinate or defecate on the altar as my offering to this supposed 'loving' God of the universe. I fucking hate God. I heard a very old woman who was a Nazi Holocaust survivor give a speech about when she was a prisoner in Auschwitz. She described in detail the horrendous tortures that many of them had received on a daily basis. When she ended her speech, she said that the only way that she could possibly believe in God was if he crawled to her on his knees and begged for her forgiveness. Well, I feel exactly the same way."

"A lot of us experience blaming and hating God for what our eyes have seen Alex. The unfairness, the abuse of children, and other innocent people. We then want to kill or torture the people who do this to them. By a show of hands can anyone else relate to this?" Everyone in the group raised their hands.

"You're not alone, 'Brother Alex.' I used to jump up and down like a raped ape with extreme rage at God for the very same things that anger you. Let's get together after group and share our anger and hatred towards God together." I suggested. (*My intent was to use a technique in psychology referred to as 'Gestalt Therapy' where the person talks or screams at an absentee person or event in an empty chair while I oversee the experience*).

"Sure," responded Alex in bewilderment.

"You're up Paul."

My name is Paul. I am a US Marine and I aint got nothin to say right now Dr. Joe. I'll pass to the next guy."

"Thank you, Paul. If you change your mind just raise your hand. I'm glad you're here buddy," I responded.

I pointed to the next student.

"Hey Gents, my name is Sergio. I am a US Army Combat Veteran from Desert Storm. I currently serve as a sergeant with the New York City Police Department. I'm putting in for a promotion to our dignitary protection unit and I am here to get the best credential in the world in executive protection. You know it's funny. I saw my fair share of shit in combat, but that doesn't bother me half as much as dealing with a bunch of ungrateful bastards who hate cops. They look at us as the enemy. I was okay being "the enemy" in another country, but it doesn't sit right with me being hated by the very people that we serve and protect as police officers. I can't believe I'm about to say this but I hate the people I serve on a daily basis. I hate the politics and the upper management that only care about themselves and don't give a rat's ass about us.

Pulling dead bodies out of burning cars, doing CPR on infants, watching criminals get put back on the street the same day I arrest them, and never being able to get my partner's face out of my head after he got shot and killed right in front of me. That's why I want off the streets and a change of scenery in a different unit. I'm done with serving the ungrateful pieces of garbage in our society who "pay our salary." Besides, I'm starting to drink way too much. I can't sleep at night, I have recurring nightmares, and I get woken up by the sound of a gunshot in my dreams. My wife says that she understands but she really doesn't. I snap at my wife and kids because they don't understand why I want to sit facing the front door in a restaurant. They ask me why I can't just leave the job at the job."

"Thanks Sergio. New York huh? That's where I was born and raised. I believe many of us here can relate to you brother. I think one of the hardest things that we deal with is to hear people say that they understand what we have been through but as you know, that's not the case. People don't understand why we are hesitant to talk about our war experiences. Some of these experiences are like swallowing bitter food that upsets our stomach. Vomiting it up only tastes ten times worse the second time so we keep swallowing until it stays down. Once we get it to stay down, we do whatever we can to keep it down. This is referred to as emotional suppression. We then sometimes avoid things that could open the lid of our suppressed emotions, so we don't have to taste that bitter vomit again. That's why we don't like to talk about our battle experiences with people who don't understand our world. It is much easier to talk about our stuff with others who have been where we have been because – "they get it." There are programs out there dedicated to helping not only us, but the spouses of combat veterans dealing with PTSD. I will give all of you guys the names of several of these programs after our meeting tonight. By the way bro, I still sit facing the front door in a restaurant myself and have taken flak for it as well."

"Group laughter."

"Rich, you're up buddy," I stated.

Thank you, Joe. My name is Rich, I'm a lieutenant colonel in the U.S. Marine Corp. I want to be considerate to my brothers sitting here with me, but I have seen a lot in my career. I've lost troops. I've second-guessed my decisions wondering if I could have changed the outcome if I had made a different decision. I was told early on to, "suck it up buttercup" and push through. So, I don't really think I have the common symptoms of PTSD."

"How about the uncommon symptoms?" I asked.

"Well, I stay to myself a lot. I refrain from watching war movies. I don't socialize or have many close friends. My wife divorced me about five years ago saying that I'm not the same man that she married. But I really don't have any feelings towards these things. I just accept it all as part of the mission fallout. I love to just be alone, drink some good whiskey, and have a cigar, unless I'm learning or teaching something. To be honest, I'm just numb and apathetic about everything in life. Is that PTSD?"

"Well Rich, yes, it is. It's like injecting Novocain into a painful tooth that needs a root canal. It numbs the pain, but the bad tooth still remains and continues to decay. Numbing the pain doesn't take away the cause. Our brain has the ability to create a similar Novocain experience so that we don't feel the pain of our suppressed emotions. It's kind of like putting a bomb blanket over a bomb. The blanket won't stop the explosion, but it will suppress it to some degree. "Numbing" as opposed to "feeling," is not an uncommon survival mechanism. Numbing can also prevent flashbacks, as well as painful thoughts and emotions. That's the upside of numbing. The downsides are, isolation, depression, loneliness, hibernating in the safety of our home, or just becoming very introverted. But the danger here is this. One unexpected life event can pierce through that emotional bomb blanket and release all that pent-up energy that has been trapped inside of us. I had numbing for a very long time. But sometimes emotions and memories pop through our numbing, especially in our dreams. I get it brother."

Rich sat back in his chair, crossed his arms in front of him, and bit his bottom lip. "Very true. That's all I have," he stated.

"Thank you for sharing, Rich. I'm sure many of us here relate to you. I know I sure do," I ended.

"Adam, you're up buddy."

"My name is Adam, and I am a former US Marine. I did four combat tours in Afghanistan. I got shot up pretty good on my last tour and was sent home with a Purple Heart and a PTSD disability rating. Yeah, I get flashbacks, nightmares, and unwanted intrusive thoughts, but you know how I handle all of that shit? I put on headphones, crank up the volume, guzzle down a Monster Energy Drink, and watch clips of war movies. I know it sounds psychotic, but putting myself back in the battle makes me feel at peace. If I lay in bed or sit in a chair, I hear all kinds of noise and my memories go at 100 miles per hour. I tried to meditate but if I lay still, I get really nervous and want to jump out of my own skin. But when I'm experiencing a war movie – that's how I stay in the game and feel normal."

"Thanks for sharing that, Adam. I've been there with the war and cop shootout movies. I used to find a weird sense of peace in that adrenaline rush myself, especially after I retired. I was an adrenaline junkie and when I started jonesing (*withdrawing*), I would look for a drug fix just like you do to get me out of the funk."

"Standby Dr. Joe, I don't take drugs, I just watch movies and take in energy drinks," replied Adam.

"Exactly Adam. By restimulating yourself by watching the movie clips, you are forcing your brain to experience a simulated "fight or flight" mode. You are engaging your combat brain just as you did when you were in actual combat. Your energy drinks contain caffeine and other stimulants. There is a certain psychological familiarity by watching battle scenes on the internet. But what you are actually doing is synthesizing battles in your brain. Your brain responds in a similar manner as to how it did in actual battle. Your brain begins to produce neurotransmitters such as Dopamine, Serotonin, Cortisol (*natural brain-produced drugs*) and then ramps up your Sympathetic Nervous System which continues to fire up your adrenal glands that causes an adrenaline dump. The same exact process of a live battle in a lesser simulated environment – and all in the comfort of your own chair in front of a computer.

What you are actually trying to experience unconsciously, is a drug rush from both your Limbic System (*survival brain*) and from your Hypothalamic – Pituitary – Adrenal Axis (*Adrenaline Dump*). This dramatically elevates our emotional moods. So, I get why you would find some sort of relief during this process, but you are further burning out your already burned-out adrenal glands. When we do things like this, we are unconsciously increasing our stress levels of both our minds and body that both work together in 'harmony' and create that "battle rush" again.

Question – do you ever feel like you have a hangover or get depressed or angry shortly after your stimulation experience?"

"All the time," responded Adam.

"And that's why you keep doing it. It becomes a vicious cycle that keeps stressing our already stressed brain and body. We become addicted to the battle stress process of our own brain and body chemistry. A similar response can be experienced from watching pornography. These things feel good at the time, but the damage and toxicity can become quite significant. We need to be careful not to burn ourselves out for good. You have survived combat tours in Afghanistan, but I'm concerned that you won't survive the addiction that you have created to deal with your PTSD (*the battle after the battle*)."

Adam just looked down in silence and nodded his head as if he had just gotten an epiphany of what he was "really" doing to himself. The next night, I took Adam out for dinner and continued our conversation trying to support him however I could.

"Frank, you're next," I stated.

"I'm Frank and I am a former Navy SEAL. I've seen a lot of combat but the incident that still haunts me to this day is when I was out on a waterborne mission, and I was attacked by a shark."

Frank was wearing shorts as he stood up and pulled up his right pant leg. He showed us all a nasty scar where a shark had bitten and ripped out a large piece of his inner thigh. Everyone in the group including me gazed at Frank's shark bite in amazement. "That beats Charlie's three bullet holes in his gut," I stated as we all began to laugh. Frank enjoyed the attention but got serious after the laughter.

"Ever since this attack, I have developed an incredible fear of swimming in the ocean. That is unacceptable and shameful for a Navy SEAL. I love to swim, surf, sail, and anything else that has to do with the ocean, but I avoid the ocean like the plague. Even when I am about to jump into a swimming pool, I have to make sure there are no sharks in it before I jump in. I hate this phobia of the water."

"Frank, I have seen a lot of things in life, but that shark bite scar puts you high on the list. It's gonna take some time and work on your part to get comfortable in the water again. But you can do it if you really want to. I crashed through a plate glass window and almost lost my hand, and for a long time had a phobia of glass. I get it bro, but it is nothing to be ashamed about. It's normal to feel that way. I think I can help you with some desensitization exercises," I replied. After that day, Frank's new endeared nickname was "*Jaws*."

"Peter, what do you have for us brother?" I asked.

"My name is Peter. I am a former Army Ranger. I've been in combat many times. My ears always ring, I have a constant buzzing in my head, and I used to be a very social person but after my last tour of duty, I have become a recluse. But I don't go to the VA Hospital, take their pills, and listen to their bullshit. I don't want any of my symptoms to be documented and I don't want a PTSD disability rating. That diagnosis will follow me for the rest of my life and could affect me getting certain jobs that I want because of what they would find in my background check. So, I aint sayin nothin to nobody at the VA. I go to the VA Hospital when I get sick, but when they try to ask how I am doing psychologically – I just say fine."

"Peter, I understand your fears, But I am gonna come right out and say this. You need to speak with someone. There are many PTSD groups for soldiers that do not keep records nor report to anyone at the VA. I strongly suggest that you join one. I suggest you contact a group named, "Mighty Oaks" or "Reboot Recovery," They would be perfect for you," I replied.

"Thank you, Dr. Joe. I will look into that."

I could go on and on with these stories. The theme is always the same, only the props change from person to person. These guys had been through hell and back. Many had bullet holes in their bodies, been injured by an IED (*bomb*) blast, watched their partners get killed, carried their dead and mangled partners off a battlefield, had traumatic brain injuries, loss of an eye or other body part, and had been bitten by a shark, etc. Yet they all seemed to have the greatest sense of humor and even a degree of spirituality to them. They were good people. I just had to watch the potential for fist fights between teammates when the stress got high – and the stress did get very high at times, especially when putting in very long hours to keep up with the curriculum. Add a little alcohol at dinner, and the potential becomes even greater. We lived and died as a team. We never left a buddy or client behind. And we all understood that for a team to be successful, there could be no "I" in the word TEAM. Most of them already understood these concepts from their prior worlds. But I pounded it into them under high-stress drills to make sure that it had become second nature to them. That we always operate as a team no matter what happens. "Two is One – One is None."

I shared with them several mental, physical, and even spiritual techniques that could help quell an episode of PTSD or a severe anxiety attack. I shared techniques and information with them that not only worked for myself but for many others as well. I also explained the connection between the brain, nervous, digestive, and endocrine systems that needed to be rebalanced in warriors who had burned-out adrenal glands. Burned-out adrenal glands are also very prevalent in law enforcement officers and other first responders and cannot be "cured" by huge amounts of caffeine, Monster Energy Drinks, Red Bulls, Ephedrine, or Five Hour Energy Drinks. They only override and compensate for an underlying deficiency in the body.

I explained that there is such a thing as a "PTSD and Adrenal Gland Diet." That there are PTSD, burned-out body, and brain-friendly foods and supplements, as well as PTSD, burned-out body, and brain non-friendly foods and supplements. There is no one size fits all. Everyone is a unique individual with a unique physiological system and background. But I strongly suggested doing some research on the internet and start rebuilding themselves from the ground up. What we eat, drink, or think can affect our mood, energy levels, and state of being. PTSD does not just affect the brain but can involve every biological and physiological system in the body. This must be considered in treating the "whole person" and not just one singular aspect. There is no such thing as a non-connected, singular aspect anywhere within the human organism. Unfortunately, they don't teach much of this if at all, at the Veteran's Administration Hospital. "Take these pills and make an appointment in three months," is usually the protocol which in my opinion – sucks.

I will say this one hundred times. "PTSD is a body, mind, and spirit issue, and the body, mind, and spirit need to be included in a holistic healing process, not just the brain. The brain is obviously an important factor, but we consist of three entities – body, mind, and spirit. Taking proper care of the body through diet, supplementation, and exercise is extremely important. Taking care of the mind and spirit through positive activities, positive thought reinforcement, as well as prayer and meditation cannot be overlooked or minimized to achieve a desired level of balance and healing (*homeostasis*) of the "whole person." Many find relief studying the martial arts, tai chi, chi gung, working with animals, or taking up new hobbies that produce pleasure and create a comfortable atmosphere. These options are definitely healthier than alcohol, drugs, pornography addiction, or sitting in a chair 'tasting gun oil' (*contemplating suicide*).

If we can find a connection with God, some form of love, and the willingness to be of service to others by turning our pain into their power and hope; then I think we stand a good chance of winning our inner battle. We do need however, to understand and become aware of this 'new theater of operation' known as the 19th Chamber and the realm of "**Spiritual Warfare,**" as opposed to only our prior missions on a physical battlefield where we were limited to guns, knives, and bombs.

Spiritual Warfare

"The Battlefield of the Mind"

> ***The Mind is a Battlefield:*** *"A war is raging, and your mind is the battlefield. Worry, doubt, confusion, depression, anger, and feelings of condemnation ... all of these are attacks on the mind. If you suffer from negative thoughts, take heart!"* ~ Joyce Meyer

As an intelligence agent for the government, I had studied the strategies and psychology of enemy combatants, criminals, and terrorists. I taught these enemy strategies to several entities of the military, tier one special operations, and intelligence groups. This training gave them the ability to not only outthink their enemies, but to anticipate the enemy's plans of attack and defeat them before their plans ever got off the ground. A physical enemy attack is strategized first in our enemy's mind before it is expressed or deployed against us with their hands. Conversely, if an enemy can penetrate our minds (*psychological warfare*) through lies, intimidation, propaganda (*fake news*), or fear, they can demoralize us. This demoralization can have a direct effect on our ability to live in truth, counterattack from a place of truth, or respond effectively by making correct defensive or offensive decisions. Perpetuating the lies of an enemy is also known as, "*a false information campaign.*"

Therefore, if a spiritual enemy can attack us with negative thoughts which cause feelings of guilt, condemnation, fear, shame, regret, anger, or any of the other "opponents" that were presented in the 19th Chamber. This attack can cause us to implode internally and make us ineffective people by convincing us that we are no good or that we have no self-worth. This is also referred to as "*the bloodless bullet.*" Nothing can take away our motivation in life more than this type of an attack of negative self-perception or self-loathing. This enemy tactic is an inner attack of our mind as opposed to an outer attack of the body. It is important to remember that words, beliefs, emotions, mindsets, and our thoughts, can become just as devastating to us as being shot with a high-powered sniper rifle; both can destroy us. Either one can attack us from a hidden, camouflaged location causing much confusion and disorientation. Lies about ourselves, negative emotions, and unresolved grief, are the spiritual equivalent to bullets fired from a gun. The Bible refers to them as, "*fiery darts from the enemy.*" These fiery darts are always aimed at our mind and thought life. A military sniper would refer to this as a "*head shot.*" Head shots are almost always fatal or at the very least, crippling. A spiritual head shot can eventually kill, or most definitely, cripple us mentally and emotionally. This is where we must cling to and meditate upon the scripture verse found in Philippians 4:8 as was told to me by the Temple Priest in The 19th Chamber. Meditating on these words will have a direct counter assault or protective effect against the fiery darts shot at us by the enemy. We must see ourselves as God sees us. Not what the enemy of our soul tells us to tell ourselves.

It is interesting to note here, that there is very little difference between human military or law enforcement warfare strategies, in comparison to spiritual warfare. The concepts between the two are at least very similar or in many cases, exactly the same. The major difference is that one enemy is visible to the human eye, while the other enemy is invisible and can only be perceived by discernment. But the battle strategies relative to camouflage, deception, baiting, propaganda, false origins of the attack, the element of surprise, demoralization, cutting off supply lines, violence of action, etc., remain parallel.

Spiritual Warfare has many levels and dimensions to it as does physical warfare. Physical warfare can be anything from a fist fight in a bar, to a full-scale military battle on the soil of a foreign country. Spiritual warfare in like manner has a scale of intensity as well. It can be anything from battling a negative inner attitude or thought, depression, or self-destructive behaviors; to struggling with character defects such as hatred, racism, unforgiveness, resentment, vengeance, severe emotional strongholds, and ultimately, the drive to murder or commit suicide.

Yes, there is the study of Demonology, Witchcraft, Satanism, Voodoo, and the like. If at some point you decide that you would like to become a demon slayer or exorcist, then go for it. Just be well prepared and anointed for that type of a confrontation. But in this section, I would like to stay within the parameters of the lessons learned within the 19th Chamber (*our inner mind and internal dialogue*).

There are physical elements involved in addictions and mental illness as well. But the real 'cure' or deliverance from these addictions and other maladies can commonly be found in a spiritual approach of working with like-minded people, such as in a twelve-step program, or similar spiritual environment. "Spiritual" doesn't always mean going to church or following a specific religion. A simplistic definition of spirituality can be a recognition or belief that there is something greater than just us in this universe – a "Higher Power" or "God" if you will, and our ability to connect with this God. This connection can be accomplished through prayer, meditation, or fellowship with people who are on the same path to recovery and growth as we are.

As previously stated, I found my spiritual connection within a Christian Church where I had accepted Jesus Christ as my "Higher Power." When I had finally established a personal connection with Jesus, my addiction to alcohol and drugs was completely and miraculously taken from me. No other spiritual or religious path that I had tried prior to this had ever been able to do that for me. That was 48 years ago and I'm still clean and sober. But I must say this – Twelve Step recovery programs have helped many people overcome addictions and have saved many lives. A Twelve Step Program kept me alive long enough until I was led to that Christian Church where I had a personal encounter with God. Twelve Step Programs are meant to save lives, not souls. Only Jesus can save a soul. Even the High Priest in the 19th Chamber stated that, "*not all philosophies or religions are equal*." It is however important to note though, that God does work through Twelve-Step Programs, medicine, psychology, and other healing arts and sciences. That's just a fact.

The primary level in spiritual warfare is to first understand and believe that there is a spiritual plane in the atmosphere all around us, that has constant vibrations of evil influence into the hearts, minds, thoughts, and intents of mankind. Some refer to this evil influence as Satan, demons, or evil spirits. But whatever you may call them, we need to know this – they can infiltrate and operate against us as *ideas, thoughts, temptations, beliefs, or emotions and inner drives.* They can also be in the form of words spoken to us that create a negative emotional reaction or a belief in a deceptive idea, *like what took place in the Garden of Eden*, as a *historical* or *metaphorical* example. You choose which one to believe in. Whether fact or fiction, it is a good example to consider.

Spiritual warfare is an art of war that must start within us and inside our own 19th Chamber (*soul*). We don't need to be perfect;

we just need to make a start at this "emotional and spiritual house cleaning." This is where we begin to develop the ability to make a difference in the lives of others as well. It no longer makes sense to me to conquer the demons in the world that operate through other people, if I haven't conquered the ones that operate within my own soul. I must first evaluate the log in my own eye before I judge the splinter in another person's eye. In other words, I must first clean my side of the street before I judge the trash on my neighbor's side.

We can master the skills of the body and we can master the skills of the mind. But if we do not consider the spiritual realm of our existence, we can easily be taken out by very formattable and ruthless enemies – God's own personal enemies, which are not made of flesh and blood – but principalities, powers, and rulers of darkness of this world, and spiritual wickedness in high places as spoken of in the sixth chapter of the Biblical Book of Ephesians.

Spiritual warfare is the ultimate form of combat against our ultimate enemies. Physical warfare is the manifestation of evil spiritual warfare operating behind the scenes. Spiritual enemies are the most dangerous enemies of our soul that hide behind the affairs of mankind. They work through and use men as puppets to achieve their evil objectives. They are extremely lethal and the most formidable opponents of all. Since the beginning of time, war began in the spirit realm and had then infiltrated its way into the human realm.

It is now time to engage in spiritual and mental warfare and teach men how to conquer their internal, unseen enemies that camouflage themselves within our minds. Enemies of the soul that not only destroy us but can destroy others as well, such as in a school or mall shooting. I honestly believe that all of the shootings that we see in recent news reports are perpetrated by people who are not only deranged themselves, but also motivated by evil and negative spiritual influences that blindly drive them. This new theater of operation (*Godly mind* versus *ungodly mind*) had become the new battlefield and final frontier for me.

> *"Finally, my brethren, be strong in the Lord and in the power of His might. Put on the whole armor of God, that you may be able to stand against the wiles of the devil. For we do not wrestle against flesh and blood, but against principalities, against powers, against the rulers of the darkness of this age, against spiritual hosts of wickedness in the heavenly places. Therefore, take up the whole armor of God, that you may be able to withstand in the evil day, and having done all, to stand. Stand therefore, having girded your waist with truth, having put on the breastplate of righteousness, and having shod your feet with the preparation of the gospel of peace; above all, taking the shield of faith with which you will be able to quench all the fiery darts of the wicked one. And take the helmet of salvation, and the sword of the Spirit, which is the word of God; praying always with all prayer and supplication in the Spirit, being watchful to this end with all perseverance and supplication for all the saints."*
>
> **Ephesians 6:10-18**

We need to put on "the whole armor of God" for this battle. And this 'armor' is quite different to that which is commonly used in military or law enforcement arenas.

THE ARMOR OF GOD
EPHESIANS 6:10-18
"... Be strong in the Lord and in his mighty power. Put on the full armor of God so that you can take your stand against the devil's schemes." v. 10, 11
The Shield of Faith (Eph. 6:16)
Faith is being sure that God will keep His promises. Faith in God protects you when you are tempted to doubt.
The Helmet of Salvation (Eph. 6:17)
Put on the Helmet of Salvation by believing that Jesus Christ died for your sins and rose again.
The Breastplate of Righteousness (Eph. 6:14)
Righteousness is being honest, good, humble, and fair to others. It means standing up for weaker people.
The Belt of Truth (Eph. 6:14)
Truth keeps us from giving in to the world's beliefs. Compare your beliefs and actions to the truth of the Word of God.
The Sword of the Spirit (Eph. 6:17)
which is the Word of God. God's Word is our offensive weapon. When we tell others what the Bible says, the Holy Spirit helps people see their bad thoughts and actions, and makes them want to be forgiven.
Feet Prepared with the Gospel of Peace (Eph. 6:15)
The Gospel of Peace is being right with God and being contented in troubled times. Jesus said peacemakers were blessed.
© Rose Publishing

"The Shield of Faith" – Having a belief system in the power and principles of God so that we can rightly divide truth from a lie and to defeat and survive the attack and fiery darts of our adversary.

"The Helmet of Salvation" – Not only to protect our thoughts and mental processes, but to have hope and assurance of spiritual deliverance and protection against our unseen enemies.

"The Breastplate of Righteousness" – Symbolizes a heart to do what is right and just, even in the face of opposition no matter what the cost, such as my Cannabis Buyers Club Investigation. It also requires us to stand up for weaker people who cannot defend themselves.

"The Belt of Truth" – Represents honesty and integrity. A commitment to live by the truth and reject lies and deceit.

"The Sword of the Spirit" – Symbolizes the only 'offensive' weapon in our spiritual arsenal. It represents the power of Divine Wisdom and the written scriptural truths, and correct teachings used to cut through confusion (*Fog of War*) and illuminate the correct path ahead to follow.

"The Shoes of Peace" – Require us to walk in peace and spread harmony to those around us.

In Brief – We define our belief system based on God's Word so that we can tell the difference between the truth and a lie. We protect our thoughts from anything that challenges that belief system. We decide to do what is right despite the possible outcome that may be in conflict with our own interests. We live by the virtues of honesty, excellence, and integrity. We study and pray for the wisdom to handle situations without immediately resorting to violence or discord. And we live in a way that spreads harmony and peace to those around us.

I have lived by many warrior codes of honor, conduct, and valor throughout my life, but this Biblical spiritual warfare code has made the greatest impact in my spiritual growth and approach to warfare.

If after attempting to live by this spiritual warfare code, our lives become endangered by a hostile enemy who refuses a peaceful resolution to a conflict; then we must consider the words spoken by Marine Corps General James Mattis: "*Engage your brain before you engage your weapon. Be polite, be professional, but have a plan to kill everybody you meet.*" Define these words for yourself (*literal or figurative*), but as I mentioned earlier – "some men only understand physical violence," because they offer us no other option. Thus, the "necessary evil of physical warfare."

Only Jesus is the true standard of righteousness, not just being a "good person" as many people claim to be. Was Jesus good by the world's standards, or good by God's standards? Our final judgement will be conducted by God – not the world's system of right and wrong. So, our definition of 'right and wrong' must be in line with God's definition of 'right and wrong' or we could be in for a *not so pleasant surprise* at the end of our earthly deployment.

> *"Not everyone who says to Me, 'Lord, Lord,' shall enter the kingdom of heaven, but he who does the will of My Father in heaven. Many will say to Me in that day, 'Lord, Lord, have we not prophesied in Your name, cast out demons in Your name, and done many wonders in Your name?' And then I will declare to them, 'I never knew you; depart from Me, you who practice lawlessness!"*
>
> **Matthew 7:21-23**

The world's definition of a "good person" will not be sufficient to survive even the fair and merciful judgement of God. That is why Jesus died for us to bridge the gap of our spiritual inadequacy from God's perspective.

But for the grace of God go I – Joe Bannon – the so called "great warrior" and "teacher of the arts of death," who was in reality "spiritually weak" inside and addicted to the lusts of the material world as the High Priest of The 19th Chamber so eloquently pointed out to me. God only knows what my fate would have been if I had not turned from my immoral and ungodly compromises before my appointed date with God's evaluation of my life. A "spiritual internal affairs" inquiry so to speak.

I have previously stated that God had spared me from death on countless occasions. This is true. But in actuality, He had spared me from countless opportunities from His judgement that I would have no justified defense against if I had died any sooner. In other words, I would have been screwed without His extreme Grace and Mercy by extending my life.

God will be much more concerned with my internal warrior rather than my external warrior at the end of my earthly deployment. He will not be impressed with the amount of people I have killed or taught to kill. He will be much more interested in how far I have grown, and the number of human souls that I have helped, fed, and given a drink of water to when they were hungry and thirsty. Warriors are necessary and commissioned by God to protect humanity from evil. That goes without saying. But there comes a time in every warrior's life, or any person's life for that matter, that he/she must look inside and face their own 19th Chamber and connect with the Temple Priest – who is Jesus Christ. This I am absolutely sure of.

"For God so loved the world that He gave His only begotten Son, Jesus Christ, that whoever believes in Him should not perish but have everlasting life." – My 'third option' as I sat on the end of my bed with a bottle of whiskey and a pistol forty-eight years ago.

John 3:16

The Prayer That Makes Us Right with God

"Dear Lord Jesus, I know that I am a sinner, and I ask for Your forgiveness. I believe You died for my sins and rose from the dead. I turn from my sins and invite You to come into my heart and life. I want to trust and follow You as my Lord and Savior and the Keeper of my inner temple (soul)."

If you have honestly said the above prayer from your heart, I encourage you to find a place where you can grow spiritually within a group of like-minded Christian people. Whether that be a church, a faith-based addiction recovery group, a military or first responder support group, or a home-based meeting of housewives. It doesn't matter where you go – just grow in truth and in faith. Really – nothing else in life matters in the big picture of eternity.

Recovery (Rebuilding) Resources:

MightyOaksPrograms.org (*PTSD*)
CelebrateRecovery.com (*Hurts, Habits, and Hang-ups common to all*)
AlcoholicsAnonymous.com (*Alcoholism Recovery*)
RebootRecovery.com (*Trauma Recovery*)
Puredesire.org (*Sexual Addiction Recovery*)
USA-NA.org (*Narcotics Recovery*)

Epilogue

"A Letter From a Police Officer"

"I have pulled dead, mangled bodies from cars. I have lied to people as they were dying. I said you are going to be fine as I held their hand and watched the life fade out. I have held dying babies. Bought lunch for homeless people who were mentally ill and hadn't eaten in a while. I have had people try to stab me and have fought with men trying to shoot me."

Do the above words sound familiar? They should. They are the same words that you read within the first paragraph of "A Letter From a Police Officer" at the very beginning of this book. The words contained in this letter at the beginning of the book had become a prophecy of my life and career to follow. Now, at the book's ending, they have become my personal testimony. I have experienced everything written within that letter and more; and more, and then some more.

At the publication date of this book (2024), it has been exactly forty years since I had crashed through Macy's plate glass door and shortly thereafter, sworn into the San Francisco Police Department. What a ride, what a miracle. Good, bad, and ugly, all in one career.

I still have dreams and nightmares now and then but for the most part, it's all just a bunch of distant memories.

As I stood on that Jamaica, New York City train station platform in 1963 and asked God, if I could become a police officer someday. I had no idea what I was asking for. Yet, I have no regrets whatsoever for Him granting me my request. If anything, I am very grateful. God had kept me alive through the impossible and miraculously spared me on more occasions than I could possibly count. Not just from hostile enemy gunfire, the Colombian Drug Cartels, murder contracts, or from corrupt cops. But from serious addictions, a reckless lifestyle, and health conditions that put me on life support on four separate occasions. Hearing the words, "I suggest that you get your affairs in order" from my doctor, weren't exactly music to my ears. But the words, "You will live and not die," whispered by God's still small voice into my dying ears were. I also cannot discount the great amount of focus and calm that I felt during some of the most horrific and violent armed and unarmed encounters that I had experienced during my missions both domestic and overseas. The PTSD that followed sucked, but I have even been able to put a good part of that to rest.

As I look back over my life, I see nothing but God's love, power, mercy, and intervention from the jaws of insanity and death. Long story short, I should have died one thousand deaths. Jesus had raised Lazarus from the dead on one occasion. There is no doubt that I have greatly surpassed Lazarus' record. I know that I had played a minor role in this script, but let's be real. God was the producer, director, and lead actor in each action scene of the movie of my life. Either directly, or by the countless people He sent to intervene along my path.

I began writing this book in July of 1976 right after I had been thrown out of the alcohol rehabilitation center as a 'hopeless case.' I wanted to memorialize the first nineteen years of my life because I believed at the time, that I would be dead before my twentieth birthday like I had been told by so many people. That obviously didn't happen, and I am now almost seventy years old, healthy, and in great physical shape. Today, I am not just surviving but thriving.

For several years I had attended and eventually led a Christian Men's Purity Group called 'Pure Desire' and have gotten out of the web of sexual addiction, pornography, and ungodly lifestyles. I went through intensive debriefing and counselling for PTSD and got involved with a trauma recovery group named, 'Reboot Recovery.' I also attend a 'Celebrate Recovery' group which addresses "Hurts, Habits, and Hang Ups" common to all men and women. Healing and recovery are a lifelong journey, not a one-time fix.

I have been able to forgive my parents and others who had wronged me in life. I am still clean and sober from drugs and alcohol. I have a men's ministry where I give presentations to military, law enforcement, and church groups relative to trauma and wounded emotions, addictions, PTSD, as well as sharing my testimony, and teaching on the subjects of Spiritual Warfare and Christian Psychology.

I had stayed single for most of my life because I had a very difficult time getting emotionally close to people. But that all changed when I met my wife that God had set aside for me in another city. For her safety and anonymity, I shall not include any of her personal information within this book other than we have been very happily married for several years.

I am writing two sequels to this book. The first is a play-by-play account of the Cannabis Buyers Club Investigation containing all of the intricate details that I was not able to include within this writing. This sequel is titled, **"Smoke Screen"** – *The Truth Behind the Cannabis Buyers Club Investigation of 1994.*

There is also a very large part of my life and former lifestyle that I did not disclose within this first book. I wrote this information in a second sequel to this writing titled, **"Secret Agent – Secret Life."** This one may shock you a bit as it addresses areas of my life that I only slightly alluded to in this book. In this sequel, I present my secret lifestyle and my involvement with the illegal, underground gambling operations and hustle rackets run by the "New York Italian Men" as a very young teenager and much more.

Both sequels will be announced on my website when published along with additional chapters of this book that are centered around the technical aspects of PTSD and addictions that I did not include in this edition. **Website: www.bannoninstitute.org**

"Secret Agent – Secret Life" is based on my Emmy Award winning interview with Mike Wallace on ***"CBS – 60 Minutes"*** and my appearance on other TV shows including, "The Phil Donohue Show."

Me and Mike Wallace of CBS – *'60 Minutes'*

"Looking Back in Hindsight" – The military reform school that I had attended was abruptly closed. There were many allegations of student abuse perpetrated by the command staff. My ex-girlfriend who invited me to the church that saved my life (*and soul*) had married the captain of my former fire department. Some of the rookies I had trained in the San Francisco Police Department are currently, assistant and deputy chiefs, commanders, and captains. But most if not all my former partners and academy classmates have retired.

My partner who was with me at the "*Machete Man*" incident retired as a homicide inspector (*detective*). The chief of police who was in office when my involvement with the Cannabis Buyers Club Investigation went public, created a new protocol that stated, "Every police officer assigned to an outside task force must continually brief the chief's office as to exactly what they were doing "***at all times***." This protocol was set in place because of me acting as a 'covert drug commando' up in the Emerald Triangle and was unofficially named, "*The Joe Bannon Rule*." The lieutenant of my narcotics division was repromoted to captain after the smoke cleared from the raid on the Cannabis Buyers Club and is now honorably retired. Dennis Peron was put on probation for his leadership of the Cannabis Buyers Club. Both he and District Attorney Terrance Hallinan both died of cancer. But Dennis Peron got his wish after his death. Marijuana is now legal in many states. RIP Dennis. We had always shared a weird type of underlying mutual adversarial respect for one another. I guess we were both just, 'doing our jobs.'

Police Commissioner Wayne Friday who was a good friend of mine committed suicide after a long battle with Parkinson's Disease. I completely severed all ties with Puerto Rico, The Caribbean, and South America. My former partner in Puerto Rico 'Airborne,' moved on to different missions in Asia and the Middle East.

Gerard Butler went on to make two sequels to Olympus Has Fallen ('*London Has Fallen*' and '*Angel Has Fallen*').

But most importantly – I have an awesome relationship with God and am finally at peace.

Many of us have experienced paths in life that led us to our own personal versions of our eighteen chambers with all our war stories, proud accolades, medals, diplomas, and awards plastered all over our "I love me" walls. But unfortunately, we can get stuck there like I had. When the real satisfaction, meaningfulness, and true eternal accomplishments are in the 19th Chamber which so few of us ever find in life.

I hope this book has become a road map to find your own 19th Chamber – however it may present itself to you.

To me – God is not just a concept or a religious figment of someone's imagination. He is the most powerful force in the universe and can be accessed and understood through the God and man of Jesus Christ. If this were not so, I would not have been around long enough to write this book. I wish you well on your journey.

Godspeed !

Special Agent Joe Bannon (Retired)
Doctor, Chaplain, and Healer of Men

The landscape of the earth and heaven is littered with the broken bodies, minds, spirits, and lives of men who have stumbled or who have been broken. The crucible that we live in, that refines us, that makes us better is often more than we can bear – and we quit, and we become part of the littered landscape. We see it all the time. But what we don't see are the hearts and individual struggles of each broken man. We only have the capacity to observe, make notes, and try to avoid the calamities we witness. Sure, we can stop to try and understand but life has a curious way of ushering us along our way and the lessons potentially learned are quickly forgotten.

In the midst of defeat and self-loathing and the ultimate destruction, there are spirits that attain a foot hold. They cling to the rocks around them for dear life. They gather themselves and take stock of where they are and what is required to stop the bleeding and move in a different direction. To say the least, the ***"rebuilding"*** process has begun.

The man who is under ***"reconstruction"*** is doing it with an eye toward never making the same mistakes again.

"Brethren, I do not count myself to have apprehended; but one thing I do, forgetting those things which are behind and reaching forward to those things which are ahead, I press toward the goal for the prize of the upward call of God in Christ Jesus."

Philippians 3:13-15

Resources

- The Vietnam Memorial Wall Painting by Lee Teter.
- The Creation Michelangelo Italy Vatican – Creative Commons Attribution 2.0 – https://creativecommons.org/licenses/by/2.0/deed.en
- Third Step Prayer used in Twelve Step program formats – "19th Chamber Scroll.
- Picture of Gerard Butler and Joe Bannon – Mother Jones / Writer Asawin Suebsaeng.
- Bannon Institute Of The Arts – Research and Training Curriculums.
- Nothing stronger than a broken man photo – X.com (twitter@wasonelegwonder), Verbiage beneath photo – Posted in general by Doug Graham / March 1, 2022 / Spartan Series #126
- Picture of Roman Soldier – Rose Publishing.
- All scripture verses taken from the NKJ Version of the Bible unless otherwise noted.

www.ingramcontent.com/pod-product-compliance
Lightning Source LLC
LaVergne TN
LVHW052224200926
848481LV00001B/211
* 9 7 9 8 9 9 0 5 0 1 2 6 3 *